LEONARDO DA VINCI
AND PERFUMES IN THE RENAISSANCE

EXHIBITION

Exhibition Curators
Pascal Brioist, Professor of Modern History at the University of Tours and member of the Centre for Advanced Renaissance Studies (CESR)
Carlo Vecce, Professor of Italian Literature at the University of Naples "L'Orientale"

Advisory Committee
Pascal Brioist, Professor of Modern History at the University of Tours and member of the Centre for Advanced Renaissance Studies (CESR)
Carlo Vecce, Professor of Italian Literature at the University of Naples "L'Orientale"
François Saint Bris, President of the Château du Clos Lucé – Parc Leonardo da Vinci

Château du Clos Lucé
François Saint Bris, President
Diane Junqua, Director of Communications and Sponsorship
Sandra Chupin, Exhibition Coordinator, assisted by Sarah Torre
Eleonora Pavesi, Italian Coordinator
Nina Germain, Communications Officer
Stéphane Darras, Head of the Technical Department, and his team

Exhibition Design
Agence NC, Nathalie Crinière, Jiebing Zhang and Élisa Laristan, scenographers
C Album, Tiphaine Massari and Jean-Baptiste Taisne, associate graphic designers
La Méduse, Édouard Lecomte, motion designer
Gelatic, Henri-Maria Leutner and Ugo Cerina, lighting
Version Bronze, pedestals

Olfactive Sensory Experiences
Givaudan, Sophie Cauchi, Head of External Communications
Givaudan, Eugénie Briot, perfume historian
Magique Studio, Mazen Nasri and Victoria Hinton-Albrieux, scenographers

Institutions Loaning Exhibits
Italy
Bergamo, Accademia Carrara
Florence, Gallerie degli Uffizi
Florence, Biblioteca Nazionale Centrale
Florence, Musei del Bargello
Florence, Museo Stefano Bardini
Milan, Veneranda Biblioteca Ambrosiana – Pinacoteca
Milan, Galleria Moshe Tabibnia
Milan, Pinacoteca del Castello Sforzesco
Pavia, Musei Civici del Castello Visconteo
Poggio a Caiano, Villa Medicea, Museo della Natura Morta
Prato, Museo del Tessuto
Pugnano, Fondazione Cerratelli
Rome, Galleria Borghese
Turin, Palazzo Madama – Museo Civico d'Arte Antica
Vigevano, Museo Internazionale della Calzatura
France
Amboise, château du Clos Lucé
Aujac, château du Cheylard d'Aujac
Blois, musée diocésain d'Art religieux
Blois, paroisse de la cathédrale Saint-Louis
Écouen, musée national de la Renaissance – château d'Écouen
Grasse, musée international de la Parfumerie
Le Mans, archives départementales de la Sarthe
Paris, Archives nationales de France
Paris, bibliothèque Sainte-Geneviève
Paris, musée de Cluny – musée national du Moyen Âge
Romorantin-Lanthenay, centre de documentation du musée de Sologne
Souvigny, commune de Souvigny
Strasbourg, bibliothèque nationale et universitaire
Tours, bibliothèque municipale
Tours, Centre d'études supérieures de la Renaissance

CATALOGUE

Project Management
François Saint Bris, President of the Château du Clos Lucé – Parc Leonardo da Vinci
Diane Junqua, Director of Communications and Sponsorship

Foreword
François Saint Bris, President of the Château du Clos Lucé – Parc Leonardo da Vinci

Essay Writers
Soline Anthore-Baptiste
Nicolas Baptiste-Anthore
Andrea Bernardoni
Marjolijn Bol
Marie-Élisabeth Boutroue
Pascal Brioist
Océane Fontaine Cioffi
Anna Messinis
Alexander Neuwahl
Nathalie Oddy
Élodie Pierrard
Jesse Rodin
Özge Samancı
Lorenzo Tunesi
Carlo Vecce
Paola Venturelli

Château du Clos Lucé – Parc Leonardo da Vinci
François Saint Bris, President
Diane Junqua, Director of Communications and Sponsorship

With the financial support of the Centre-Val de Loire Region
With the financial support and expertise of Givaudan

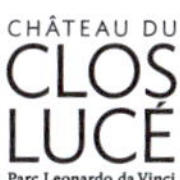

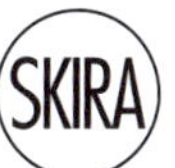

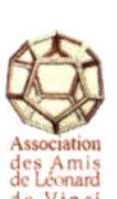

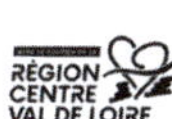

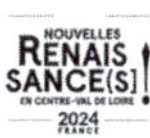

Givaudan

Cover illustration:
Leonardo da Vinci, *Study of Flowers*, 2nd half of the 15th c., pen, brown ink, mostly over a preceding sketch in metalpoint, paper slightly browned, 18.3 × 20.1 cm, Gallerie dell'Accademia di Venezia, inv. 237

LEONARDO DA VINCI
and Perfumes in the Renaissance

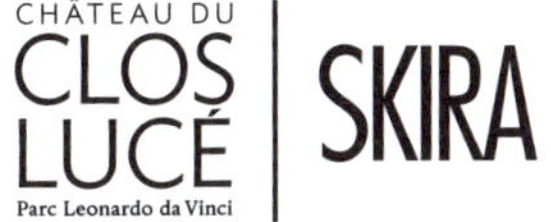

CONTENTS

IV. At the Sforza Court in Milan

V. Perfumes at the Court of Francis I

Annexes

Essay writers

François Saint Bris, President of Château du Clos-Lucé – Parc Leonardo da Vinci

Pascal Brioist, Professor of Modern History at the University of Tours and member of the Centre for Advanced Renaissance Studies (CESR)

Carlo Vecce, Professor of Italian Literature at the University of Naples "L'Orientale"

Marie-Élisabeth Boutroue, CNRS Research Fellow at the Centre for Advanced Renaissance Studies (CESR)

Nathalie Oddy, Postdoctoral Researcher in the History of Philosophy at Oxford University

Özge Samanci, Lecturer at the Department of Gastronomy and Culinary Arts at Özyeğin University, Istanbul

Anna Messinis, Independent Researcher and author of the book *The History of Perfume in Venice* (2017)

Alexander Neuwahl, founder of the interdisciplinary research group Artes Mechanicae (Florence), collaborator at the Museo Leonardiano in Vinci, expert in 3D reconstructions

Andrea Bernardoni, Professor of History of Science and Technology at the University of L'Aquila, and Consultant at the Museo Galileo in Florence

Jesse Rodin, Associate Professor of Music at Stanford University

Lorenzo Tunesi, doctoral student in Musicology at Stanford University

Marjolijn Bol, Associate Professor of Art History at the University of Utrecht

Paola Venturelli, Scientific Director at the Gianmaria Buccellati Foundation in Milan and Curator at the Museum of Jewellery in Vicenza

Soline Anthore-Baptiste, Doctor of Modern History at Grenoble-Alpes University and "Ca' Foscari" University in Venice

Nicolas Baptiste-Anthore, Doctor in Medieval History at the University of Savoie-Mont-Blanc

Élodie Pierrard, doctoral student in History at the University of Tours and member of the Centre for Advanced Renaissance Studies (CESR)

Océane Fontaine Cioffi, doctoral student in History at the University of Tours and member of the Centre for Advanced Renaissance Studies (CESR)

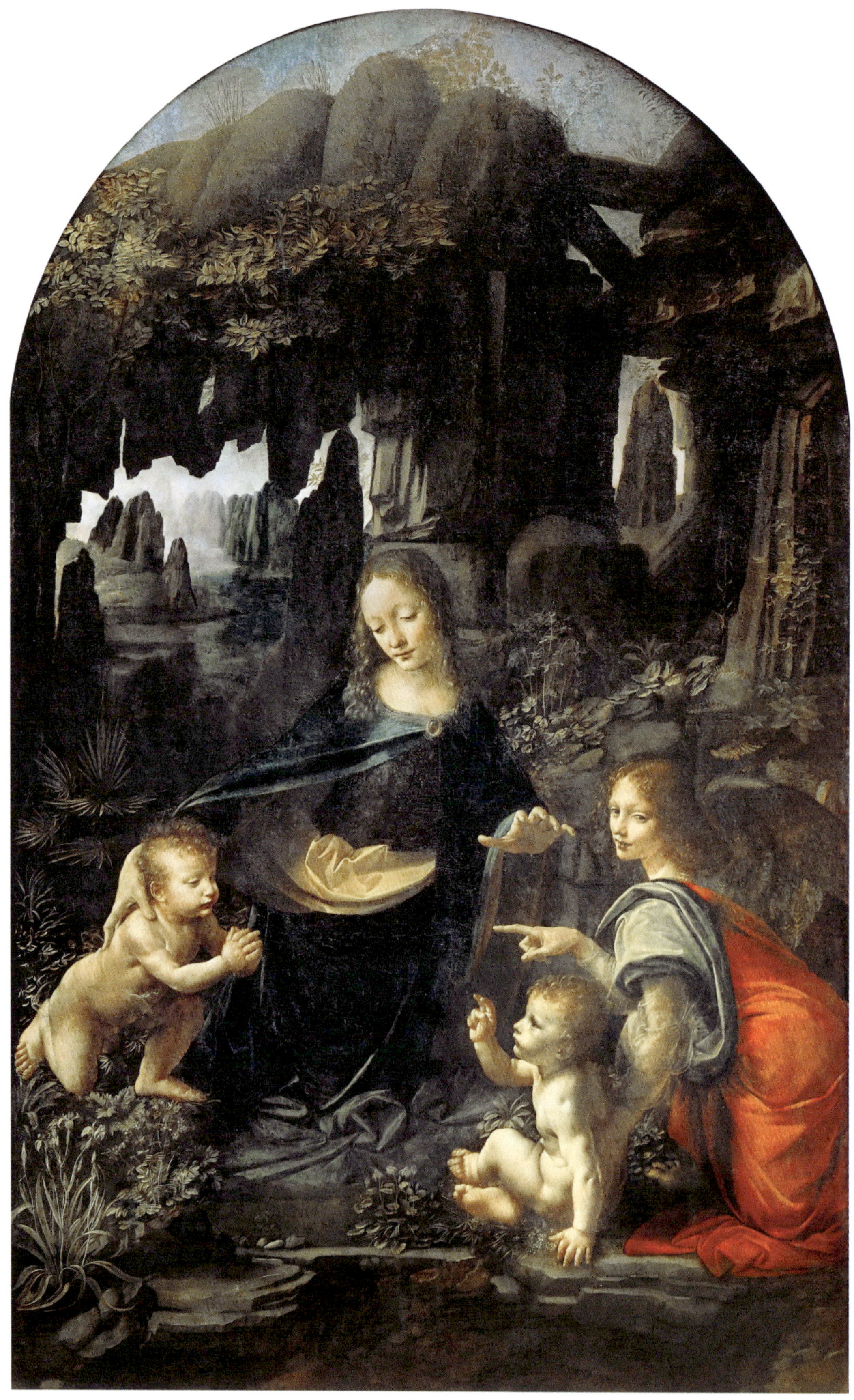

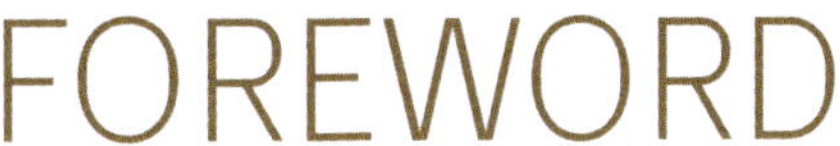

FOREWORD

François Saint Bris

Château du Clos Lucé, the artist's final residence, is presenting a new exhibition from 7 June 2024 to 15 September 2024: "Leonardo da Vinci and Perfumes in the Renaissance". It takes visitors right to the heart of Leonardo's experiments and discoveries relating to perfume in the Renaissance, and also presents his research on the sense of smell. For example, Leonardo recorded perfume recipes that made use of the techniques of maceration and distillation, a little-known facet of his brilliance.

Clos Lucé's mission is to pass on the heritage, memory and universal knowledge of Leonardo da Vinci. The exhibition focuses on an unusual subject: perfumes, an integral part of our intangible and artistic cultural heritage.

The art of making perfume dates back to ancient times, to the civilisations of Mesopotamia and Egypt, then to those of Greece and Rome. Perfume is linked to the history of civilisation, to the history of cultures, to the sacred and the profane, to therapeutic practices designed to protect against disease, to purifying and healing. And it satisfies needs, such as for the pleasure of giving, the wish to please and seduce, and the desire for well-being.

The word "perfume" comes from the Latin *per fumum*, which literally means "through smoke". This refers to the religious rituals involving incense, resins and aromatics, used since ancient times as offerings to divinities. Perfume is a symbol of aspiration and of communicating with the divine spirit.

Left
Leonardo da Vinci, *The Virgin, the Christ Child, St John the Baptist and an Angel*, known as *The Virgin of the Rocks*, 1483–94, oil on canvas, 199.5 × 122 cm Paris, musée du Louvre, inv. 777

The Renaissance, a vast intellectual, artistic and humanist movement, originating in Italy and Flanders, confirmed a return to the founding roots of ancient Greece and Rome and spread across the whole of Europe. It reached France under the successive reigns of three kings, from 1494 to 1547. Fascinated by Italy, the Valois kings were constantly crossing the Alps and, campaign after campaign, sought to entice architects, artists and craftsmen into building and embellishing cities, castles and gardens for them and to promote a new art of living. Great discoveries,

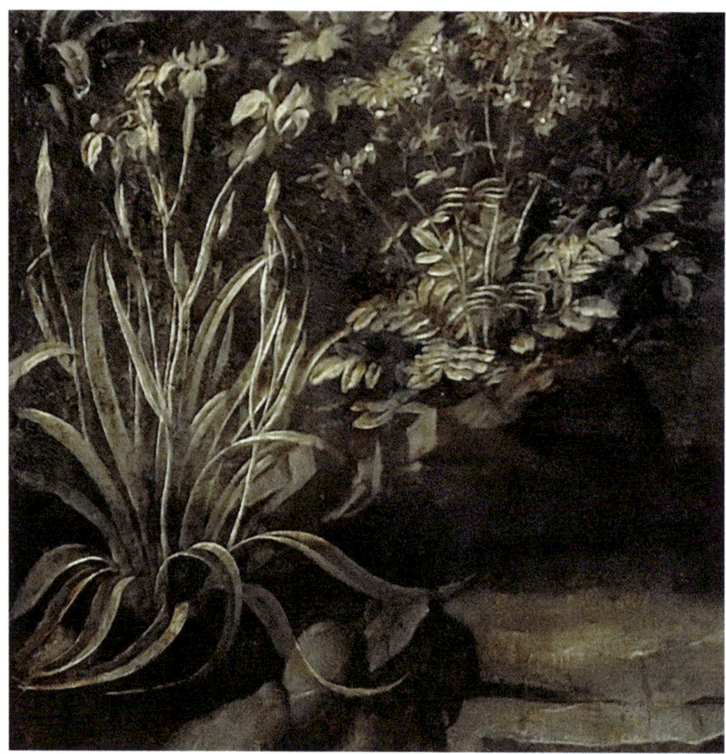

Leonardo da Vinci, *The Virgin of the Rocks* (detail)

bringing massive quantities of gold, spices and aromatics from the New World, contributed to the prosperity and rapid development of the whole of Europe. Amboise became the cradle of the French Renaissance.

Organised by Château du Clos Lucé, this major exhibition was devised and produced in collaboration with curators Carlo Vecce, professor of Italian literature at the University of Naples "L'Orientale", and Pascal Brioist, professor at the Centre for Advanced Renaissance Studies (CESR) at the University of Tours, a historian specialising in Leonardo da Vinci, the Renaissance, science and technology. Clos Lucé is most grateful to them for their outstanding teamwork and the expertise they shared with us.

The main aim of our exhibition is to introduce visitors to the world of perfume during the Renaissance, through the extraordinary odyssey of two intersecting destinies: those of Leonardo da Vinci and his mother, Caterina. By tracing their adventure-filled journey, the same route followed by perfumes in the Renaissance, this exhibition invites visitors on a multi-sensory journey filled with sensations and emotions. It is as much a historical and cultural journey as it is an immersive olfactory investigation, designed to appeal to all ages and to all the senses, allowing visitors to learn as well as experience.

The journey takes us from the mountains of the Caucasus to the Black Sea, and on to Constantinople; from the Mediterranean to Venice, gateway to the Orient; from Leonardo's native Tuscany to Lombardy; and finally, from the Duchy of Milan to the court of the Valois in the Loire Valley.

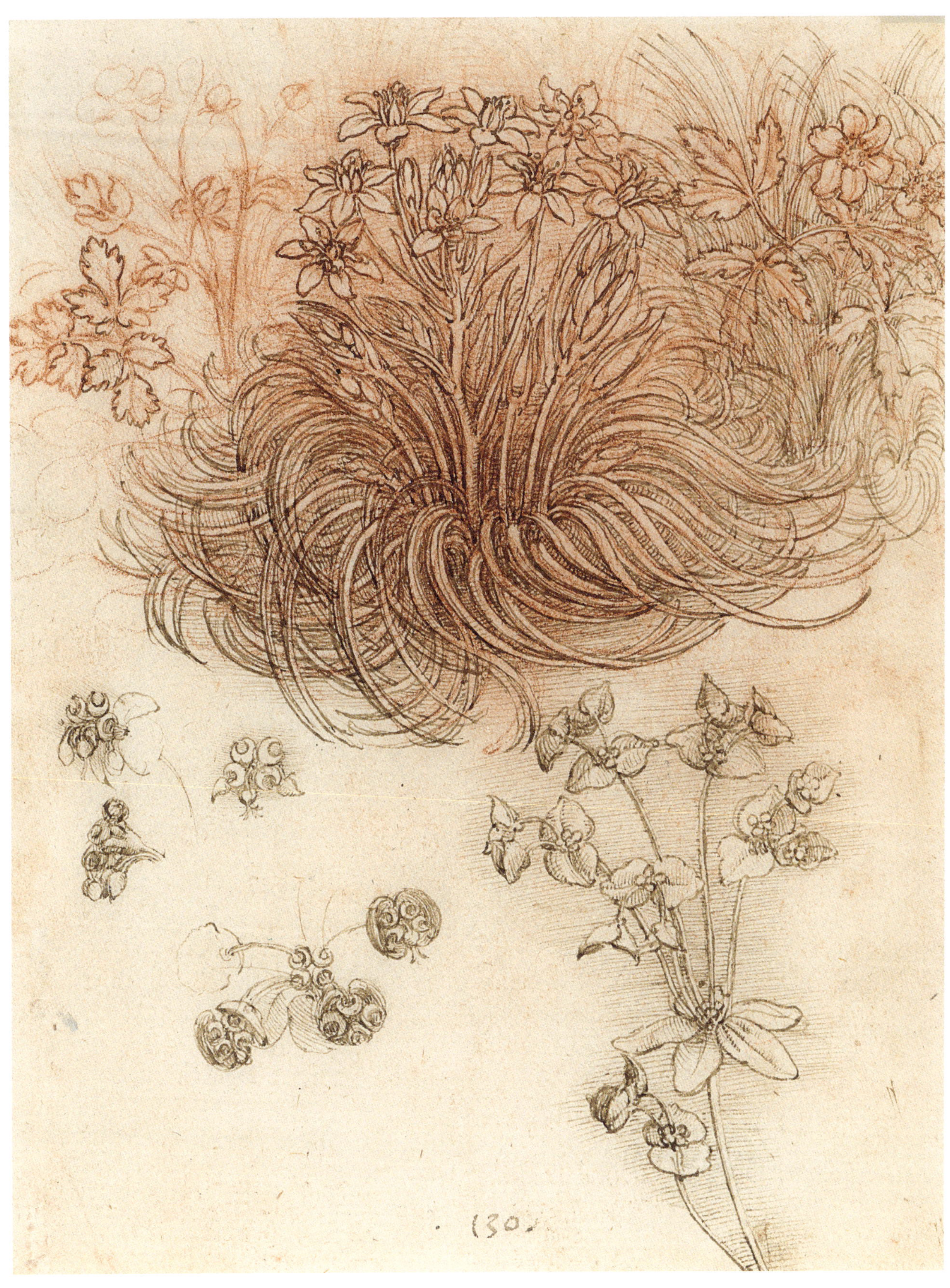

Leonardo da Vinci, *A Star-of-Bethlehem and Other Plants*, ca. 1506–12, red chalk, pen and ink, 19.8 × 16 cm, Windsor, Royal Collection Trust, RL 12424

The exhibition presents sixty original works from French and Italian state museums and private art collections. The didactic tour includes original drawings by Leonardo da Vinci; paintings by his pupils; court paintings from the Quattrocento; Florentine and Venetian manuscripts; books by Leonardo's contemporaries from the 16th century; reconstructions – including an alembic based on an original drawing by Leonardo, who was experimenting with the art of perfume in Florence around 1480; and *albarello* apothecary jars. It also features objects associated with perfumery: *cassoni* or chests, caskets, bottles, pomanders and *oiselets de Chypre* (Chypre birdies), censers, incense burners and rosaries, and perfumed costumes, jewellery and gloves. Visitors will also find a spice stall, a maceration and distillation workshop complete with excipients, raw materials of animal origin (musk, civet and ambergris), plant and mineral ingredients, and audiovisual and olfactory exhibits.

This exciting presentation draws on Professor Carlo Vecce's recent discoveries about the origins and early life of Caterina, Leonardo da Vinci's mother. Originally from Circassia, the northern region of the Caucasus Mountains to the west of the Caspian Sea, she was abducted and sold several times as a slave, in Constantinople, Venice and finally Florence, where she met Piero da Vinci, a young notary and father of Leonardo. Shortly after the birth of their child, Piero da Vinci notarised the deed that freed Caterina, allowing her, according to Carlo Vecce, to "regain her freedom and dignity as a human being".

In Constantinople, amidst the hustle and bustle of the noisy, fragrant markets, Caterina discovered, as did the merchants from Genoa and Venice, exotic perfumes and the scent of spices, cinnamon and pepper, amber and musk, incense and myrrh. At the time, perfumes had a wide range of uses, from dietary and religious to therapeutic.

In Venice, Caterina, who was still in her teens, was sold to a wealthy Florentine family, manufacturers of *cassoni*, or chests. The city, at the junction of shipping routes, had become the most important centre for the trade in oriental spices and perfumes. Aromatics and the raw materials used in perfumery – Aleppo soap, essential oils, but also the first perfumes diluted in alcohol and a wide range of scented articles, including gloves and shoes – passed through the city of the doges before being distributed throughout Europe, while the glassmakers of the island of Murano, with their unique skills, exported their blown glass creations throughout the West.

The exhibition then takes us to Tuscany, where Leonardo spent his childhood and adolescence. The young Leonardo was free to roam the hills of Vinci, the village where he was born, dotted with vineyards and olive groves, immersing his senses in the smells, colours and sensations of stone pines, cypresses, jasmine and orange blossom, amongst other plants. Self-taught, Leonardo grew up in the school of nature, which inculcated in him the importance of observation, experimentation and knowledge of the cosmic universe, while his grandfather, Antonio, instructed him in the importance of "keeping his eyes open" ("*Po l'occhio*").

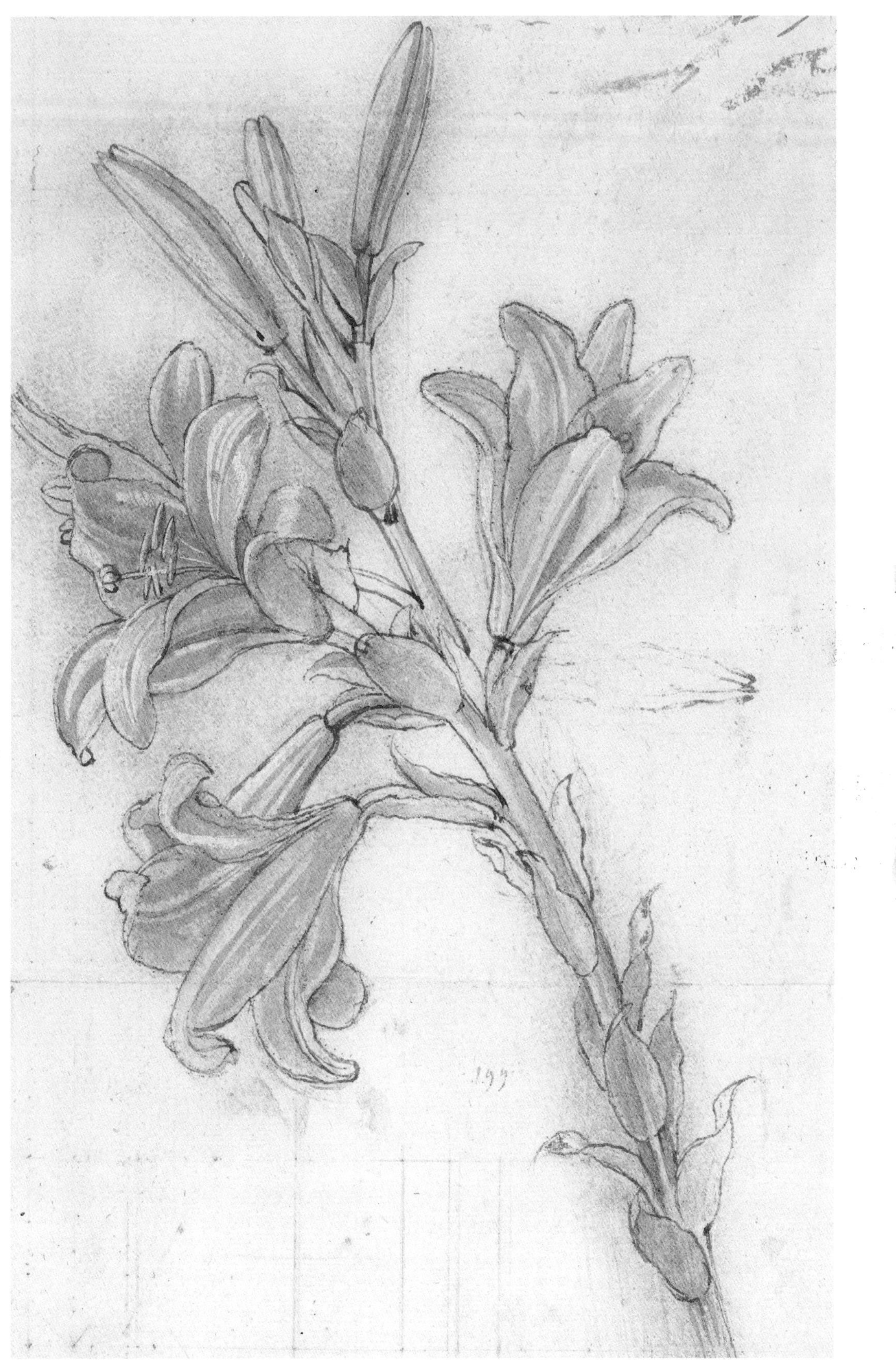

Attributed to Andrea del Verrocchio, *A Lily*, ca. 1475, stylus, pinpointing, leadpoint, pen and ink, brown wash, ochre wash and rubbing, white heightening (partly discoloured), pricked through, 31.4 × 17.7 cm, Windsor, Royal Collection Trust, RL 12418

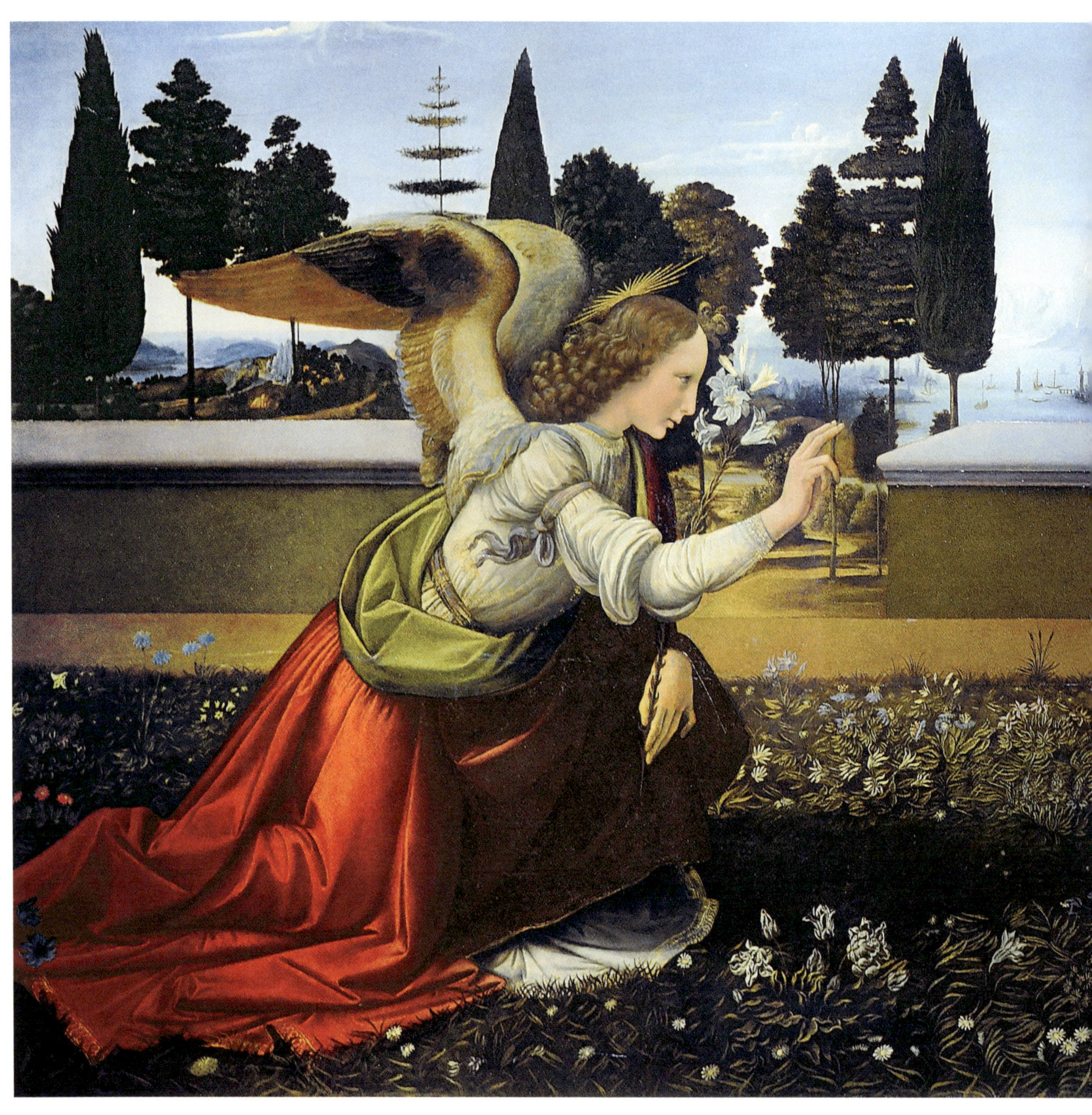

Leonardo da Vinci, *Annunciation*, 1472–75, oil on canvas, 90 × 222 cm, Florence, Galleria degli Uffizi, inv. 1890, no. 1618

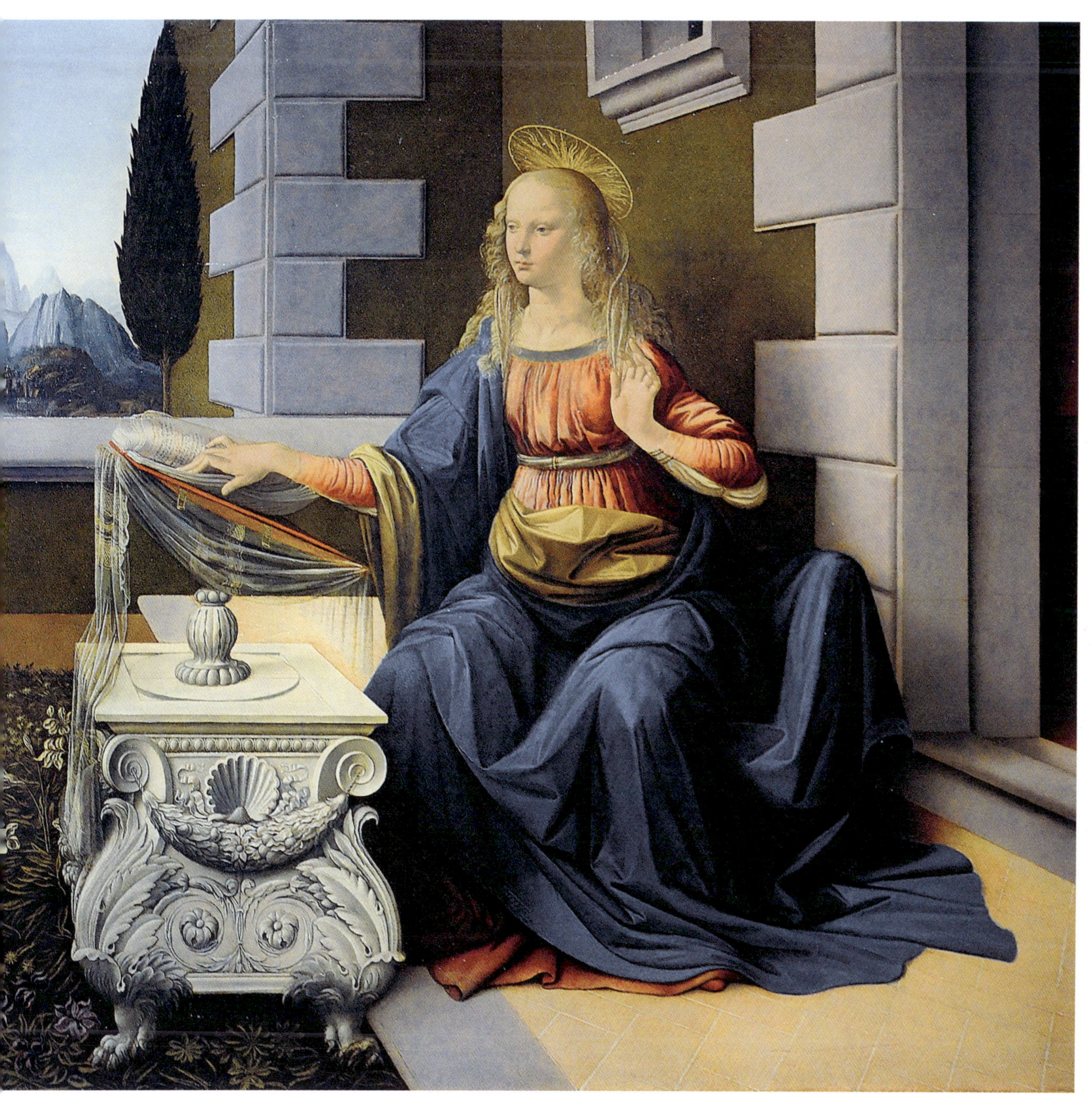

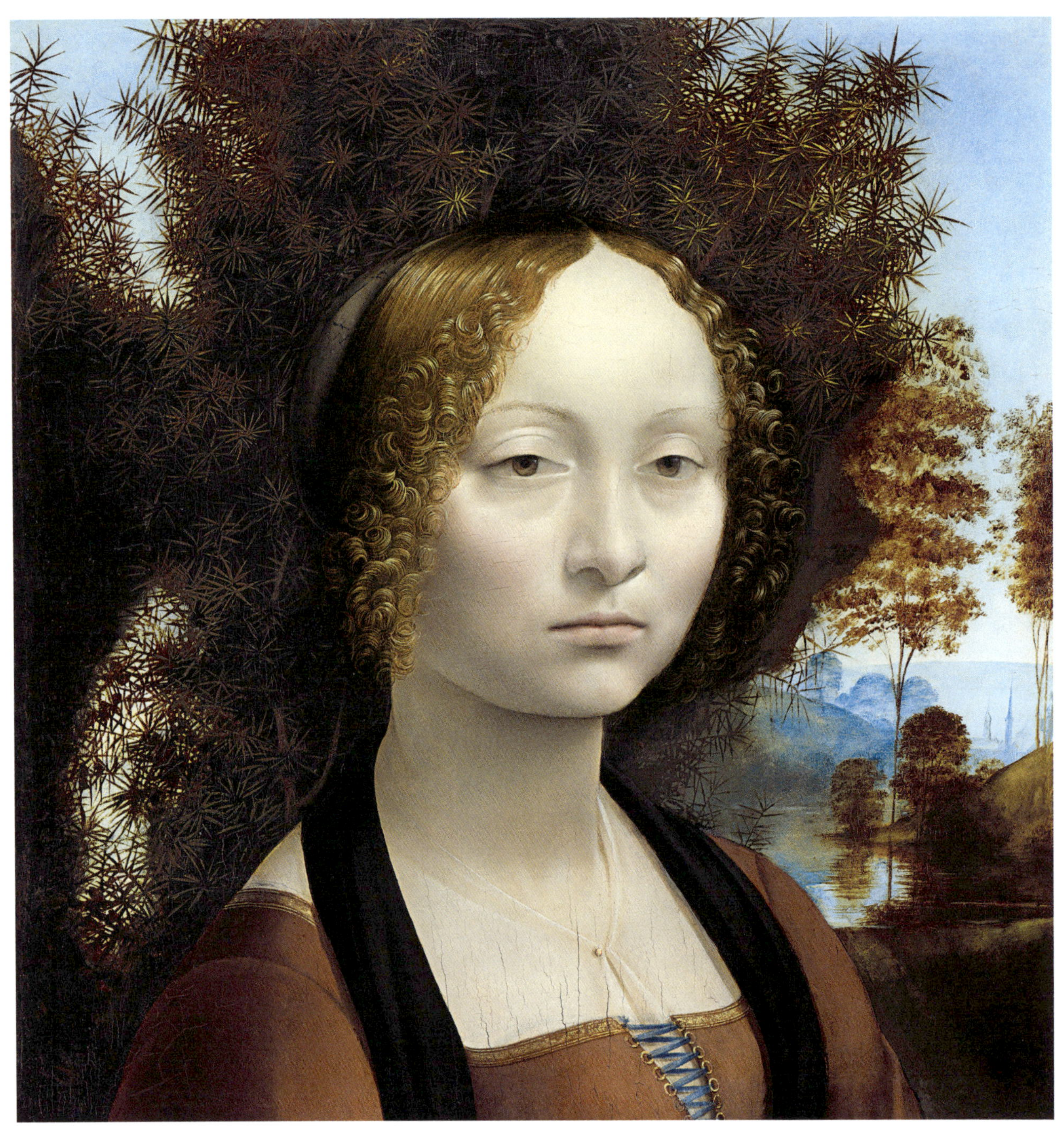

Leonardo da Vinci, *Ginevra de' Benci*, ca. 1474–78, oil on canvas, 38.1 × 37 cm, Washington, D.C., National Gallery of Art, inv. 1967.6.1.a

Leonardo da Vinci's passion for nature and botany became the source of all his inspiration as an artist and his insights as a man of science. For him, nature was a guide and a permanent framework for observing and representing the phenomena and mysteries underlying the living world. The study of plants, flowers and rocks was at the heart of his work. As a painter, he achieved a new degree of perfection in the rendering of landscapes, mountains, rivers and even the rustling of leaves in the trees. His landscape paintings revolutionised the notion of perspective and the use of light and shadow. As a man of science, he studied natural phenomena and uncovered many of their interactions in the fields of botany, geology and hydrology. On nature, he commented: "Everything is there".

In Florence, Leonardo discovered the excitement and splendour of the City of Lilies, Florence's symbol, as is mentioned in the "Song of the Perfumers", which references Chypre birdies and other fragrant products. A cradle of art and architecture, Florence enjoyed a golden age during the rule of Lorenzo de' Medici, known as the Magnificent, who was instrumental in developing the city. This was fertile ground for the art of perfumery, which aroused Leonardo's curiosity. It was in Florence that, at the age of fourteen, he joined Verrocchio's polytechnical workshop as an apprentice. There he learned drawing, painting, sculpture, architecture, goldsmithing and the art of casting, as well as how to grind colours and mineral and vegetable pigments.

Later, in his own workshop, his experiments helped him discover the relations between colours and fragrances: "Note how *aqua vitae* collects in itself all the colours and scents of the flowers. If you want to make azure, put cornflowers in it; and wild poppies for red" (manuscript B, folio 3v). Two original drawings by Leonardo da Vinci, on loan from the Biblioteca Ambrosiana in Milan, are featured in the exhibition, along with botanical books he owned, such as the *Natural History* by Pliny the Elder and Johannes de Cuba's *Ortus Sanitatis*. The exhibition also offers a glimpse into his workshop, filled with the scents of plants, minerals and animals: excipients, vegetable oils, animal fats and *eaux de vie* (distilled spirits) used to make perfumes.

For Leonardo da Vinci, "The five senses are the ministers of the soul". Curious about the sense of smell, Leonardo described the different types of nose in his *Treatise on Painting* (folio 108v). He also wrote several texts describing maceration techniques for jasmine and citrus fruits, and how to remove the smell of walnut oil, which he found "sad". In his workshop, he developed techniques involving maceration and distillation, for which he designed an alembic, the original drawing of which – on special loan from the Biblioteca Ambrosiana in Milan – is on display in the exhibition.

Leonardo da Vinci joined the court of the House of Sforza at the age of thirty, after offering his services to Ludovico il Moro, the all-powerful Duke of Milan. The art of perfuming played a role in defining the social status of the Milanese aristocracy, both male and female, and perfume was as much a luxury item as the clothes, accessories and finery of the great aristocratic families of the time. Cecilia Gallerani's magnificent necklace of fragrant black amber, seen in the painting *Lady with an Ermine* and recreated as if it had been "extracted" from the painting for this exhibition, offers a glimpse of the seductive and beautiful finery of Milan's nobility.

Towards the end of his life, Leonardo da Vinci joined the French court at the invitation of Francis I. In the autumn of 1516, he undertook his final journey and crossed the Alps, taking with him his three masterpieces, the *Mona Lisa*, the *Saint Anne* and the *Saint John the Baptist*, which he continued to work on in his workshops at Clos Lucé. Appointed "First Painter, Engineer and Architect to the King", he was involved in everyday life at court, as organiser of royal festivities, and worked on major town-planning and hydraulic projects for the kingdom until his death at Clos Lucé on 2 May 1519.

France had its own traditions in perfumery, and the court perfumers helped Leonardo expand his sensory world. The king even had his own perfumer, François d'Escobart, from Valencia in Spain. Perfumes also travelled across Europe as diplomatic gifts: in 1516, a Venetian embassy arrived at the court of Francis I laden with sumptuous perfumes. Owing to French military campaigns in Italy, the trends of Italy's renowned perfumers were soon to spread across the country, particularly the trend for perfumed gloves, promoted by Catherine de Médicis, wife of Henri II – the son of Francis I.

What art and science have in common is that they extend the limits of our knowledge and question the world by making the "invisible" visible. Bringing Leonardo da Vinci's work to light means that his artistic and scientific discoveries can be shared with as many people as possible.

The exhibition catalogue, co-published by Éditions Skira and the Château du Clos Lucé, brings together important and previously unpublished contributions from numerous international specialists in the work of Leonardo da Vinci. The Château du Clos Lucé extends its heartfelt thanks to the exhibition curators, Carlo Vecce and Pascal Brioist, and to all the authors whose research continues to advance knowledge of Leonardo da Vinci and his work:

Carlo Vecce, Professor of Italian Literature at the University of Naples "L'Orientale";
Pascal Brioist, Professor of Modern History at the University of Tours and member of the Centre for Advanced Renaissance Studies (CESR);
Soline Anthore-Baptiste, Doctor of Modern History at Grenoble-Alpes University and Ca' Foscari University in Venice;
Nicolas Baptiste-Anthore, Doctor in Medieval History at the University of Savoie-Mont-Blanc;
Andrea Bernardoni, Professor in the History of Science and Technology at the University of L'Aquila, and consultant at the Museo Galileo in Florence;
Marjolijn Bol, Associate Professor of Art History at the University of Utrecht;
Marie-Élisabeth Boutroue, CNRS research fellow at the Centre for Advanced Renaissance Studies (CESR);
Océane Fontaine Cioffi, doctoral student in History at the University of Tours and member of the Centre for Advanced Renaissance Studies (CESR);
Anna Messinis, independent researcher and author of the book *The History of Perfume in Venice* (2017);
Alexander Neuwahl, founder of the interdisciplinary research group Artes Mechanicae (Florence), collaborator at the Museo Leonardiano in Vinci, expert in 3D reconstructions;

Nathalie Oddy, post-doctoral researcher in the History of Philosophy at Oxford University;
Élodie Pierrard, doctoral student in History at the University of Tours and member of the Centre for Advanced Renaissance Studies (CESR);
Jesse Rodin, Associate Professor of Music at Stanford University;
Özge Samancı, lecturer at the Department of Gastronomy and Culinary Arts at Özyeğin University, Istanbul;
Lorenzo Tunesi, doctoral student in Musicology at Stanford University;
Paola Venturelli, scientific director of the Fondazione Gianmaria Buccellati in Milan and curator of the Museo del Gioiello in Vicenza.

Clos Lucé would also like to thank the French and Italian museums that have loaned works:

Bergamo, Accademia Carrara;
Florence, Gallerie degli Uffizi;
Florence, Biblioteca Nazionale Centrale;
Florence, Musei del Bargello;
Florence, Museo Stefano Bardini;
Milan, Veneranda Biblioteca Ambrosiana – Pinacoteca;
Milan, Galleria Moshe Tabibnia;
Milan, Pinacoteca del Castello Sforzesco;
Pavia, Musei Civici del Castello Visconteo;
Poggio a Caiano, Villa Medicea, Museo della Natura Morta;
Prato, Museo del Tessuto;
Pugnano, Fondazione Cerratelli;
Rome, Galleria Borghese;
Turin, Palazzo Madama – Museo Civico d'Arte Antica;
Vigevano, Museo Internazionale della Calzatura.

Aujac, château du Cheylard d'Aujac;
Blois, paroisse de la cathédrale Saint-Louis;
Blois, musée diocésain d'Art religieux;
Écouen, musée national de la Renaissance – château d'Écouen;
Grasse, musée international de la Parfumerie;
Le Mans, archives départementales de la Sarthe;
Paris, Archives nationales de France;
Paris, bibliothèque Sainte-Geneviève;
Paris, musée de Cluny – musée national du Moyen Âge;
Romorantin-Lanthenay, centre de documentation du musée de Sologne;
Souvigny, commune de Souvigny;
Strasbourg, bibliothèque nationale et universitaire;
Tours, bibliothèque municipale;
Tours, Centre d'études supérieures de la Renaissance.

This exhibition has been made possible by the financial support of the Centre-Val de Loire region, for whose generosity and trust the Château du Clos Lucé is grateful.

Château du Clos Lucé would like to thank Givaudan, the world leader in the creation of fragrances and flavours, and its staff, who have contributed through their financial sponsorship and expertise to the olfactory interpretation of Renaissance fragrances and to the production of this exhibition: Gilles Andrier, its CEO; Sophie Cauchi, Head of External Communications; and Eugénie Briot, "History & Transmission" Project Manager.

Lastly, the Château du Clos Lucé would like to thank the members of its own team, who have worked with enthusiasm, professionalism and dedication to bring this wonderful cultural project to fruition, in particular Michaël Petitjean, General Secretary; Diane Junqua, Director of Communications and Sponsorship; Sandra Chupin, Exhibition Coordinator, assisted by Sarah Torre; Nina Germain, Communications Officer; Eleonora Pavesi, Translator and Italian Coordinator; Jordane Mourgues, Executive Assistant; Stéphane Darras, Head of the Technical Department, and his entire team; and Agence NC represented by Nathalie Crinière, interior architect and exhibition designer, and Studio Magique, in charge of olfactory systems, represented by Mazen Nasri.

This exhibition testifies to the richness and vitality of European relations and illustrates our ability to share and spread a common culture inherited from the humanism of the Renaissance.

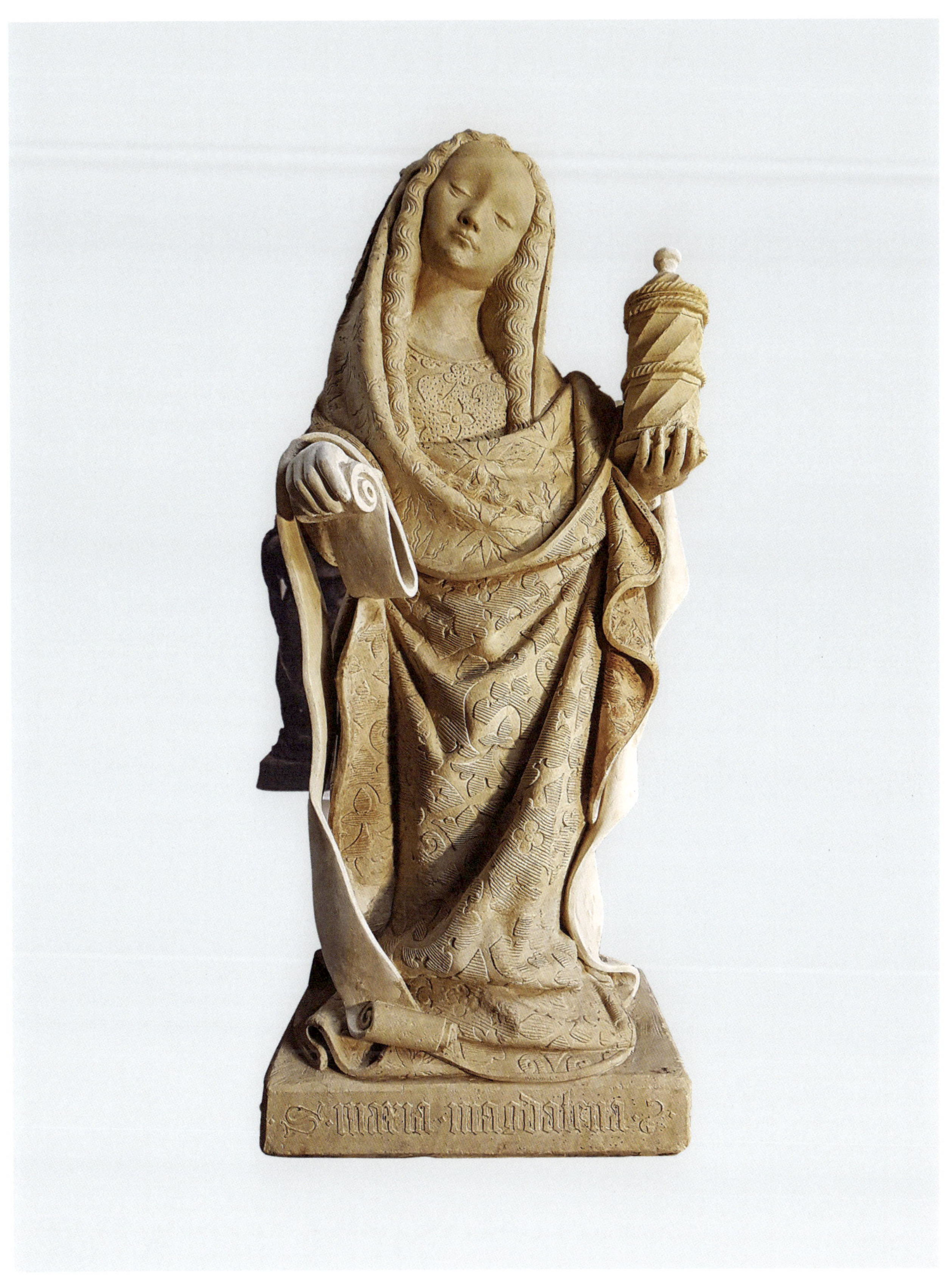

St Mary Magdalene, late 15th c., carved stone with traces of polychromy, 61 × 28 cm, commune de Souvigny. Work classified as a historical monument on 7 April 1902

A WORD FROM THE CENTRE-VAL DE LOIRE REGION

FRANÇOIS BONNEAU, PRESIDENT OF THE CENTRE-VAL DE LOIRE REGION

The Centre-Val de Loire region created the "Nouvelles Renaissances" (New Renaissances) programme to promote an innovative cultural dynamic, highlight the energy of the Centre-Val de Loire and connect our present with the region's universal history.

There could be no finer embodiment of this desire than this new exhibition, which invites visitors on a journey through the fragrances and intertwined histories of two remarkable individuals: Leonardo da Vinci and his mother, Caterina.

At the heart of the exhibition is Leonardo da Vinci's fascination with perfume, an often overlooked aspect of his multi-faceted genius. Through his writings and scientific research, we discover a man who was driven by an indefatigable curiosity to explore the mysteries of the sense of smell and the secrets of perfume-making. His sketches of alembics, his perfume recipes, everything testifies to his commitment to this emerging science, whose uses were not merely aesthetic.

But behind every great man there is often a great woman, in this case Caterina, Leonardo's mother. Originally from the Orient, having been freed from slavery, she left an indelible mark on the life and work of her son. This exhibition offers a fascinating insight into the influence of this mother figure, connecting us in a new and personal way to the almost legendary figure of Leonardo.

In a year marked by the exploration of new horizons, the exhibition at Château du Clos Lucé offers an inspiring reminder of the richness and diversity of our cultural heritage, while encouraging us to embrace curiosity and explore the unseen worlds around us. As such, I welcome an exhibition that appeals to the sense of smell and offers a different way of discovering the courts of the Renaissance.

A WORD FROM GIVAUDAN

Gilles Andrier, CEO

For more than 250 years, Givaudan has been at the heart of the major innovations in perfumery. Whether it be the extraction of natural materials or the synthesis of new substances for perfumers, Givaudan has initiated and supported the industry's leading breakthroughs to provide perfumers with the finest raw materials.

More than 500 years ago, perfume making, amongst many other subjects, was also of interest to Leonardo da Vinci. He was fascinated by botany and tried to capture the scent of flowers through maceration and distillation at a time when the latter was still in its early days. At the dawn of the first great technical revolution in perfumery – the production of essential oils by distillation – he devised new methods, stimulated by his insatiable curiosity.

For over 100 years, in addition to its role as a supplier of raw materials for the perfume industry, Givaudan has developed primarily into a creator of its own fragrances, relying on the expertise of its 120 perfumers to produce original creations that delight millions of people every day, bringing them joy and confidence, or transporting them on olfactory journeys.

The emotional dimension of perfume was not unfamiliar to Leonardo. His whole life was infused with powerful fragrances, from the orange blossom and jasmine of Tuscany in his youth to the invigorating scents of his residence at Clos Lucé, not forgetting the heady perfumes of Venice, Florence, and the courts of the House of Sforza in Milan and of Francis I in the Loire Valley. Perhaps also, deep within himself, he was influenced by the scents of the Orient, from where his mother Caterina originated.

It is the intellectual path of the engineer and the aesthetic journey of the artist that the exhibition "Leonardo da Vinci and Perfumes in the Renaissance" aims to retrace in olfactory terms, like an intimate journey that gathers together the different threads of the genius of this universal man.

Givaudan is delighted to support Clos Lucé in this endeavour. Perfumes speak to the mind and the heart, as do the works of Leonardo.

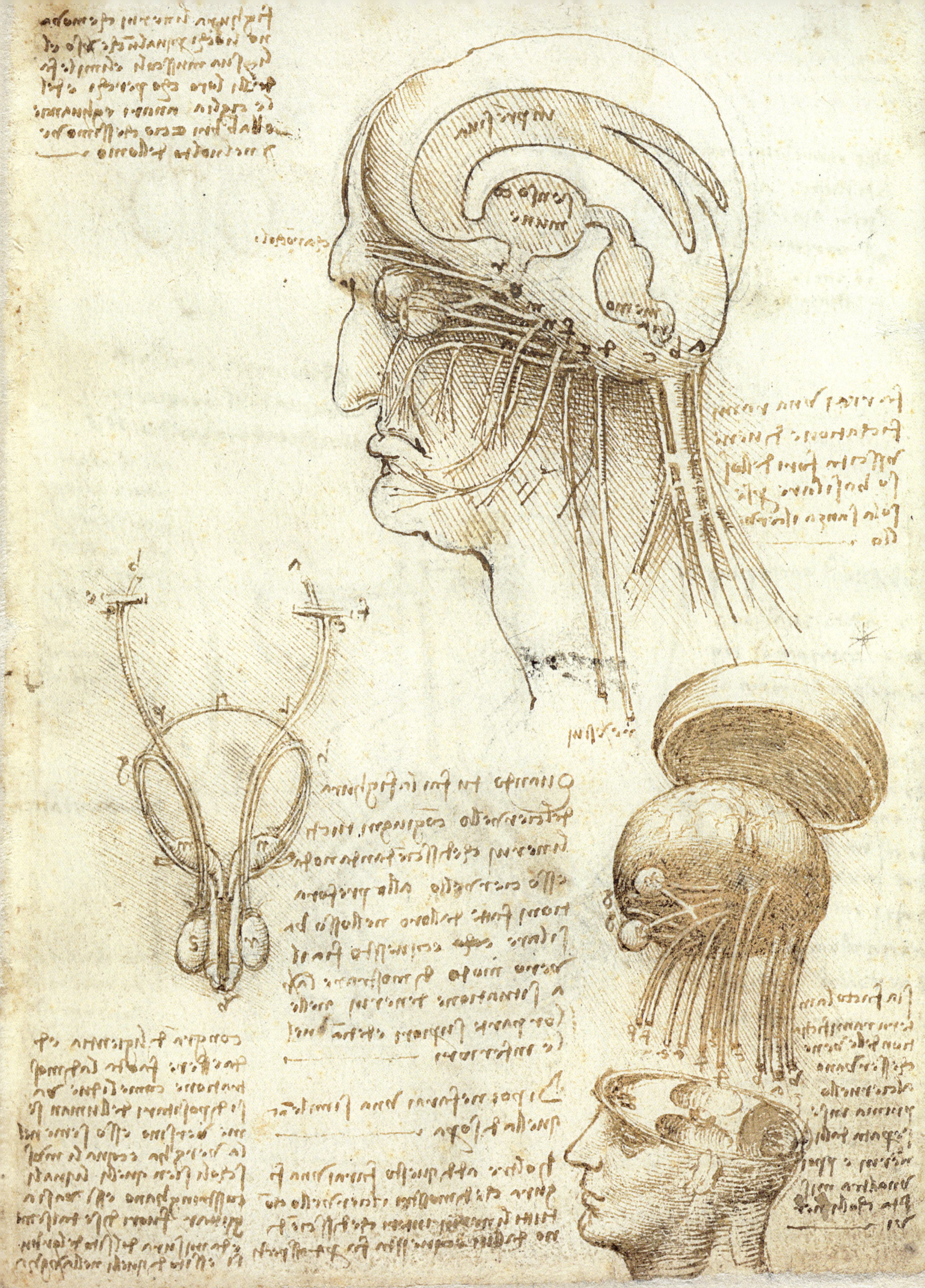

INTRODUCTION

Carlo Vecce and Pascal Brioist

Some scents are cool as children's flesh is cool,
Sweet as are oboes, green as meadowlands,
And others rich, corrupt, triumphant, full,
Expanding as infinity expands:
Benzoin or musk or amber that incenses,
Hymning the ecstasy of soul and senses.
Charles Baudelaire, *Correspondances*

Epigraphs in an indecipherable language, half their
Letters rubbed away by the sand-laden wind...
Italo Calvino, *The Name, the Nose*

Fragrances and memory

What was Leonardo seeking in a fragrance? What did he feel when he closed his eyes and listened to the silent music of his earliest memories?

Before answering, we need to understand that for him, the sense of smell, like the other senses, was a fundamental instrument in the relationship between man and the world. A complex relationship, between the internal and external, between darkness and light, with its many issues that may never be resolved. As a solitary child in the countryside, he began to explore the depths of his soul at a very early age, but also, at the same time, to open his eyes to the immensity of creation, to the beauty and variety of forms in nature. In this journey of discovery of the world, it is the eye that is our noblest sense, the "window of the soul", but full knowledge of the reality that surrounds us is only possible with the help of all the other senses, the "servants of the soul", guided by the common sense that is their "captain" (Windsor, RL 19019r). Without their support, our soul would remain locked in a dark prison, without knowledge (science) of external reality.

It is a poetic vision, of course, but it is also based on a specific philosophical doctrine, that of Aristotle's *De Anima*, conveyed to Leonardo through one of the books in his library, *Philosophia Pauperum*, attributed to Albertus Magnus. It is here that Leonardo learned Avicenna's distinction

LEFT
Fig. 1. Leonardo da Vinci *Manuscript Sheet With Anatomical Drawings and Notes*, 1506–08, pen and two different coloured inks, shades of brown 19.3 × 14.1 cm, Klassik Stiftung Weimar, Bestand Museen, KK 6287

between the "vegetative soul", the "perceptive soul" and the "rational soul", signifying respectively: common sense or imagination; the capacity to conceive and perceive; and, lastly, memory.

While sight and hearing are considered the fundamental senses for our apprehension of reality, the sense of smell seems less necessary:

> Smell, of all the senses, is the least necessary: although it contributes to the health of an animal, as the animal senses a corruption of the air, the acuity is lost. This corruption, as the doctor says, is more harmful to the animal than spoiled food. Similarly, the sense of smell contributes to knowledge by chance or circumstance, as scents, when smelt, comfort the brain and do much to help us reason better. (Giorgio Arrivabene, *Philosophia Pauperum*, Venice, 1496, folio e3r: part V, chap. 5)

Further on, in the chapter *De Obiecto Olfatus*, Leonardo read that smell is a kind of smoke or vapour, emitted by an odorous substance through the effect of heat or following a process of corruption, which is diffused by the medium of air and sensed by two nerves, the "*carunculae*", fleshy excrescences which, in anatomical dissection, seem to protrude from the frontal sinuses, similar to the teats of udders:

> The object one smells in a perfume is the odour in a medium called "smoke" or "vapour", which heat transforms into an odoriferous substance. The same applies when heat accelerates the corruption of a scented object, an apple for example, as the most delicate humours in a preserved object are attracted by odours. The medium of odour is air, but the organs that convey it are two nerves that come down from the brain, similar to two nipples through which the odorous spirit that produces the sensation arrives. (*Philosophia Pauperum*, folio e4r: part V, chap. 7)

A more detailed description can be found in *Anatomy*, by Mondino de' Luzzi, translated into the vernacular by Sebastiano Manilio and published in the *Fasciculo de Medicina*, another book that Leonardo owned and read: "two caruncles similar to the nipples of the breasts, which in substance are close to the substance of the brain".

At the beginning of his anatomical studies in Milan, around 1489–90, Leonardo took up Avicenna's taxonomy, simplified it into a more manageable tripartite scheme (common sense, the *imprensiva*, or the ability to apprehend, and "memory"), and then translated this into drawings (Windsor, RL 12602r, 12603r, 12626r, 12627r, 19127r, 12602r). A few years later, at the time of his Florentine dissections at the Santa Maria Nuova hospital, in 1507–1508, he produced his famous drawing of the anatomy of the head: inside the cranium, we can see the location of the faculty for processing sensory information, and also of the common sense and memory, as well as a detailed, labelled representation of the optic and olfactory nerves in the branches descending from the brain. The *caroncoli* represent the olfactory nerves [fig. 1]. In another drawing, the relationship between the optic and olfactory nerves is defined: "The nerves are the optic nerves, which are situated beneath the nerves called 'caruncules', but the optic nerves serve the visual power; the caruncules the olfactory power." (Windsor, RL 19052r) [fig. 2]

In practice, Leonardo discovered that the sensations produced by the sense of smell, perfumes and odours all follow the same path as other sensations, from the exterior to the interior, when, after initial contact with the sensory organ, they are transmitted to be imprinted, processed by the common sense, and finally entrusted to memory: "From thence, being judged, they are transmitted

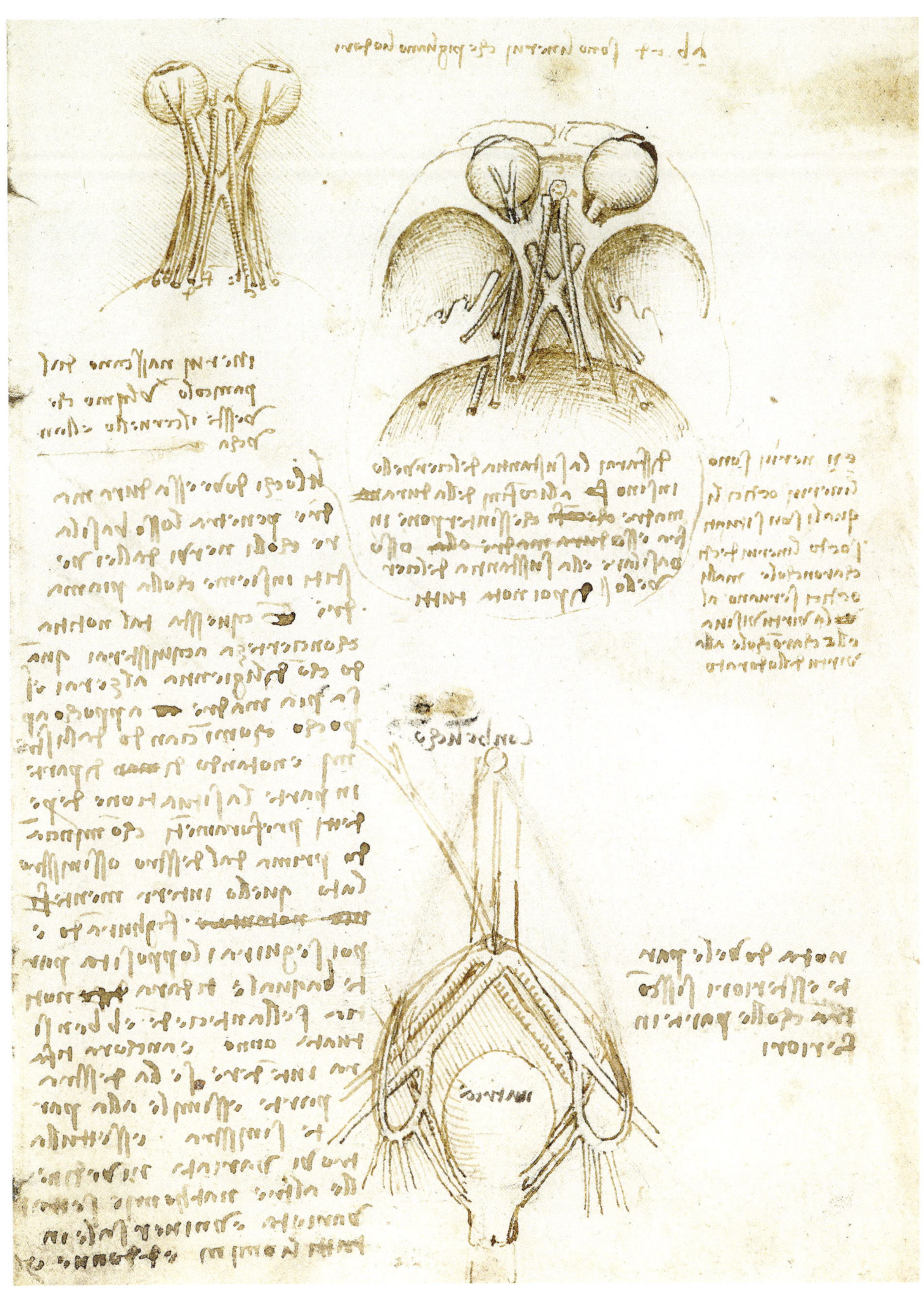

Fig. 2. Leonardo da Vinci, *The Cranial Nerves*, ca. 1508, pen and ink over traces of black chalk, with scratching out, 19 × 13.6 cm
Windsor, Royal Collection Trust, RL 19052

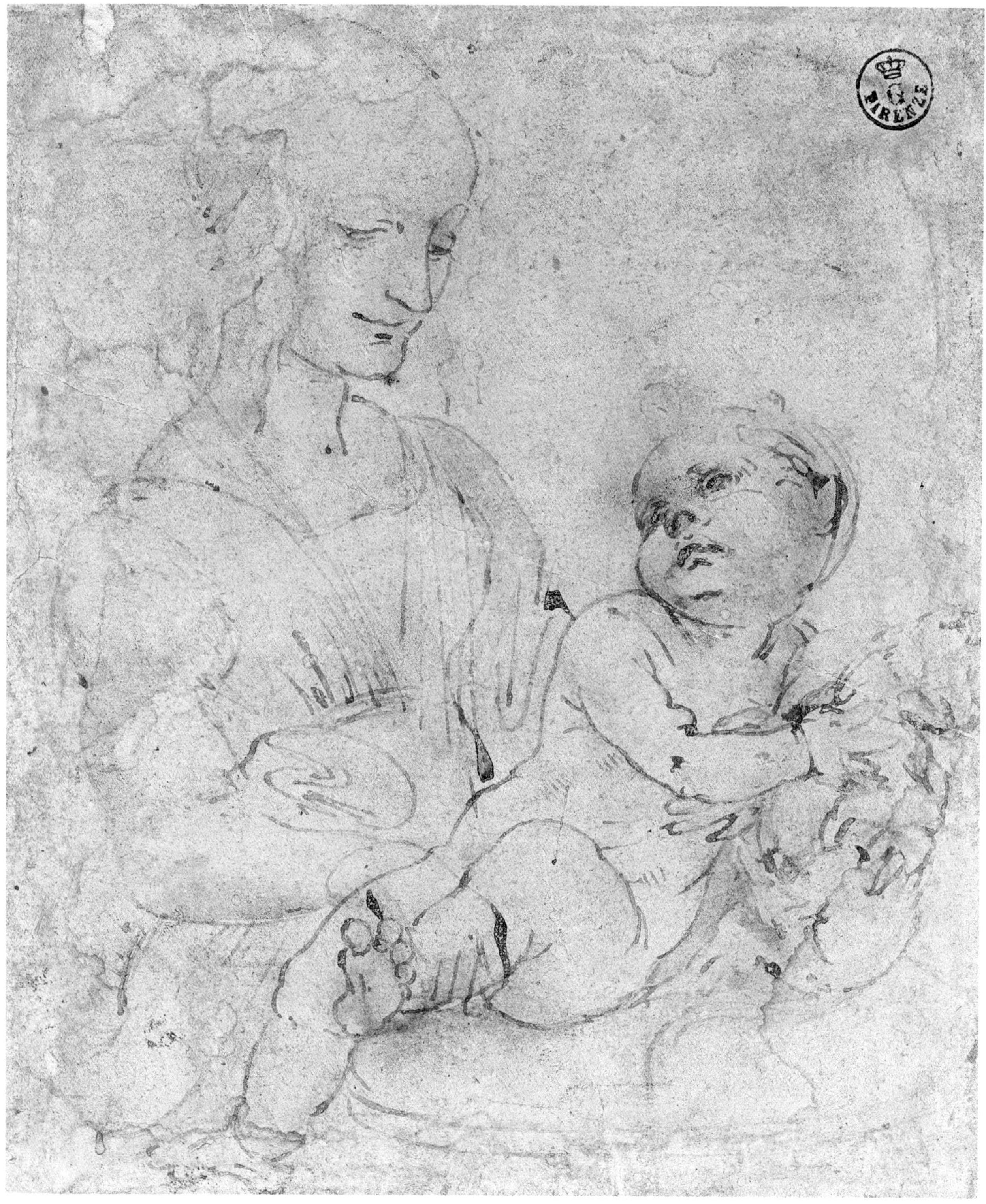

Fig. 3. Leonardo da Vinci, *Virgin and Child with Cat*, 15th–16th c., drawing, azure prepared paper, pen and ink, brush and diluted ink Florence, Gabinetto dei Disegni e delle Stampe, Galleria degli Uffizi

to memory, in which according to their power they are retained more or less distinctly." (*Codex Atlanticus*, folio 45r)

The memory chamber, on the other hand, closed and dark, is perceived by Leonardo as a prison in which sensations are like wild animals pursued and captured by hunting dogs (*Codex Atlanticus*, folio 729r). It is a prison of images, sounds, tastes, and even smells and perfumes, which can suddenly resurface, even years later, when evoked by a similar smell or taste. An involuntary memory, like that evoked by Proust's famous "madeleine".

This is probably the deep memory of Leonardo's childhood [fig. 3]. Jumbled recollections of gestures, words, sounds, glances and smiles. And, above all, smells, an "infinite mixture of smells" (Windsor, RL 19045v). These are the smells of the countryside where da Vinci and his mother, Caterina, lived: the smell of her body, of her sweat, of the milk congealed around her nipple. The old farmhouse with its fireplace, the burning wood, the hens and pigs in the barnyard, the hay and manure, the flowers of the fields in spring, the jasmine, juniper and elder trees, the freshly cut wheat and dry grass in summer, the rain absorbed by the parched earth, the strong, intense smells of the oil mill and wine press. In short, the smells of life, of real life, which Leonardo would never find again during the long journey that saw him move from Florence to Milan, to the court of the Sforza family; then to Amboise in France, to the court of Francis I.

After Vinci, his birthplace, the smells the boy discovered in Florence were those of Florence's paper-making district, the world of his father Piero, a notary: the smells of booksellers' workshops, of macerated rag paper, still slightly damp, brought in from paper mills in the countryside or from Val d'Elsa, the metallic smell of ink and lead from the first printing works, wax and parchment; then, in Verrocchio's studio, the "sad smells" of the studio of the painter and creator of new formulations of varnishes, oils and colours. These included walnut oil, linseed oil, turpentine, rabbit-skin glue, resins, waxes and fats, as well as "acqua ardente", or alcohol. At the court in Milan, Leonardo was intoxicated by the sophisticated and intense perfumes of the princesses and ladies of the aristocracy, their dresses, veils, gloves and perfumed jewellery, such as Cecilia Gallerani's necklace of spherical black amber beads, which he included in *Lady with an Ermine*, or the enchanting *oiselets de Chypre* (Chypre birdies). In contrast, in the hospitals where he performed dissections – Santa Maria Nuova in Florence, the Ospedale Maggiore and Santa Caterina in Milan – Leonardo experienced the "fetid stench" of death and putrefaction (*Codex I*, folio 67r), the smell of infected blood, and of excrement in the intestines (Windsor, RL 19020r, 19051v, 19053v).

Returning to Florence in the early 16th century, Leonardo resumed work on his *Treatise on Painting* with the aim of unifying all forms of knowledge and communication. In one of his most interesting texts, dating from around 1504, he declared that he wanted to base his work on the "mathematical sciences", i.e. "those which, by means of the senses, represent the highest degree of certainty": arithmetic and geometry, which apply respectively to continuous and discontinuous magnitudes, and which are the basis of the perspective seen by the eye, and therefore of painting. After painting comes music, perceived through the sense of hearing, which sends to the common sense "a great variety of consonant sounds from different instruments"; then comes the sense of smell, considered capable, surprisingly, of creating "harmony" through the concord of different perfumes, as if they were musical chords in an instrumental concert or a polyphonic musical composition, or proportional relationships and tonal harmonies in a pictorial composition:

Next comes the sense of smell, which, with its different odours, delights the common sense. Even if these smells give rise to a *refraganza*, a concord similar to music, it is however not within man's power to explain this. (*Codex Madrid II*, folios 67r, 66v, 62r.bis)

Although Leonardo concluded that it is impossible to derive clear knowledge of reality from smell, and that it is therefore impossible to "make a science of it", his intuition is nonetheless extraordinary. In Italian literature, the word *concento* ("harmony"), applied mainly to music, defines the harmony that results from the concordant sound of voices and instruments. For Marsilio Ficino, the very movement of the cosmos – the harmony of the celestial spheres – was a *concento*. Leonardo used this term in some of the most beautiful texts of the *Paragone delle Arti*, the first part of his *Treatise on Painting*: "the proportionality called 'harmony', which delights the sense with sweet concord, no differently than the proportionality made by different musical notes to the sense of hearing" (*Treatise on Painting*, chapters 21 and 23).

Perfume is indeed like a sound, spreading through the air with a defined, almost sensual movement (*Codex Atlanticus*, folio 543v). The skilful combination of essences is therefore capable of creating a kind of music. It is music (of sounds and scents) that acts at the deepest level of bodily communication, in the dark prison of memory, and summons the sensory ghosts locked therein.

So what was Leonardo looking for in a perfume?

Perhaps the lost scent of his mother's body.

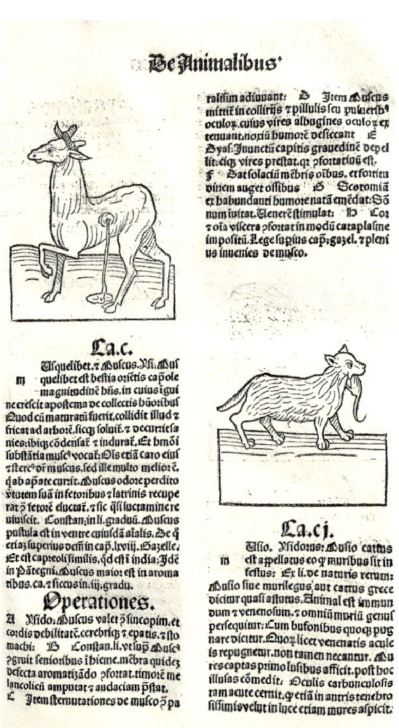

De Animalibus

Ca.c.

Operationes.

Ca.cj.

Fig. 4. Johannes de Cuba (presumed author)
Ortus sanitatis, 1491, printed text, 32 × 22.7 cm
Strasbourg, bibliothèque nationale et universitaire, réserve Joffre K.2.057, page E ii r

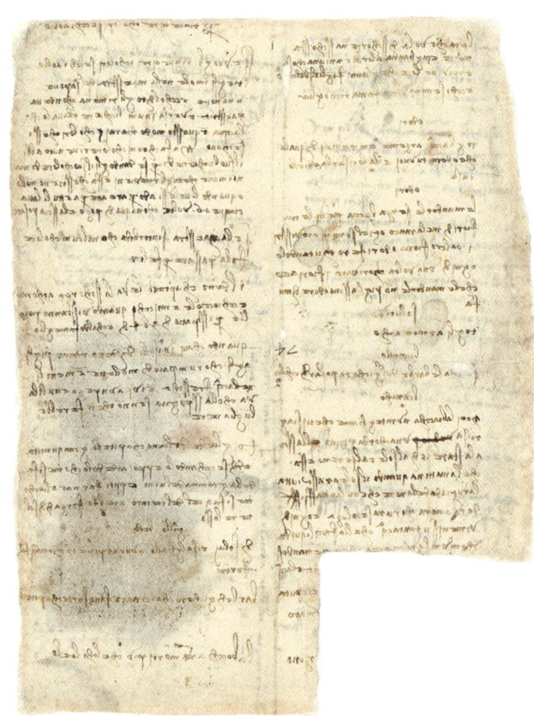

Fig. 5. Leonardo da Vinci, *Codice Atlantico* (*Codex Atlanticus*), f. 195v
"Ricetta per la composizione di colori; nota per la composizione di essenze; sentenza morale", ca. 1480
Milan, Veneranda Biblioteca Ambrosiana – Pinacoteca

In Leonardo's research into the five senses, the world of perfume occupies a special place, one that has remained virtually unknown until now. His manuscripts, however, reveal a constant interest in the olfactory realm. His interest was also linguistic, as demonstrated by the words recorded in the *Codex Trivulzianus: perfumare, odorifera / aulente, refragantia, macierato / lacierato, putride / puzolente / putrefatto, fetulente / fetore / fetido* (folios 5r, 13v, 17v, 23r, 43r-v, 44v, 46v). In practice, Leonardo wondered how to talk about substances as intangible and elusive as perfumes, and which words to use to describe them.

He studied in depth the properties of substances of animal, vegetable and mineral origin, also using the books in his library: Marbode of Rennes's *De Lapidibus*; the *Herbarium Apulei*; the bestiary in *Fiore di virtù*; Pliny the Elder; and Cecco d'Ascoli. One of his most beautiful books was the large folio volume of the *Ortus Sanitatis*, which was printed in Strasbourg in 1497 with a magnificent set of illustrations: it tells the extraordinary story of the origin of musk, a secretion from the glands of the musk deer native to Tibet and Central Asia [fig. 4].

The scent of musk is so intense that it can spread through the air over very long distances. In his treatise on the movement of sounds, odours and flavours, Leonardo recalls the power of this fragrance: "What will they say of musk, which holds large swathes of the atmosphere charged with its scent and, were it to be carried through air over a thousand miles, would permeate a thousand miles with the heavy air of its scent, without any diminution of itself?" (*Codex Atlanticus*, folio 729v; *Codex A*, folio 0r).

In his manuscripts, Leonardo often included recipes for perfumes, which are generally delicate, subtle and not too intense, based on plant essences such as orange blossom, jasmine and elderflower, rose water, juniper and cypress (*Codex Atlanticus*, folios 195v, 807r; *Codex B*, folio 3v; *Codex Forster I*, folio 43r).

These recipes include techniques already in use in Venice: for making almond essential oil and for distillation. In the *Codex Atlanticus* (folio 195v), for example, Leonardo makes the following recommendation:

> Add peeled almonds together with the flowers of bitter orange, jasmine, privet or other fragrant flowers and change the water each time you have to change the flowers, so that the almonds do not take on a musty smell. Solvents. Remove the ammonia. [fig. 5]

This is a fairly primitive method, not quite the same as enfleurage, a process that uses the ability of fats to capture odours through maceration. Known since antiquity, it involves placing flowers, jasmine for example, in animal fat. For three months, the fat captures the floral scents, then the resulting ointment is decanted into alcohol to dissolve the fragrant essence. Here, however, instead of animal fat, the Tuscan uses a decoction made from peeled almonds. This method is similar to later recipes by the Venetian Fioravanti. In 1564, in his *Dello Specchio di Scientia Universale*, he explains how clove, nutmeg, cinnamon, mace and sesame oils are obtained by mixing these substances with sweet almonds crushed with a pestle and then left to stand for several days.

The Secrets of Alexis of Piedmont, dating from 1557, gives details on the use of almonds in a recipe for clove oil:

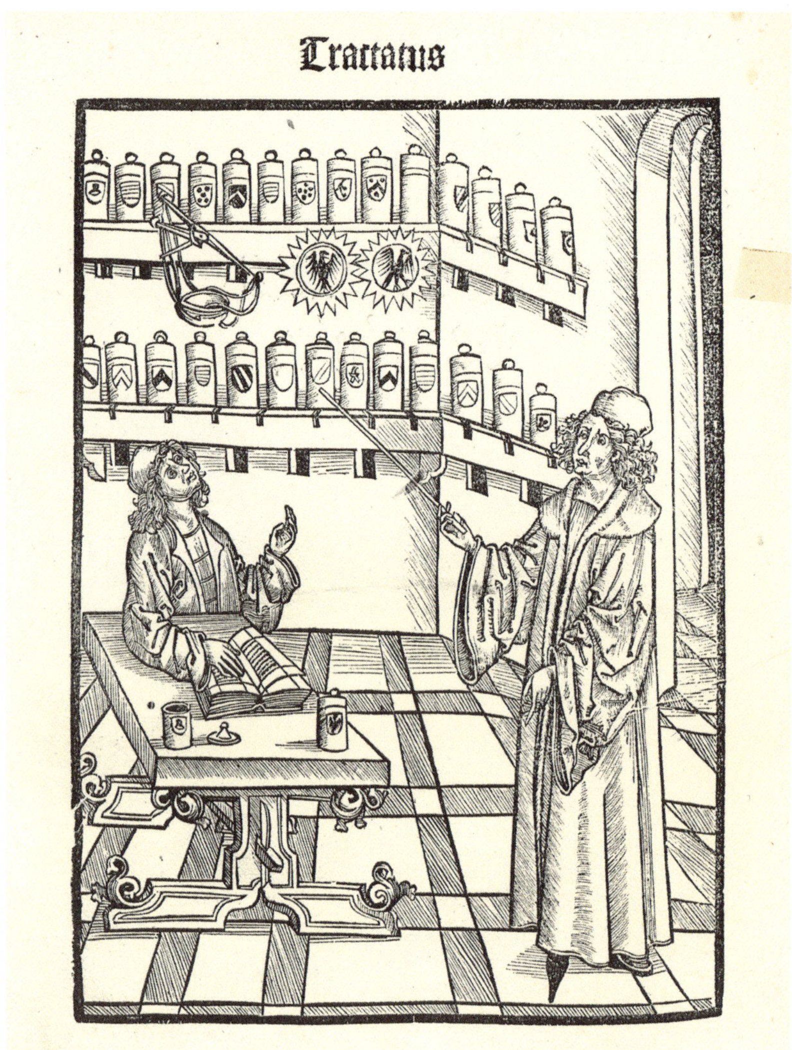

Fig. 6. Johann Prüss, *Ortus Sanitatis*, f. 325v, ca. 1497, Munich, Bayerische Staatsbibliothek

> Oile of Cloves very noble. – Take almonds mundified, and made cleane with a knife, and broken into pieces, steepe or temper them in rosewater, then dress them in this maner. Take cloves stamped, and temper or laie them in rosewater, and cover the vessell viligentlie, leaving them so, until the water have taken the vertue of the cloves: put also the almondes in the saide water. And after you have taken them out, and dried them in the sunne, laie them in the water againe to swell: and afterward let them drie well as before, continuing this five or six times. Then put them in a presse, and presse out the oyle, which you shall keepe in a cleane vessell well stopped. In this maner may you make oile of muske, of amber, of bengewine [benzoin]...

The almonds are regularly removed from the rose water, where they have taken on the scent of cloves. Then, by grinding them, the desired essential oil is obtained. We can see that Leonardo must have experimented with this recipe when he mentions that the almonds can take on a musty smell.

We should compare what Leonardo says about another technique, not mentioned here, that of hot enfleurage, which spread from Constantinople and Venice from the 15th century onwards.

With this technique, flowers and aromatic plants could be infused or macerated in vegetable fats (olive oil, almond oil) that had been heated in pots or warmed in the sun.

In manuscript B, folio 3v, Leonardo mentions the possibility of putting flowers in alcohol, which produces a colouring effect while preserving the fragrance: "Note how *aqua vitae* collects in itself all the colours and scents of the flowers. If you want to make azure, put cornflowers in it; and wild poppies for red."

Indeed, Leonardo also explored the more complex techniques of the art of perfumery stemming from the great Arab tradition, which involve the distillation of essences using ovens and alembics: a process of transforming substances that brought the perfumer's and apothecary's workshops closer to that of the alchemist [fig. 6]. Numerous manuscript texts and drawings bear witness to this interest (*Codex Arundel*, folios 145v and 170r; *Codex Atlanticus*, folios 912r, 1114a-b.r, 216r, 989r; *Codex F*, folios 73v and 96r; *Codex Leicester*, folio 3v). This curiosity goes back to his Florentine apprenticeship: the young Leonardo had attended a centre of excellence for glasswork, the convent of San Giusto dei Gesuati, which also specialised in the preparation of the pigments and colours that he used in *The Adoration of the Magi* and the *Saint Jerome*.

In truth, he used these techniques more for the distillation of oils and paints than for the composition of perfumes. In the *Codex Forster* I, folio 44v, there is a specific reference to distillation: "Remove the yellow surface covering the orange and distil it in an alembic until the extract may be said to be perfect".

The recipe, which is very brief, does not indicate which solvent should be used in the alembic to preserve the scent. Is it water, oil or spirit? The *Codex Atlanticus* suggests that it is most likely to have been spirit. But what kind of alembic was used? We have drawings of distillation apparatus made by Leonardo in Florence in the 1480s (*Codex Arundel*, folio 145v; *Codex Atlanticus*, folios 912r and 1114 a-b.r). We understand that the heated product (the solvent as well as the flowers or bark) is transformed into vapour and condensed again, passing into a liquid state in the spout of the device, allowing the essential oil to be recovered in the collector on the surface of a hydrosol. Renaissance recipes are always difficult to interpret, given the tacit knowledge hidden within them.

Another perfume used in Florence appears in a drawing in the *Codex Atlanticus*, folio 190v [fig. 7], namely the *oiselet de Chypre* (Chypre birdie), a kind of perfumed resin moulded into the shape of a bird, which was burnt in a cage that served as a censer. The inspiration for Leonardo's design came from the *Fior di Virtù Historiale*, printed by Bartolomeo di Libri [fig. 8]. In it, the caged bird symbolised the virtues of love, capable of healing the sick with just a glance. Leonardo's drawing differs slightly from the illustration in the *Fior di Virtù*: the spherical cage can be placed on a piece of furniture, but is also shown attached to an interlaced belt, suggesting it might be used as an accessory. Venetian treatises of the 16th century, such as Rosetti's *Notandissimi Secreti de l'Arte Profumatoria* and Isabella Cortese's *Secreti* (1561), give recipes for Chypre birdies (see also the recipe on page 177).

What products were used to make perfumes during the Renaissance? There are many details open to interpretation here. Understanding perfume recipe collections from the Renaissance is a difficult task, requiring a mastery of philology and a sound knowledge of botany. We should start by noting that the substances used were of animal, plant and mineral origin. Among the

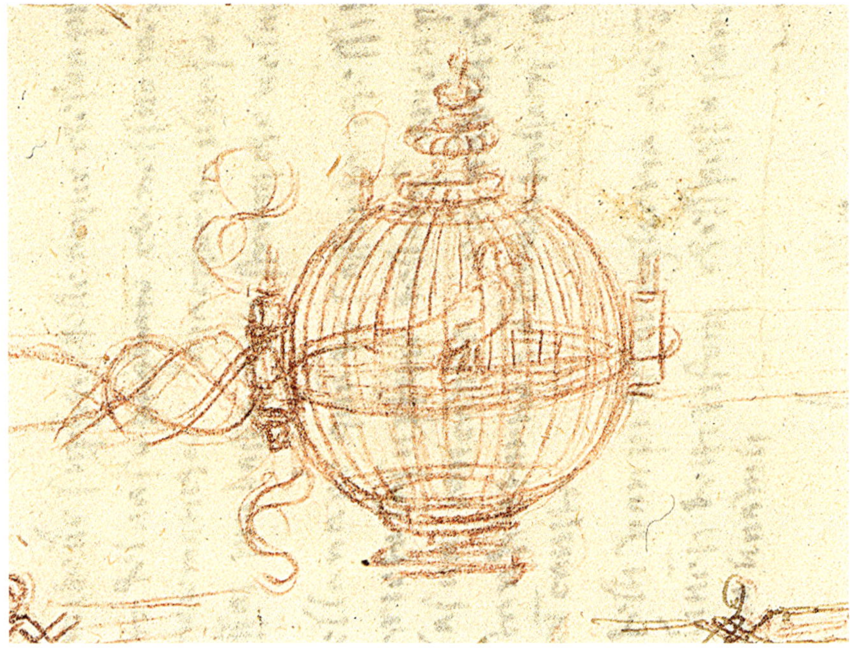

Fig. 7. Leonardo da Vinci, *Codice Atlantico* (*Codex Atlanticus*) , f. 190v, "Motto e motivi decorativi", 1508–10
Milan, Veneranda Biblioteca Ambrosiana – Pinacoteca

substances of animal origin were musk, well known to Leonardo, a product derived from the glands of Siberian or Tibetan musk deer; civet, obtained by curettage from a carnivorous mammal closely related to the cat, and native to Abyssinia; and ambergris (or *ambracan)*, a kind of renal calculus excreted by sperm whales. In the 15th century, these products, known since antiquity, were exported to Europe from Alexandria, Aleppo, Constantinople and Damascus.

Plant substances were much more numerous. *Storax calamita*, for example, which was used to make Chypre birdies, is a shiny resinous substance. It is the sap of a tree which, when thrown into the fire, produces an odour similar to benzoin, and is found in Greece, Asia Minor and Syria. Mastic is a resin native to the island of Chios, while tragacanth is a viscous liquid that hardens into resin and was imported from Greece, Crete, Cyprus and Asia Minor. Labdanum is a gum obtained from the leaves of the cistus, a Middle Eastern or Mediterranean flower. Lemon balm and hyssop also come from the shores of the Mediterranean. Myrrh is the resin of a thorny plant from the Arabian Peninsula, as is frankincense. Camphor is a substance obtained from the leaves of Asian trees. Aloeswood is native to China, India and the Arabian Peninsula. Sandalwood (white, red or yellow) comes from India.

Mineral substances used in perfumery are rarer: the only example is alum, used in the manufacture of ointments and tinctures, but also in perfumes such as orange blossom oil [fig. 9]. Alum was produced in Europe, particularly in Italy, and was found on board Genoese and Venetian galleys.

The manufacture of perfumes involved long-distance trade, and it is not easy to reconstruct a map detailing the trade in the products needed to make perfumes in the 15th and 16th centuries. Modern historical sources, which can be cross-referenced with the writings of Galen or Pliny in antiquity, include treatises such as Mattioli's, which specify the origins of particular plants, and perfumers' commercial archives. These show that Giacomo Badoer, a Venetian merchant in

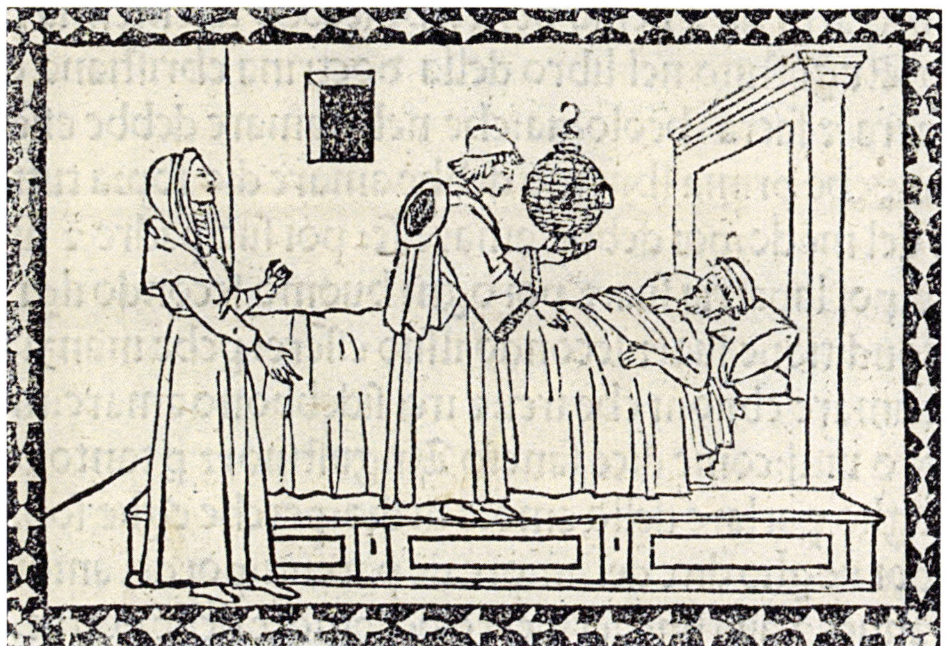

Fig. 8. Bartolomeo de' Libri, *Fiore di virtù*, carta a3r, 1491, Washington, D.C., Library of Congress (Lessing J. Rosenwald Collection)

Constantinople between 1436 and 1440, bought cloves, frankincense, ginger, alum and musk, among other things.

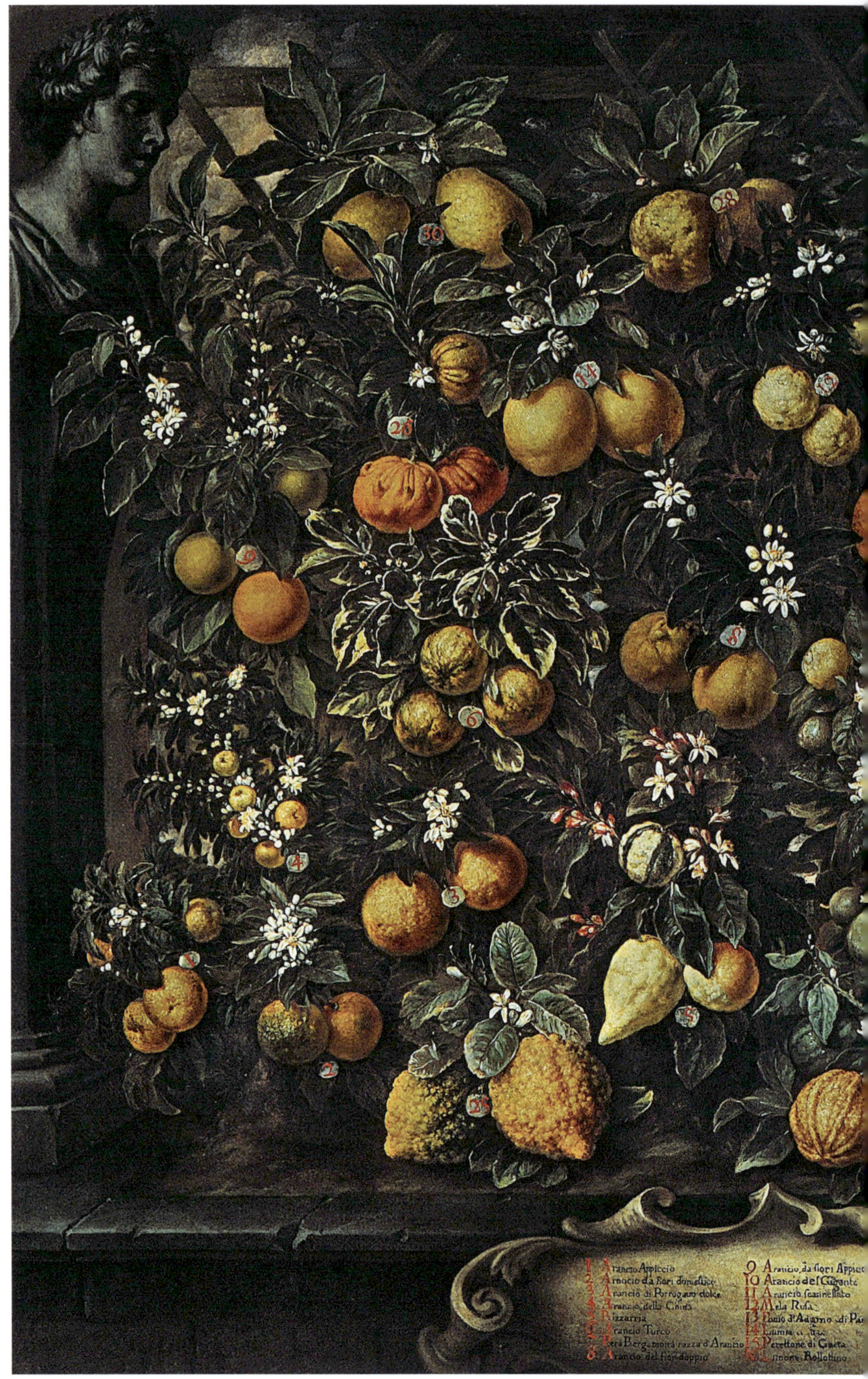

Fig. 9. Bartolomeo Bimbi, *Oranges, Limes, Lemons and Citrus lumia*, 1715, oil on canvas, 198 × 257 cm, Poggio a Caiano, Villa medicea – Museo della natura morta (Direzione regionale musei della Toscana), inv. Castello no. 594

mone dolce di Spagna
mone dolce di Portogallo
mone dolce di Napoli
a falsa
oncello di Napoli
mone scannellato Tondo
tta di S. Domenico
mone spinoso
25 Lumia Cedrata
26 Arancio a Berretta di Prete
27 Portogallo di Spagna
28 Lumia Cedrata di quarta Classe
30 Lumia fatta a Pera di seconda Classe

BIBLIOGRAPHY

GREPPI Caterina, *Profumi ed essenze alla corte dei califfi* (Palermo: Dario Flaccovio Editore, 2023).

MARITANO Cristina, *Profumo. Origini, storie, confezioni* (Cinisello Balsamo: Silvana Editoriale, 2018).

MESSINIS Anna, *Storia del Profumo a Venezia* (Venice: Lineadacqua, 2017).

PAZZANESE Michela, *La Profumeria del Rinascimento tra igiene, medicina e seduzione* (Florence: EBS Print, 2020).

PEDRETTI Carlo, *Il tempio dell'anima* (Campi Bisenzio: CB Edizioni, 2007).

ID. (ed.), *Léonard de Vinci et la France* (Amboise: Cartei & Bianchi Éditeurs, 2009).

ROQUES Dominique, *Il cercatore di essenze. Viaggio alle origini del profumo* (Milan: Feltrinelli, 2021).

VECCE Carlo, *Il sorriso di Caterina, la madre di Leonardo* (Florence: Giunti, 2023).

ID., *Leonardo, la vita. Il ragazzo di Vinci, l'uomo universale, l'errante* (Florence: Giunti, 2024).

ID. (ed.), *La Biblioteca di Leonardo* (Florence: Giunti, 2021).

DE VINCI Léonard, *Carnets* (Paris: Gallimard, 2019).

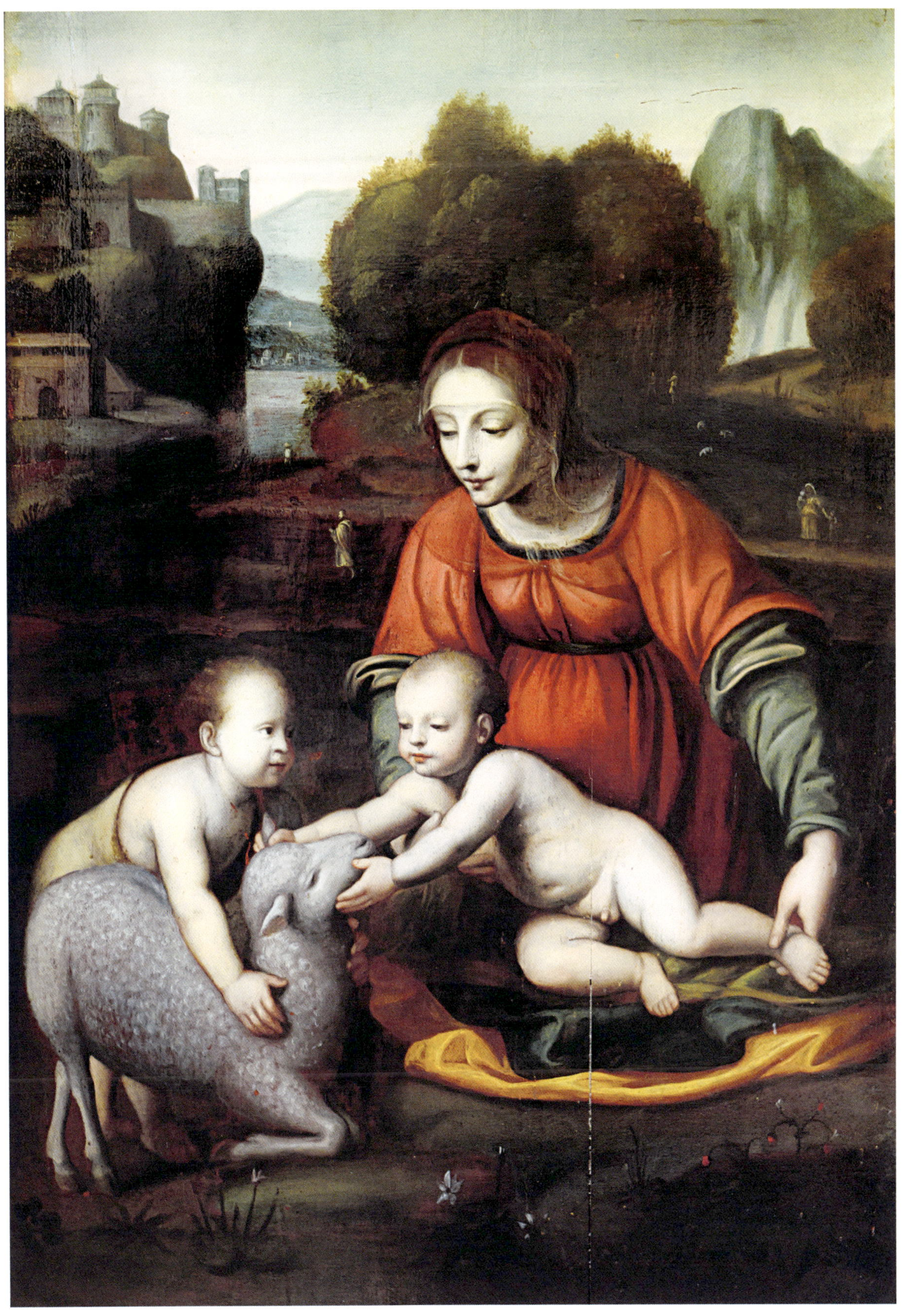

Milanese school, disciple of Bernardino Luini, *The Virgin and Child with Saint John the Baptist and the Lamb in a Landscape*, ca. 1600, oil on canvas, 91 × 63.5 cm, Amboise, château du Clos Lucé

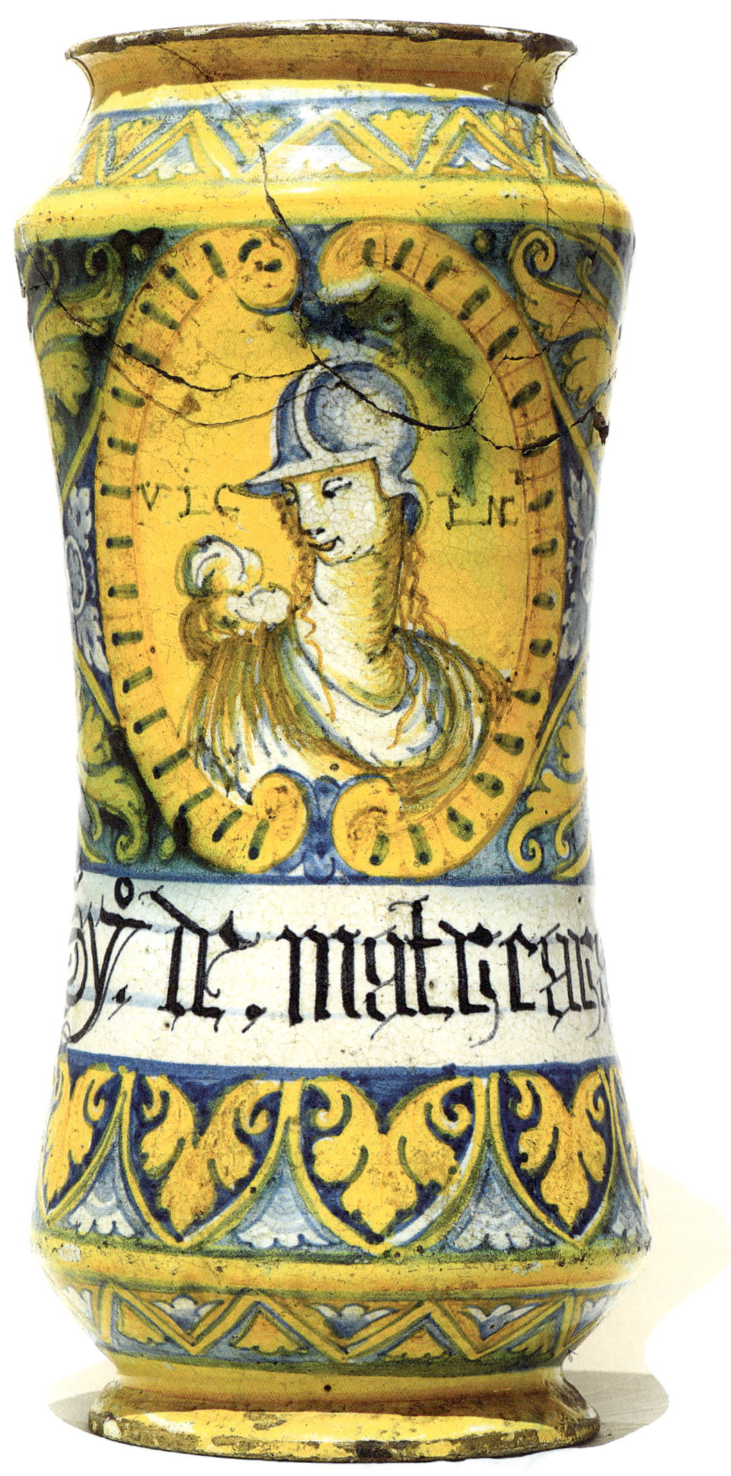
VIC
EN

FRAGRANT PLANTS IN BOTANICAL BOOKS

Marie-Élisabeth Boutroue

At the time of the Renaissance, knowledge of plants, and particularly of fragrant plants, was based partly on practices that could be described as "artisanal", and partly on a series of ancient texts that passed on scholarly knowledge directly derived from classical civilisations and its transmission during the Middle Ages.

From the 15th century onwards, but especially in the 16th, the challenge of botany consisted in classifying all the information needed to create a theoretical framework for a field of knowledge with numerous practical applications, from documentation that had sometimes been handed down in a rather erratic manner.

The books that convey this knowledge fall into three different categories.

First, the various editions, commentaries and translations of classical texts. These were published by humanists, who were experienced Latinists and Hellenists. In the case of scientific texts, these were mostly written by physicians, more rarely by apothecaries.

The second category consisted of printed herbaria. The plants they contain were generally classified in a range of different ways: Pietro Andrea Mattioli followed the order used in the text by the Greek physician Dioscorides; garden inventories were in alphabetical order; as for the Pinax by the Swiss naturalist Gaspard Bauhin, its classification is closer to a taxonomy.

The picture is completed by pharmacopoeias. Whereas editions of classical texts leaned towards theory, pharmacopoeias took the opposite approach, placing emphasis on practical applications, including the preparation of perfumes or scented ointments.

Knowledge from antiquity

As in other cases involving technical knowledge, understanding of perfumery was initially derived from what ancient authors had to say about them. In this particular instance, the information was based primarily on two ancient texts: Pliny the Elder's *Natural History* and a short work by Theophrastus, with the Latin title *De Odoribus* (*On Odours*). Transmission of *De Odoribus* took a relatively short time: it was published with other botanical texts by the same author and was the subject of an important commentary in 1556. Adrien Turnèbe, the commentary's author, was a brilliant Hellenist, well versed in all the difficulties involved in publishing and translating texts. Above all, he was familiar with the works of both the Greek Theophrastus and the Roman Pliny the Elder. His commentary is, therefore, first and foremost a comparison and bringing

LEFT
Albarello, 16th c.
Polychrome earthenware,
45 × 14 cm, Amboise,
château du Clos Lucé

together of his readings of the two authors, from which, through a process of compilation and synthesis, he arrived at a modernised knowledge base that was valid for that time.

In his *Natural History*, Pliny the Elder attempted to describe everything of note in the world, a very large proportion of which (around a third) concerns plants. At the beginning of Book 13, he describes several perfumes and offers a history of their uses. He then addresses the names of the perfumes in a manner similar to his explanation of the etymology of plant names at the start of Book 25. Renaissance commentators made extensive use of this part of the Plinian encyclopaedia. In 1530, one of the most curious of them, Étienne de Laigue, took up Pliny's exposition and added other examples in a disquisition that falls somewhere between commentary and paraphrase. Unsurprisingly, he is mindful of the futile nature of cosmetic perfumes, of which he seems to disapprove.

In addition to these two ancient authors, the Greek physician Dioscorides was the subject of a wide variety of commentaries during the Renaissance.

Which plants ? Which fragrances ? Which illnesses ?

Certain fragrant plants are frequently mentioned in herbaria. The way in which these books are organised varies from author to author, but they always mention the names of the plants, the place where they are to be found, their flowering and fruiting seasons and their properties. Although fragrance does not generally constitute a taxonomic characteristic of plants, ancient herbaria do sometimes group fragrant plants together. This is the case, for example, in the treatise published by the physician Rembert Dodoens, first in Flemish in 1554, before being translated into French by Carolus Clusius in 1557. Book 2 of his *Histoire des Plantes* (*A New Herball, or Historie of Plants*) contains ninety-five chapters on as many plants. They are not all fragrant plants, but it is important to understand that, following a practice that already existed at the time of Pliny the Elder, botanical thinking in the Renaissance happily classified a fragrant plant with other plants belonging to the same group, whether they are fragrant or not. The grouping of plants should be thought of as a game of dominoes in which a piece can be played provided it has a feature in common with the previous piece. Occasionally, the naturalist will specify the part of the plant that carries the scent: for example, it is the flower in the case of the yellow gillyflower (*Erysimum cheiri*).

The most commonly mentioned fragrant plants include French lavender (*Lavandula stoechas* or "butterfly lavender"), rose and honeysuckle, violet and jasmine, myrtle and benzoin.

Occasionally – as in the case of butterfly lavender – Amatus Lusitanus (João Rodrigues de Castel Branco) mentioned the practices of Portuguese merchants of his time and the trade routes by which this plant passed. In 1566, Garcia de Orta also devoted many pages to the perfumes of the Orient, which he saw in Goa.

The brain, the nose and smell

Perfumes can be administered in a number of ways, but they were mainly used in two situations: when hunting venomous animals and when treating ailments, often gynaecological. Perfumes were used in this instance as pessaries. Physicians explained how scents could be effective: this was not a matter of indicating which plants might be used, but of demonstrating how scents can affect the womb. The basis for this reasoning was Hippocratic: the only organ in the human body that can "understand" odours is the nose. The physician André du Laurens, for example, stated that it is the internal parts of the nose that are concerned, an analysis of the relationship between odours and the sense organs that continued into the 17th century. The physician Jacques Rohault took up the same idea, extending it to all the sense organs. André du Laurens, in his *Œuvres*, also described the process by which odours reach the brain, based on the authority of Hippocrates:

> When a man breathes in air through the mouth and nose, it goes first to the brain. Now this inhalation of air which takes place in the superior ventricles, and the exhalation of the same, is not done by the arteries, but by the mammillary processes which are the organs for smelling: and therefore the movement by which the brain inhales and exhales depends on the brain and not on the arteries. The fact that air is inhaled and carried by these apophyses to the brain is proven in this way. Both air and odour are carried together by the same conduits; for odour can never be smelt, however forcefully it is pushed into the nostrils, unless the air is drawn to the brain by inhalation.

It is also in pharmacy books that we find certain well-known perfumes, including the celebrated *oiselet de Chypre* (Chypre birdy), for which Léonard offered a recipe. Contemporary pharmacists explained the benefits of this fragrance, and in 1625 the physician Louis de Serres mentioned this fragrance in his writings on sterility.

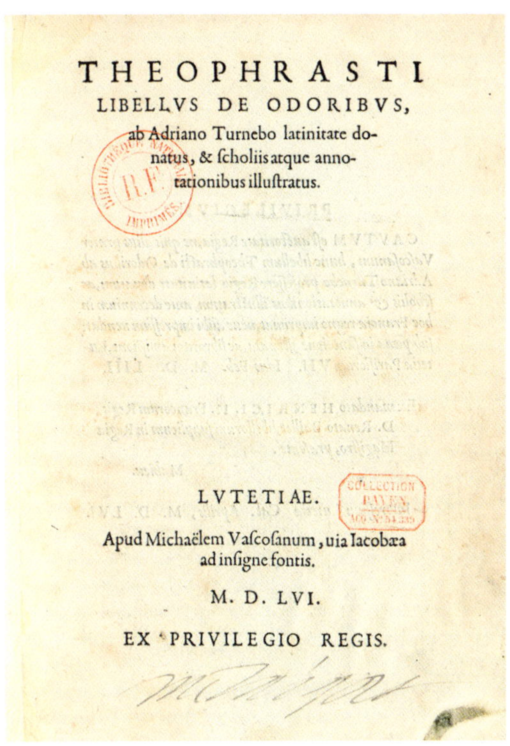

THEOPHRASTI
LIBELLVS DE ODORIBVS,
ab Adriano Turnebo latinitate donatus, & ſcholiis atque annotationibus illuſtratus.

LVTETIAE.
Apud Michaëlem Vaſcoſanum, uia Iacobæa ad inſigne fontis.
M. D. LVI.
EX PRIVILEGIO REGIS.

Theophrastus, *Enquiry into Plants. Excerpt* (ancient Greek-Latin), 1556, Paris, Bibliothèque nationale de France

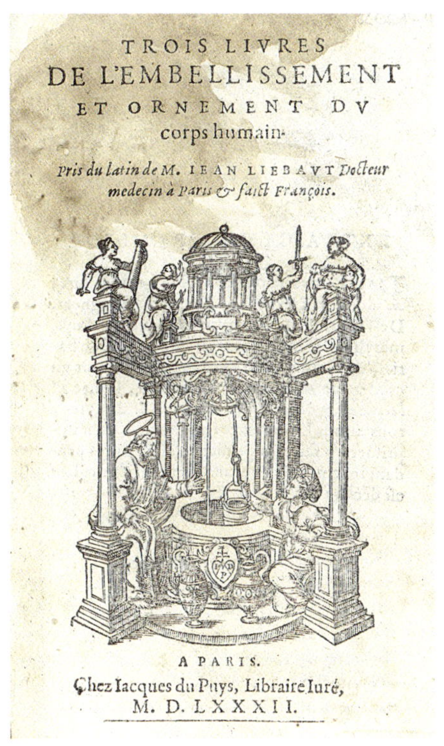

TROIS LIVRES
DE L'EMBELLISSEMENT
ET ORNEMENT DV
corps humain.
Pris du latin de M. IEAN LIEBAVT Docteur medecin à Paris & faict François.

A PARIS.
Chez Iacques du Puys, Libraire Iuré,
M. D. LXXXII.

Jean Liébault, *Three Books on the Embellishment and Adornment of the Human Body*, 1582, 16.7 × 11.1 cm
Grasse, musée international de la Parfumerie,
inv. M08770149

fois qu'il retient quelque odeur du Styrax calamita, mais il eſt beaucoup pl⁹ penetrãt & d'odeur plus forte, qui me faict penſer que ce pourroit eſtre la Reſine plus liquide du Styrax, auec laquelle on eut demeſlé de la Myrrhe, comme ſouuẽt d'vn meſme arbre, il en coule Reſine l'vne plus liquide que l'autre.

Il ſ'en trouue auſsi vn qu'ilz appellent *Storax rubra* és Boutiques de France & de baſſe Alemaigne. C'eſt l'eſcorce de quelque arbre, aſſes eſpeſſe, de couleur rouſſatre tirãt ſur le noir. Il en arriue beaucoup en Anuers, & eſt achetée des Iuifs pour ſ'en ſeruir és perfums, voyla dequoy elle eſt appelée d'aucuns en Brabant *Thus Iudæorum*, & d'aucuns *Thymiama*. Selon toutesfois l'opinion de gens Sçauans ce n'eſt autre choſe que le Narcaphthõ des Anciens, lequel, ſelon le teſmoignage de Dioſcoride, eſtoit apporté des Indes, & reſemble à l'eſcorce d'vn Sycomore, duquel on faict perfum à cauſe de ſon odeur plaiſante. Car il dit ainſi. *Narcaphthum ex India defertur, corticoſum; ſimile Sycomori libro, quod iucundi odoris gratia ſuffitur: miſcetur thymiamatis compoſitis:* laquelle deſcription conuient au *Styrax rubra* des Boutiques de ce païs, ioinct que (ſelon que nous auons deuant dit) les Iuifs l'achettent pour ſ'en ſeruir en perfums.

Styrax. L'arbre portant le Storax.

LE LIEV.

Il croiſt en Piſidie, Cilicie, & Cypre, & en Crete pareillemẽt, mais l'autre eſt meilleur, & celuy principalement qui croiſt au tour de Gabala de Syrie, dond il a prins le nom Gabalites.

LES NOMS.

Ceſte gomme eſt appelée en Grec ϛύραξ: en Latin *Styrax*: és Boutiques *Storax calamita*.

LE TEMPERAMENT.

Le Styrax eſt chaud & ſec, emollitif & maturatif.

LES VERTVS ET OPERATIONS.

Le Styrax eſt bon contre la toux, contre defluxions tombans du cerueau és parties plus baſſe: & contre enroueure.

Beu ou appliqué par bas, il prouoque les fleurs aux femmes. Il eſt vtile aux femmes qui ont l matrice fermée & endurcie.

Il lache le ventre tout doucemẽt, prins en petite quãtité auec terebinthine, en forme de pilule:

On le meſle vtilement parmy emplaſtres qui ont vertu de reſoudre & digerer.

Inſtillé dans les oreilles, il guerit bourdonnement d'icelles: & induit ſur les ſtrumes & nodoſités des nerfs, il les reſout.

Il profitte contre venin qui nuit à cauſe de ſa froideur, comme Cigue & autres ſemblables.

LE CHOYS.

Dioſcoride dit qu'il faut eſlire celuy qui eſt gras, rouſſatre, reſineux, qui a quelques fragment blancs, demourãt long tẽps en ſa bonne odeur, & qui rend vne liqueur comme miel quand on l'a mollit: Il faut reietter celuy qui eſt noir, & comme plein de ſon, friable, & comme moyſi.

De Sarcocolla. Chap. VI.

SArcocolla eſt la gomme d'vne plante eſpineuſe croiſſant en Perſe. Et la meilleure eſt celle qu eſt iaulnatre, amere au gouſt, & qui reſemble aux fragments & petis loppins d'Encens: Pline to tefois au li.13.cha.11. de ſon Hiſtoire prefere la blanche à l'autre, & pareillement au li.24.chap.14.

Rembert Dodoens, *A History of Plants, containing a full description of herbs…not only those that grow in this country, but also other foreign herbs used as medicine*, 1557, printed monograph, f. 556, Paris, Bibliothèque nationale de France

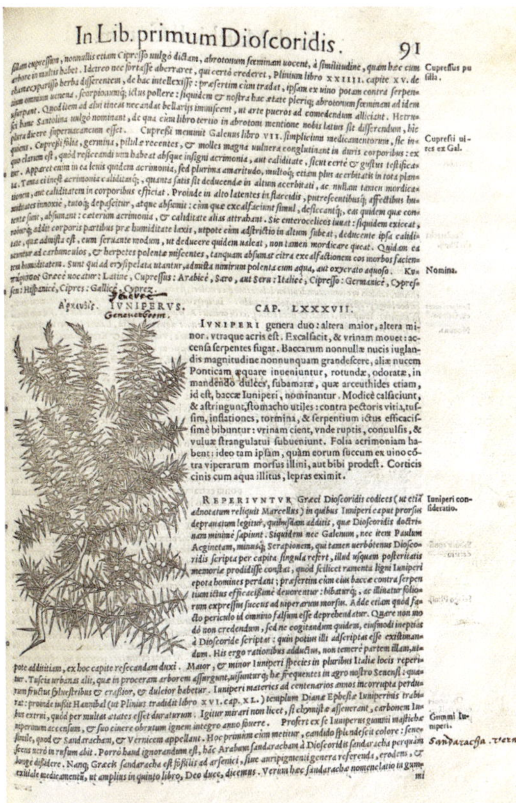

In Lib. primum Dioscoridis. 91

IVNIPERVS. CAP. LXXXVII.

IVNIPERI genera duo: altera maior, altera minor. vtraque acris est. Excalfacit, & vrinam mouet: accensa serpentes fugat. Baccarum nonnullæ nucis iuglandis magnitudine nonnunquam grandescere, aliæ nucem Ponticam æquare inueniuntur, rotundæ, odoratæ, in mandendo dulces, subamaræ, quæ arceuthides etiam, id est, baccæ Iuniperi, nominantur. Modicè calfaciunt, & astringunt, stomacho utiles: contra pectoris vitia, tussim, inflationes, tormina, & serpentium ictus efficacissimè bibuntur: vrinam cient, vnde ruptis, conuulsis, & vuluæ strangulatui subueniunt. Folia acrimoniam habent: ideo tam ipsam, quàm eorum succum ex uino cōtra viperarum morsus illini, aut bibi prodest. Corticis cinis cum aqua illitus, lepras eximit.

Pietro-Andrea Mattioli, *Commentarii secundo aucti, in libros sex Pedecii Dioscoridis anazarbei de Medica Materia*, 1558, printed text, 33.3 × 22.5 cm, Romorantin-Lanthenay, centre de documentation du musée de Sologne, inv. FM 254, p. 91

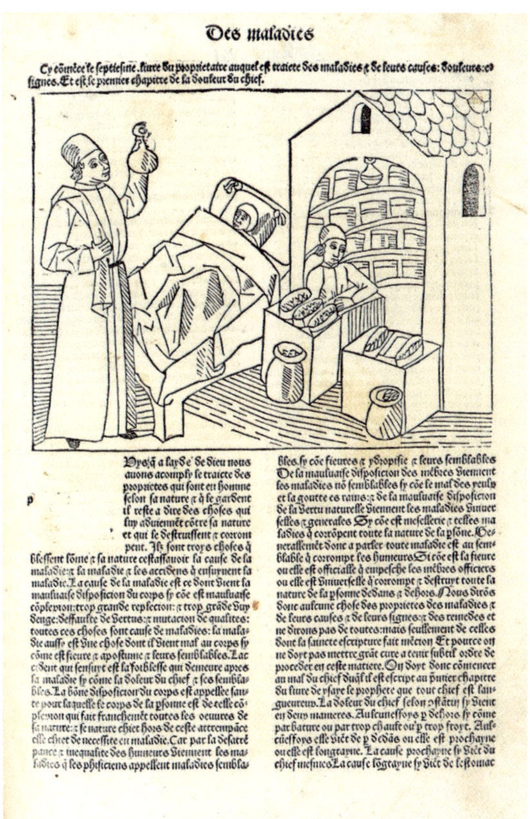

Des maladies

Bartholomaeus Anglicus, *Le Proprietaire en françoys* (French translation of *On the Properties of Things*), 15th c. Bound paper work, 35.5 × 26 cm, Tours, bibliothèque municipale, Rés. 7573, f. 111

Conclusion

As well as being the organ for perceiving fragrances and bad smells, the nose was also a focus of aesthetic considerations. While educational treatises focused on hygiene and how to help small children blow their nose, other medical treatises emphasised the beauty of the nose and the opposite: its aesthetic or functional defects. This is the case of Jean Liébault, author of the treatise *Trois Livres sur l'embellissement et ornement du corps humain* (*Three Books on the Embellishment and Adornment of the Human Body*), who discusses at some length the defects of a nose that is too short or too flat:

> Together with these marks of beauty, you will compile a list of its defects, whether it is too large, too small, pug-nosed, sunken, too prominent: such defects in truth are not easy to correct, whether natural or through accident: all the more so as the natural structure and composition of the nose is more cartilaginous, bony, and membranous than fleshy: I cannot, however, accept the fantastic stories of those who say they have seen pug-noses develop and become larger.

On occasion, noses and their anatomical perfection even became the subject of jokes. This is demonstrated by one published by Poggio Bracciolini, summarised here from the French version of 1514: a Franciscan had noticed a beautiful young woman, married (alas!) to a neighbour.

The neighbour begged the monk to be godfather to the first child to be born to the young woman, who was already pregnant. The monk looked at the mother-to-be with a sorrowful gaze that eventually caused her to become afraid. When pressed, the monk replied that she was to give birth to a son "who would have no nose, the worst thing that can happen to the human face." Understandably worried, the poor woman enquired if there was any means of averting such a cruel misfortune. The monk then explained that the absence of the nose was due to a deficiency in her husband, and offered a remedy: "I shall have to sleep with you to make good your husband's deficiency and put a nose on the child's face."

Despite some reluctance, the young woman consented to the remedy suggested by the monk, and when at last she was brought to bed of a boy, as chance would have it, the child was blessed with "a long and beautiful nose." Naturally, the young woman was most grateful for the good offices of this monk; her husband too, against all expectations, "thanked him sincerely for the excessive pains he had taken".

Bibliography

Texts from antiquity

Pliny the Elder, *Naturalis Historia* (Paris: Collection des universités de France, Les Belles Lettres, 1951-2015).

Theophrastus, *Theophrasti Libellus de Odoribus, ab Adriano Turnebo latinitate donatus et scholiis atque annotationibus illustratus* (Paris: Michel Vascosan, 1556).

Dioscorides, *Pedanii Dioscoridis Anarzabei De medica materia libri sex, Joanne Ruellio, Suessionensi, interprete, nunc primum ab ipso Ruellio recogniti et suo nitori restituti* (Paris: Simon de Colines, 1537).

Ancient herbaria

Dodoens Rembert, *Histoire des plantes, en laquelle est contenue la description entière des herbes (Éd. 1557)*, "c'est-à-dire leurs espèces, forme, noms, tempérament, vertus et opérations : non seulement de celles qui croissent en ce païs, mais aussi des autres estrangères qui viennent en usage de médecine (By Rembert Dodoens...translated from Low German into French by Carolus Clusius, Antwerp, J. Loe)" (Paris: reprint, Hachette Livre/BnF, 2012).

da Orta Garcia, *Colloques des simples et des drogues de l'Inde*, translated from Portuguese by Sylvie Messinger Ramos and António Ramos (Arles: coll. "Thesaurus", Actes Sud, 2004).

Classical sources

Liébault Jean, *Trois Livres de l'embellissement et ornement du corps humain. Pris du latin de M. Jean Liebaut, docteur medecin à Paris, et faict François* (Paris: Jacques du Puys, 1582).

du Laurens André, *Les Œuvres de Mr. André Du Laurens – traduites de latin en françois par Theophile Gelee, medecin ordinaire de la ville de Dieppe* (Paris: Augustin Courbe, 1639).

Poggio Bracciolini Gian Francesco, *Les Facecies de poge florentin* (Lyon: Olivier Arnoullet, 1514).

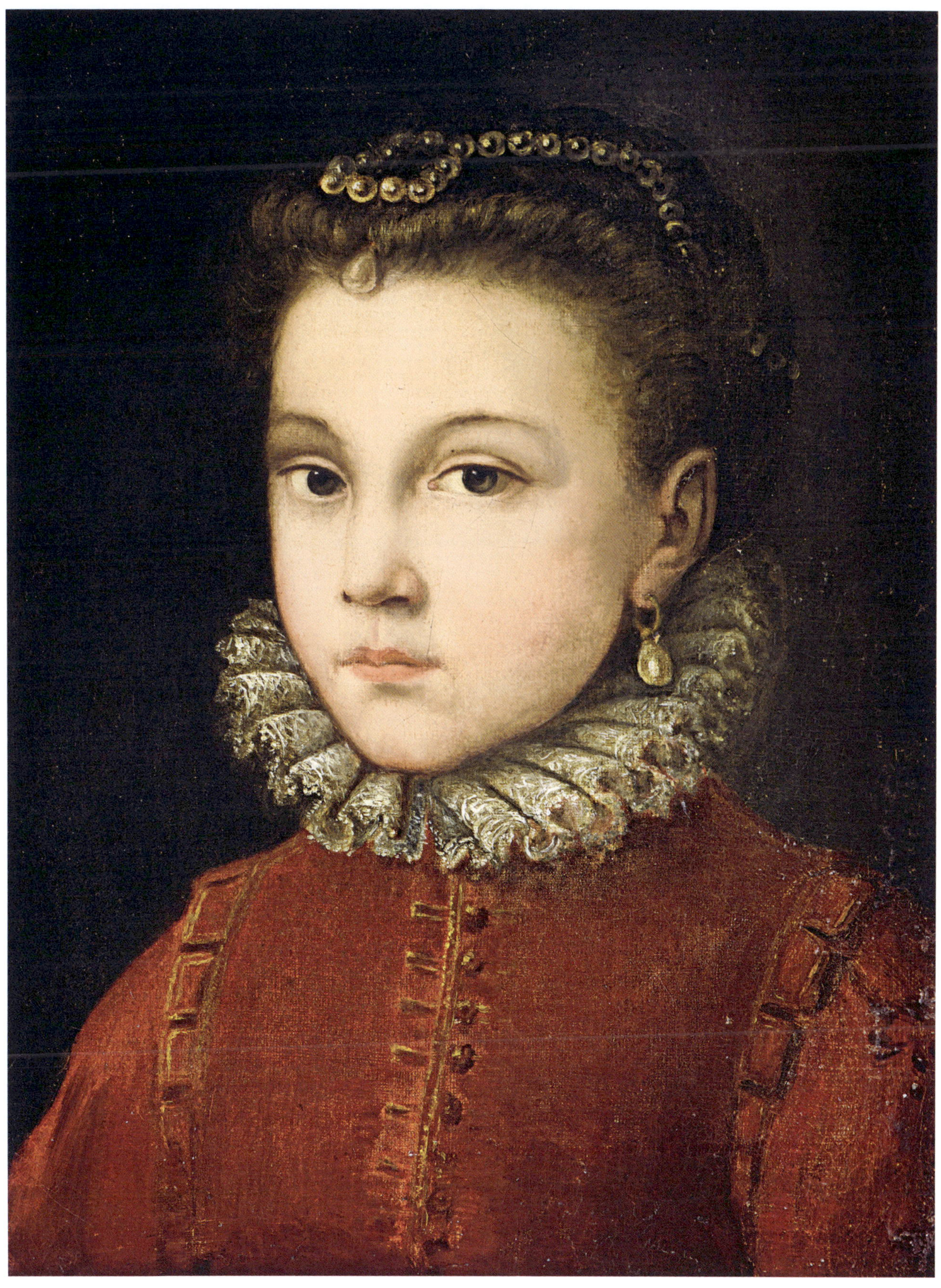

Attributed to François Clouet, *Portrait of Marguerite of Navarre as a Child*, 16th c., oil on canvas, Amboise, château du Clos Lucé

Carlo Pedretti's dating of this folio to between 1506 and 1508 is based partly on stylistic elements in the writing, and partly on the quick topographical sketch which appears to show the loops of a river, and which should be compared with folios 765v and 766r (ca. 1507), dedicated to the study of the canalisations of the Adda River. The two columns of writing, on the other hand, deal with an entirely different subject: Leonardo discusses here the usefulness of glasses when, as eyesight declines "with age", one is obliged "to move the object further away." However, "by placing glasses between the eye and the object, vision regains the sharpness of youth, and the object becomes discernible again at a normal distance".

The drawing of the flowers, done in black chalk, represents, as it is botanically defined, an *Asphodelus luteus*, i.e. the inflorescence of a lily. It is not drawn by Leonardo, as the cross-hatching on the right shows, but it is of a much higher quality than the folios mentioned above. Carlo Pedretti has suggested that it should be attributed to Cesare da Sesto, certainly one of Leonardo's most gifted disciples. It does not seem, however, that this artist was sufficiently close to Leonardo for the Tuscan master to allow him access to his notes, let alone to use them for his personal drawings. Among the few people authorised to do so were Francesco Melzi and Gian Giacomo Caprotti, known as Salaì. While Salaì's artistic style, which was not yet fully developed, makes it impossible to attribute authorship of the drawing to him with any certainty, Melzi's possible involvement cannot be ruled out. Indeed, Melzi began exchanging views with Leonardo in 1508, a date that is not incompatible with the one attributed to this folio.

Maria Teresa Fiorio

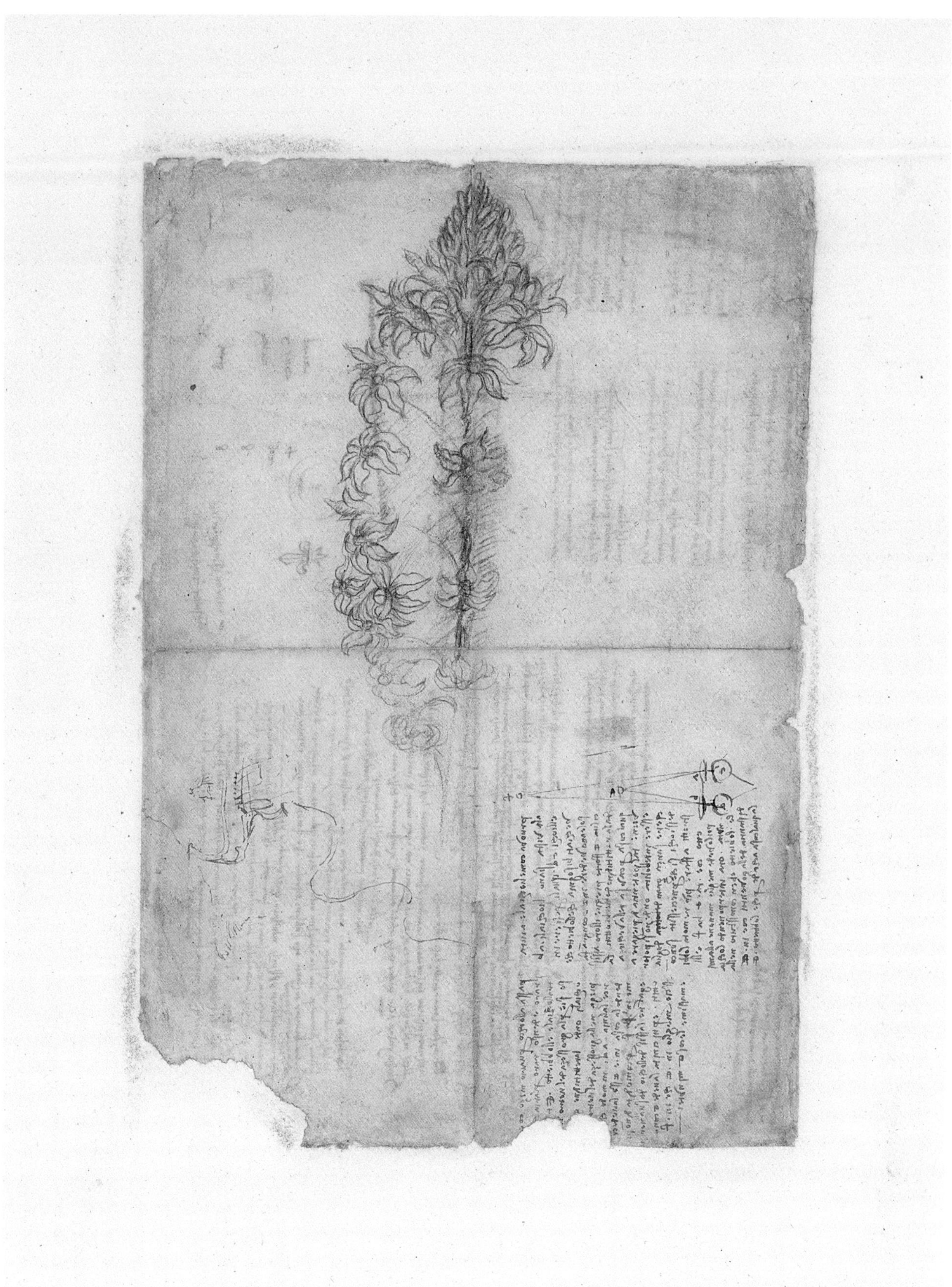

Leonardo da Vinci, *Notes on the usefulness of spectacles, and study of an asphodel* (leaflet by Leonardo, drawing by Francesco Melzi?), *Codex Atlanticus*, fol. 663r, ca. 1508, 34.7 × 24.2 cm, Milan, Veneranda Biblioteca Ambrosiana – Pinacoteca

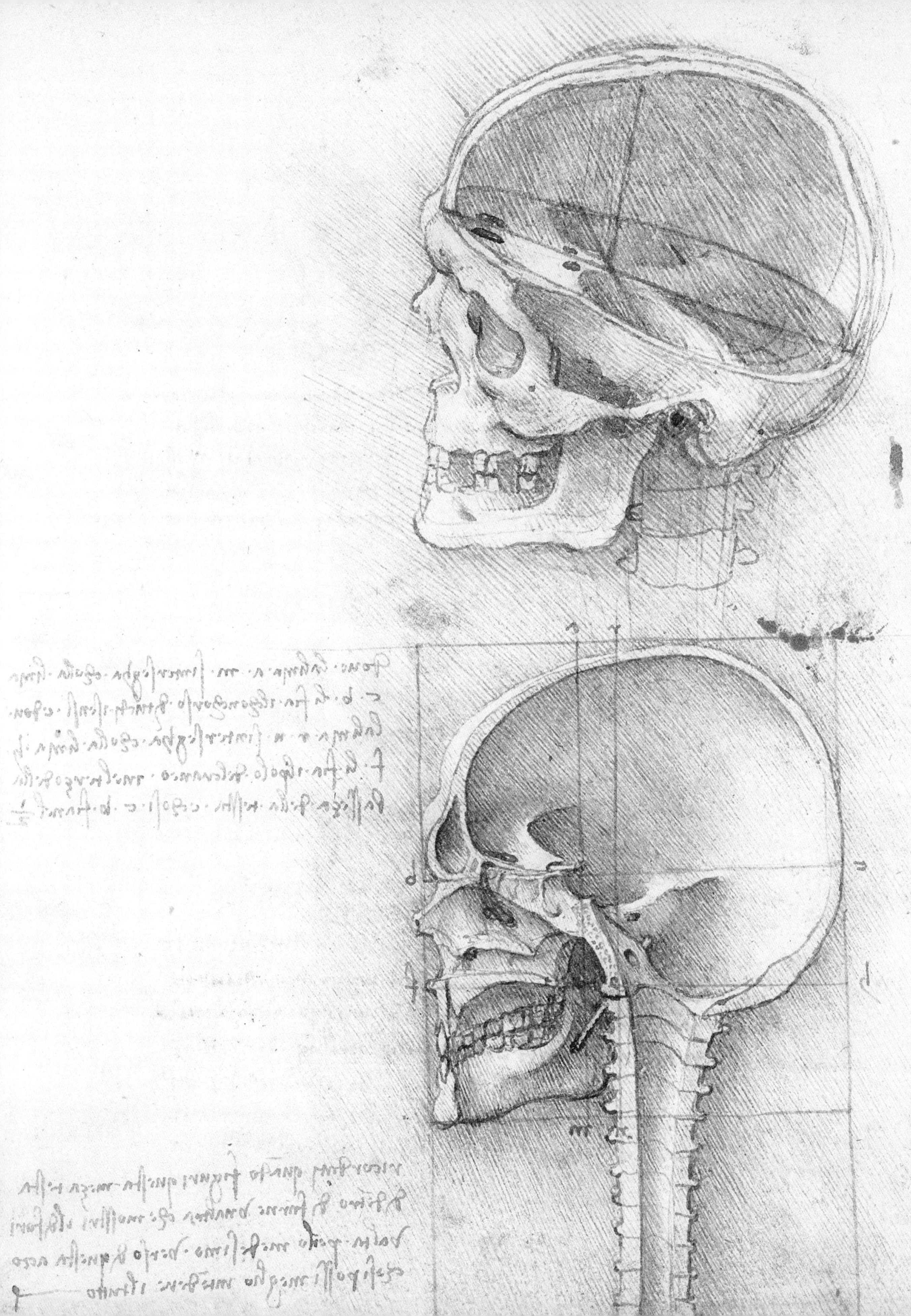

(AL)CHEMICAL SENSIBILITY: HISTORICAL AND PHILOSOPHICAL PERSPECTIVES ON OLFACTION

NATHALIE ODDY

"Physicians might, I believe, extract greater utility from odours than they do, for I have often observed that they cause an alteration in me and work upon my spirits according to their several virtues." (Montaigne, "On Smells", *Essays*, I, 55)

The enduring fascination with olfaction – the chemical sense that makes it possible to perceive volatile molecules – and smells stems in part from a number of tensions and contradictions inherent in the latter.

One of the main tensions is linked to temporality: smells are fleeting, but as literary and neuroscientific sources attest, they can encode deep memories that transport us, transcending and subverting linear time.

Another tension relates to the question of materiality: smells, perceived as vapours, seem to occupy a space between the immaterial and the material, the corporeal and the spiritual. The history of this intermediate state can be traced back to the Platonic conception of smells, which describes them as arising in a transitory state, an impermanent stage in the passage from air to water and vice versa.

By examining premodern and contemporary perspectives on olfaction, this article will outline some of the ways in which sensory and olfactory modality has been understood scientifically and philosophically.

Fragrances are both sensual and abstract, atmospheric in nature, and the expression of a poetic quality that lies somewhere between the physical and the metaphysical. This quality gives scents a symbolic role, that of intermediary and bridge between heaven and earth.

From a philosophical point of view, the places of smell in epistemology, and that of perfumes in aesthetics, are far from straightforward. Until recently, it was common to consider olfaction as a sense that needed to be restored to favour in a world dominated by the sense of sight, and in which the "lesser" senses of olfaction and taste – which belong to the chemosensory system – were considered secondary, vestigial and subjective.

LEFT
Fig. 1. Leonardo da Vinci, *The Skull Sectioned*, 1489, traces of black chalk, pen and ink, 18.8 × 13.4 cm Windsor, Royal Collection Trust, RL 19057r

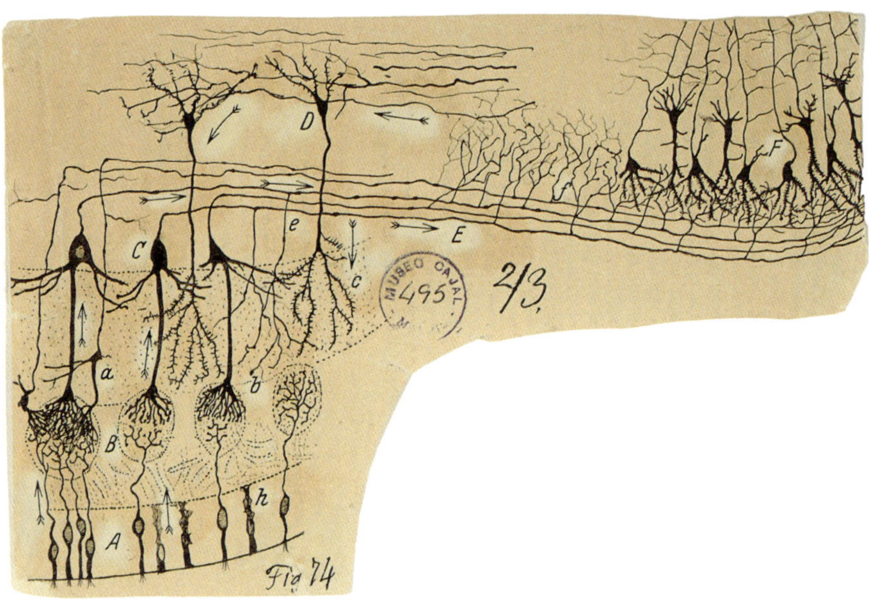

Fig. 2. Santiago Ramón y Cajal, *Diagram of the structure of the olfactory bulb and the sphenoidal cortex of the brain*, 11 × 16.5 cm, Madrid, Instituto Cajal, Cajal legacy, inv. CV03740

The etymology of two closely related concepts, "sagacity" and "flair", however, underlines, from an epistemological, cognitive and ethical point of view, the historical relevance of olfaction as a means of acquiring knowledge and orienting oneself effectively in one's environment. "Flair", derived from the Latin *fragrare* (to smell sweet), is a natural aptitude or ability; "sagacity", from *sagax* (a person with a keen sense of smell), denotes subtlety and acuity of understanding and judgement. In *De Rerum Natura*, Lucretius's poem on the atomist physics of Epicurus, the sagacity associated with the olfactory sense is presented as a model of cognitive science: a person described as "sagacious" is able to detect by smell what is invisible, to glimpse what escapes sight.

Historically, the sense of smell was regarded as an indicator of truth, revealing the invisible essence of things, and smells as a "moral signature" that circumvented cognitive and linguistic processes, allowing impressions to be registered directly in the brain without the need for language. This concept is reinforced by the semantic coincidence of the word "essence", the use of which expanded considerably over the course of the 17th century. Although the term originally meant "that which constitutes the being of a thing", this ontological meaning was complemented, most probably in the 1660s, by an olfactory meaning: "Among chemists, it means a spirit or extract that can be obtained from any substance, chiefly flowers and aromatic drugs", according to the Académie Française's dictionnary of 1694. To this definition one should add the notion of *quinta essentia*, the substance of which celestial bodies are composed and which alchemists believed to be latent in all bodies and could be extracted from them, notably by distillation. The senses, and olfaction in particular, were considered to be pathways to the sacred, a means of theological understanding: they enabled us to apprehend divine intelligence through the created world, and offered a means of knowing things that might be immediate or transcendental. The symbolic association of a pleasant odour with virtue (*odor suavitatis*) and a foul-smelling odour with vice

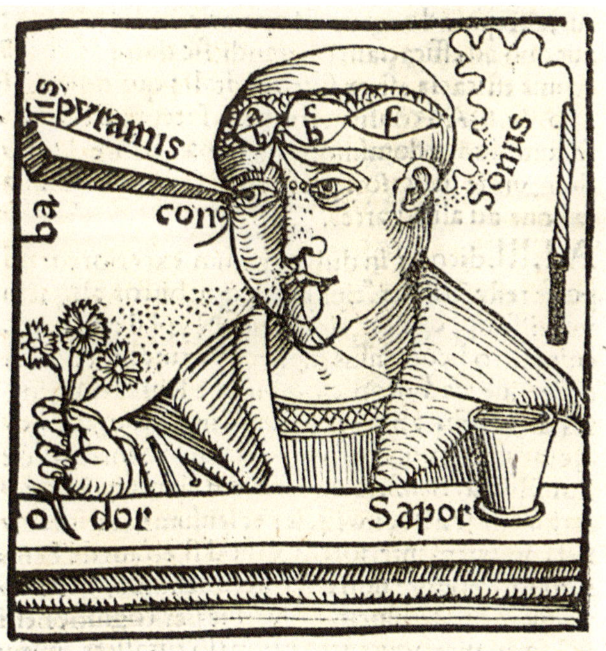

Fig. 3. Johann Maier von Eck, *Aristotelis Stagiritae Philosophi De anima Libri III*, 1520, woodcut, Munich, Bayerische Staatsbibliothek, f. 81

and corruption gave rise to the expression "odour of sanctity".

Until the end of the 19th century, and the discovery of scientific works such as those by Santiago Ramón y Cajal, the father of modern neuroscience, relatively little was known about the olfactory system and its physiology, although Galen had discovered the olfactory nerves and Hippocrates and Leonardo da Vinci had produced anatomical drawings of the base of the nasal cavity [fig. 1, fig. 2]. Premodern notions of olfaction are rooted in the writings of a number of philosophers and physicians, including Plato, Aristotle, Theophrastus and Galen. For Plato, olfaction is a sense of "vapours", and odours have an intermediate, hybrid character that cannot be described as concrete. In his *Timaeus*, odours are described as a "half-formed class": they always come from bodies that are either moist, or being putrefied, liquefied or vaporised, and are only perceptible in the intermediate state in which water is transformed into air and air into water, and in which they all manifest themselves in the form of vapour or mist. In *De Sensu et Sensibilibus*, Aristotle places olfaction between the senses, arguing that odours are not objects in themselves or even half-formed objects, but rather immaterial forms or "species" that emanate from an object. By examining the way in which air (normally imperceptible to the nose) is "affected" by these forms (and becomes perceptible to the nose), Aristotle recognises that odours have an influence, which can even be exerted on inanimate objects.

Although smells are ambiguous by nature, Theophrastus concluded that unpleasant smells came from bad things, and pleasant smells from good things, thus establishing an important olfactory model that developed throughout medieval Europe following early Christian practices. In ancient medicine, smells were considered essential diagnostic tools, enabling doctors to detect disease, a practice that continued into the Renaissance. Galen took Aristotle's implications about the organ of smell a step further, concluding that it had nothing to do with the nose or nostrils, but rather with the brain. The sense of smell was therefore considered to be unique among the five senses, since it had no secondary organ of perception and the brain, in the case of olfaction, was itself a sensory organ. It was then established that small teats or papillae extending down from the brain were located at the top of the nose and collected the odours present in the air. Bartholomaeus Anglicus, an erudite Franciscan monk of the 13th century, took up this concept of the principle of olfaction, stating that when in contact with the teats or "mamillary projections", the vapours inhaled took on a spiritual dimension. This physiological and metaphysical concept of olfaction spread throughout medieval and early modern thought. Anatomical representations of the olfactory pathways, which were printed in the form of woodcuts, are based on the medieval cellular doctrine, a neuroanatomical model according to which the various cognitive faculties are located in particular ventricles of the brain [fig. 3].

The close relationship between olfactory experience and memory seems to be confirmed by certain parallels between the olfactory pathway and the forming of memory impressions, as understood by the ancients: in both cases, the "image" acts in some way directly on the mind. This immediacy establishes a powerful link between memories – particularly those of an emotional and autobiographical nature – and the particular smells associated with those experiences. In more modern language, the limbic system refers to a structural system of the brain that involves many different functions, including emotion, behaviour, motivation, long-term memory and olfaction.

Pre-modern conceptions clearly cannot simply be "translated" into a contemporary neuro-scientific idiom. Olfaction is now considered to be a chemical sense in the same way as taste and the trigeminal chemosensory system, a system that enables organisms to interpret chemical signals from our environment. The process by which volatile molecules become an integral part of our sensory experience is now akin to an electrophysiological process: these three chemosensory systems rely on receptors located in the nasal cavity, in the mouth or on the face, which interact with the molecules concerned and generate receptors and action potentials. In this way, they transmit the effects of chemical stimuli to the appropriate regions of the central nervous system.

Olfaction is a particularly intriguing subject for philosophers because the same stimulus from volatile molecules suspended in the air can give rise to very different olfactory experiences.

In a conceptual landscape where vision is the dominant paradigm of perception, what is the place of olfaction and what knowledge of the world does it provide? Typical philosophical questions about olfaction are epistemological – What can the nose know? Is olfaction a perception or a sensation? – and ontological – What kind of entity is an odour? What is an olfactory image? What does it represent or to what does it refer? In some studies, olfaction is proposed as an alternative model of perception with the aim of displacing or decentralising the notion of "mapping" stimuli, which was at the heart of sensory neuroscience in the 20th century. Talking about mapping obscures what perception is: a skill involving context-dependent decision-making.

Although olfaction remains an enigma for philosophers and neurobiologists alike, considering it as a kind of measurement of the environment rather than as a map may help to challenge our thinking about the sense of smell, both in contemporary times and throughout the evolution of sensory history.

Bibliography

Albert Jean-Pierre, *Odeurs de sainteté : la mythologie chrétienne des aromates* (Paris: Éditions de l'EHESS, 1996).

Barwich Ann-Sophie, *Smellosophy: What the Nose Tells the Mind* (Cambridge, MA: Harvard University Press, 2020).

Bhushan Nalini, Rosenfeld Stuart (eds.), *Of Minds and Molecules: New Philosophical Perspectives on Chemistry* (New York: Oxford University Press, 2020).

Dugan Holly, *The Ephemeral History of Perfume* (Baltimore: Johns Hopkins University Press, 2011).

Jaquet Chantal, *Philosophie de l'odorat* (Paris: Presses universitaires de France, 2010).

Read Sophie, "What the Nose Knew: Renaissance Theologies of Smell", in *Literature, Belief and Knowledge in Early Modern England: Knowing Faith*, Mukherji Subha, Stuart-Buttle Tim (eds.) (Basingstoke: Palgrave Macmillan, 2018), pp. 175–93.

Roch Martin, *L'Intelligence d'un sens. Odeurs miraculeuses et odorat dans l'Occident du haut Moyen Âge (vᵉ-viiiᵉ siècles)* (Turnhout: Brepols, 2009).

Rouby Catherine (ed.), *Olfaction, Taste and Cognition* (Cambridge: Cambridge University Press, 2002).

Salesse Roland, Gervais Rémi (eds.), *Odorat et Goût. De la neurobiologie des sens chimiques aux applications* (Versailles: Éditions Quæ, 2012).

Smith Mark M., *Sensing the Past: Seeing, Hearing, Smelling, Tasting and Touching in History* (Berkeley: University of California Press, 2007).

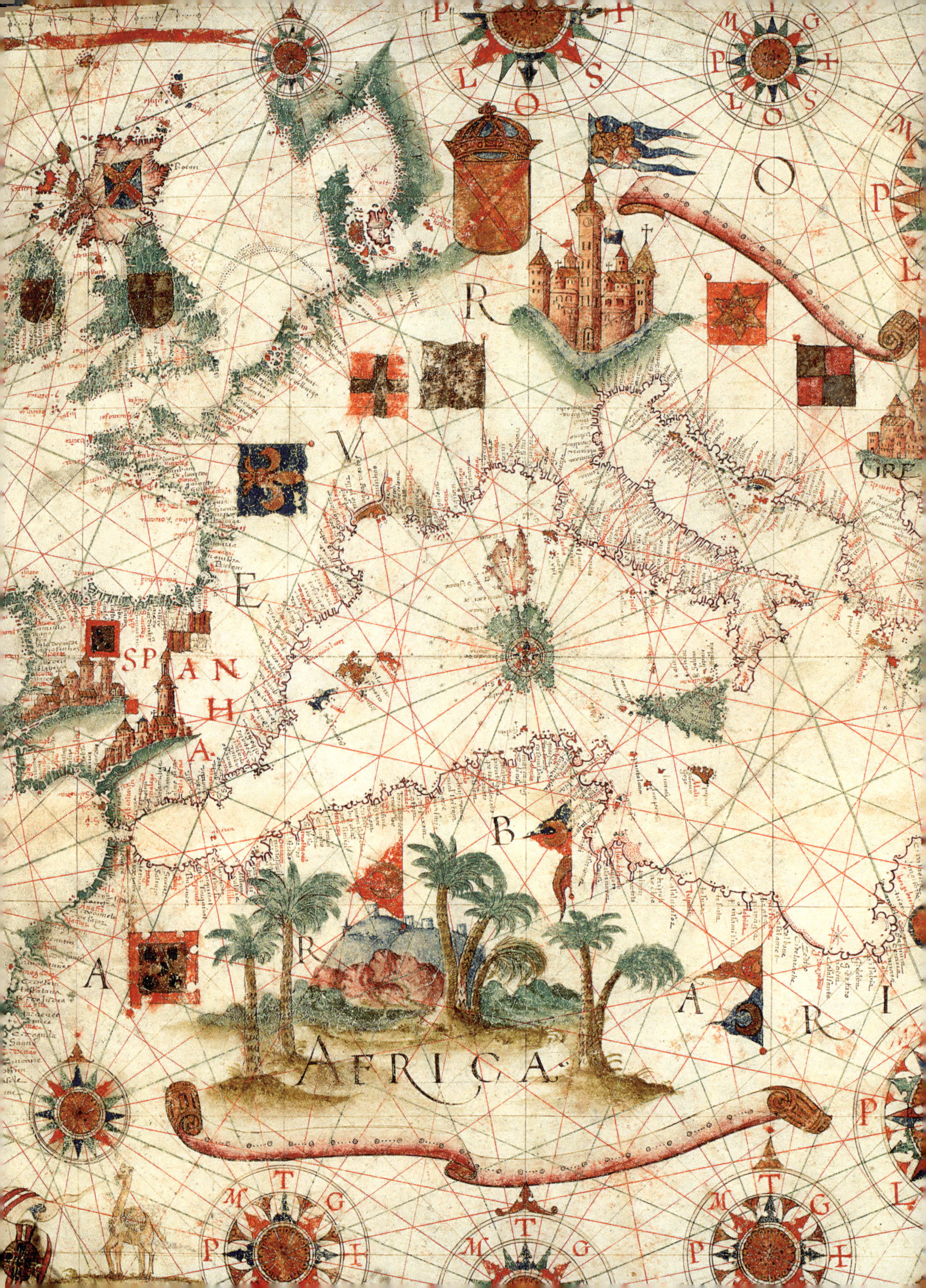
SPANHA
GRE
AFRICA

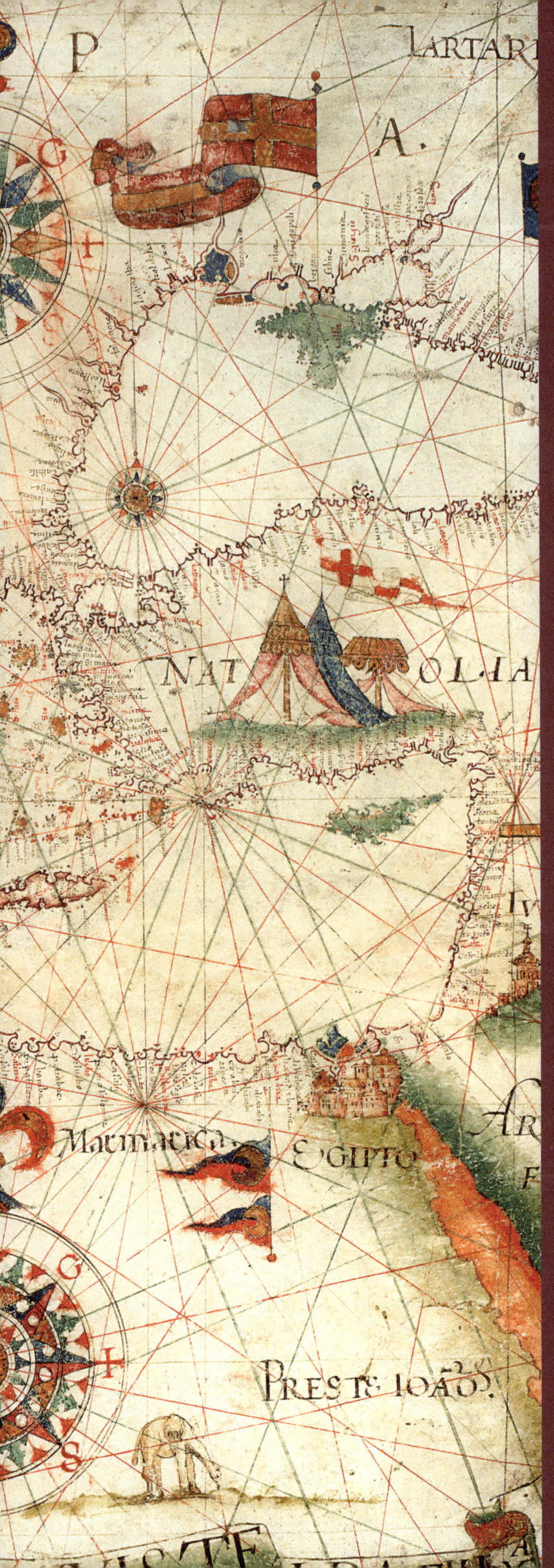

The Orient and the Sea

Chapter I

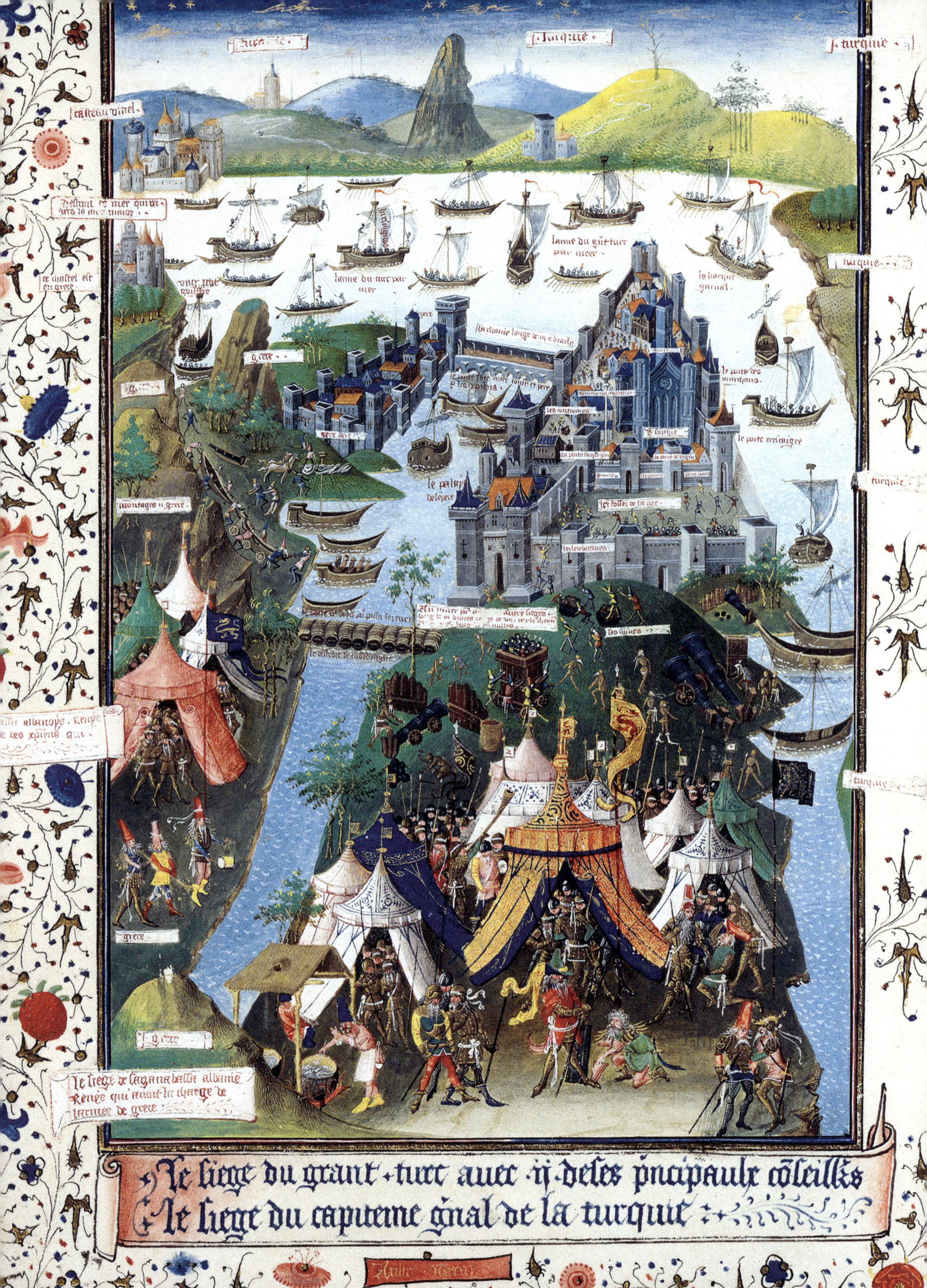
turquie
turquie
turquie
turquie
grece
grece
Le siege du grant turc auec .ij. de ses pncipaulx cõseilles
le siege du capitene gñal de la turquie

CATERINA, SCENT OF THE WILDS

Carlo Vecce

Who was Caterina, the mother of Leonardo? A young girl from the Tuscan countryside? A peasant girl? A servant? Following ardent research, she can finally be introduced: Caterina was born in Circassia, in the highlands of the North Caucasus, and kidnapped and sold into slavery in Constantinople, Venice and Florence. Thanks to the man who loved her, the notary Piero da Vinci, she was finally freed; this man would also become the father of Leonardo da Vinci.

Her extraordinary story is only recorded from the time of her arrival in Florence. Although there is no written record of events prior to this period (her origins, birth and childhood in the Caucasus, her journey to the Mediterranean), they can be reconstructed from the chronicles of the time and the ample archaeological and ethnographic documentation on the history and customs of the Circassian people. Nevertheless, Caterina's early life remains shrouded in mystery and belongs to legend. Above and beyond historical documents, it is perhaps only imagination and creative writing that will enable us to understand this woman's story, and to capture all its beauty.

In my novel *Il sorriso di Caterina, la madre di Leonardo* [Caterina's Smile, the Mother of Leonardo], I imagined that Leonardo, as a young apprentice in Florence, tried his hand at the art of extracting essences and creating perfumes in order to rediscover something of the olfactory world of his childhood and his mother, with Caterina being the first beneficiary of his experiments:

> Leonardo would always bring his mother something as a present: [...] a piece of sweet-smelling ambergris, stolen from who knows where, a small phial of orange blossom perfume distilled in an alembic. Caterina, however, would tell him that these perfumes were too strong, that she preferred the ones she made herself, with her ancient, rustic art, by macerating shelled almonds in cold water, together with rose flowers, jasmine, lavender or wild herbs that only she knew. Like a sorceress, she would collect them from the fields at dawn, when the stems were still damp with dew. (Chap. 11)

Caterina seems to have continued to live in harmony with her body in the most natural and free way possible, following the education she received as a child. The fragrances she obtained using the simple, age-old techniques of maceration and enfleurage came from animal and plant

PREVIOUS PAGE
Luís Teixeira
Nautical chart of the Mediterranean area, including Europe with British Isles and a portion of Scandinavia, ca. 1600, manuscript, 59.5 × 95 cm
San Marino, Huntington Digital Library, HM 1549

LEFT
Bertrandon de la Broquière
The Siege of Constantinople (1453) – Le Voyage d'outre-mer (Overseas Voyage), Lille, 1458 (?), parchment, f. 207v
Paris, Bibliothèque nationale de France

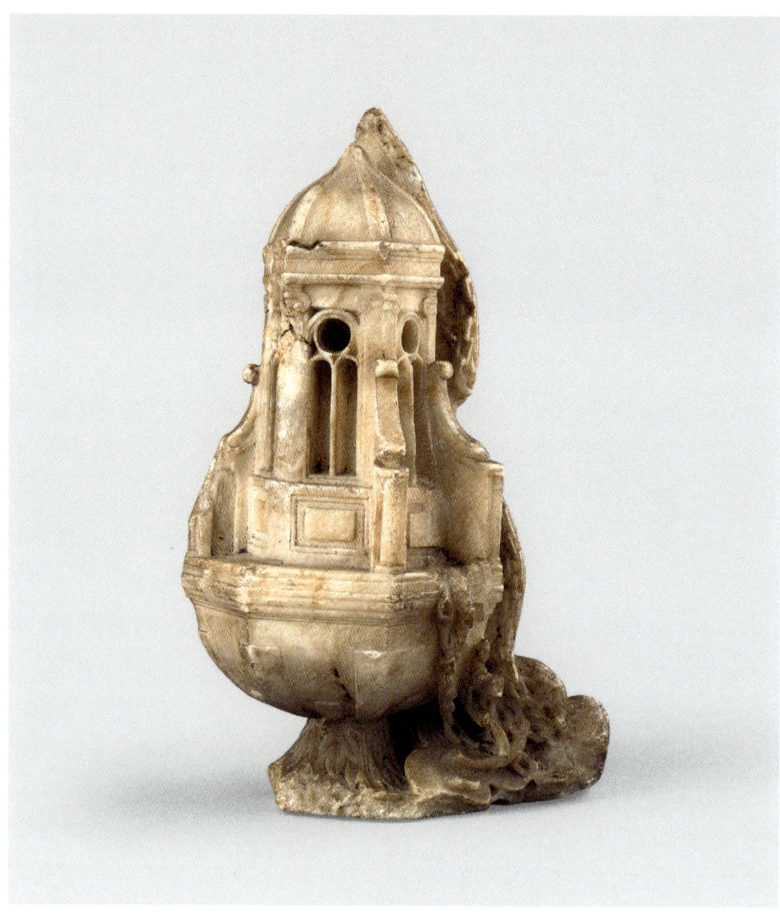

Censer, 16th c., alabaster, 19 × 12.4 cm, musée national de la Renaissance – château d'Écouen, inv. E.CL. 19310

essences gathered in the mountains and forests of her homeland: wild herbs, resins, the effluvia and secretions from animal glands, the smell of menstrual blood. Her earliest childhood memory, and also the most delightful, was olfactory, of the arrival of her father, the warrior-prince Yakov, returning to the village:

> She remembered the warrior who dismounted in front of the porch and touched her face with his rough hand, but also the acrid, bad smell of that dirty body, sweating after the journey, and all the other smells, those of the metal of the chainmail, the leather of the boots, the horses nervously beating their hooves in the mud and their own excrement. (Chap. 1)

When Caterina was a little girl, she may already have been familiar with the essences transported from the trading centres to her village, to the north of which ran the final stretch of the Silk Road – joining the Caspian Sea to the basins of the Volga and Don rivers – that linked Samarkand to the Venetian port of Tana, or from the Genoese ports on the coasts of the Sea of Azov and the Black Sea. The few merchants who were brave enough to travel to the mountain villages brought with them very rare essences, still in their raw state, in paste or grain form, from Central Asia, India or the Far East, such as musk, aloe and camphor; and others from the South, the Middle East, Africa, the Red Sea and the Indian Ocean, such as ambergris and civet, frankincense tears and

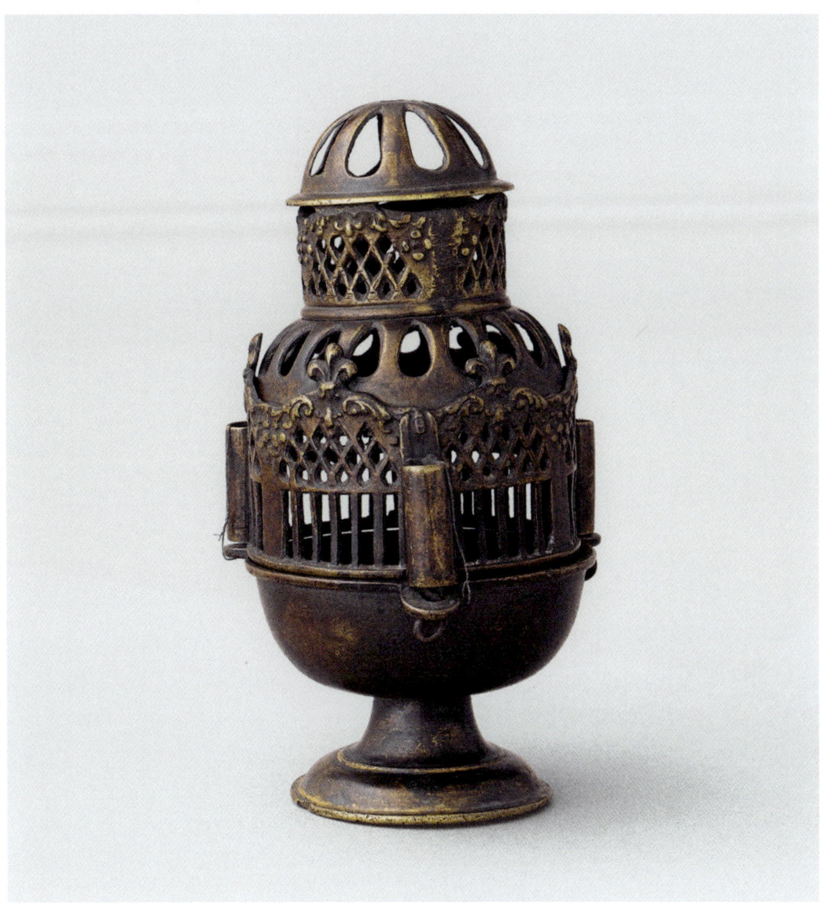

Censer, first quarter of the 17th c., copper, 19.3 × 11 cm, musée national de la Renaissance – château d'Écouen, inv. E.CL. 1007

fragments of aloeswood, to be burned so as to perfume the closed, smoke-filled rooms of the Circassian huts, ointments and pastes to apply to skin chapped by the sun and the cold, powders to sprinkle on clothes on feast days, and distilled oils and waters scented with rose and saffron.

And then came the great leap, the journey across the Mediterranean, with its smells of boats and of human bodies brought together on the crossing, odours that Caterina experienced when she embarked for the first time:

> She struggled to her feet, wobbled and leant against the bulkhead. She took a long breath, as if she wanted to breathe in the air filled with smells and perfumes she had never known: salt, encrustations of lichen, remoras, guano on the sides of the boat, dried fish, human sweat, urine, damp wood. (Chap. 2)

Later, she experienced the musty, heady scents of the wonderful spice market in Constantinople, the Byzantine capital, on the verge of falling to the Turks at the end of its thousand-year decline; the intoxicating, seductive fragrances of musk, cinnamon, pepper, myrrh and hyssop, and the smell of incense that filled the immense, sacred space of Hagia Sophia.

When she arrived in Venice, Caterina lost herself in the labyrinth of spice and perfume shops,

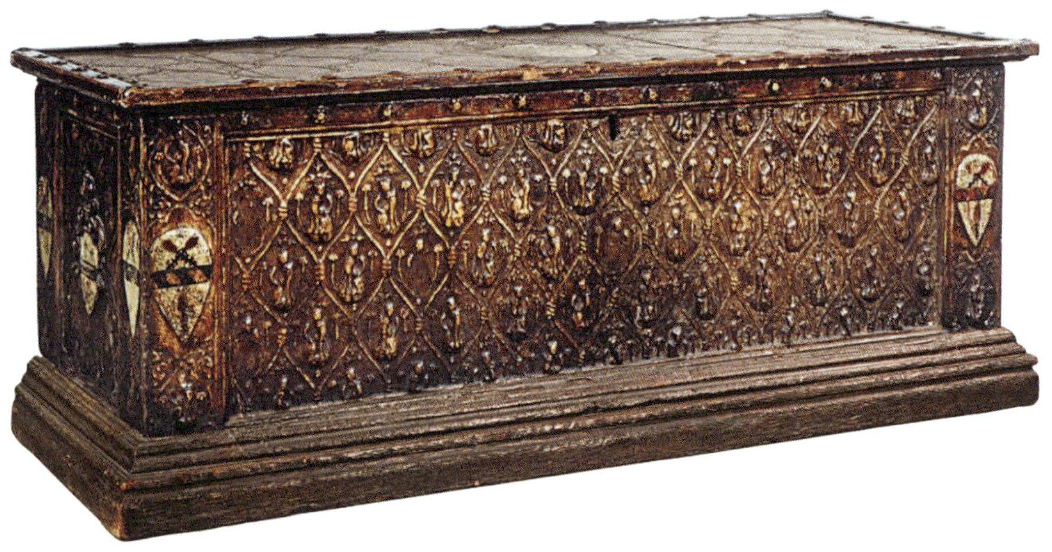

Cassone with noble coat of arms of the Segardi-Cristofori family, ca. 1460, polychrome pastiglia decoration, 186 × 71 cm
Amboise, château du Clos Lucé

among courtesans, workshops and factories. Finally, when she arrived in Florence, she was placed as a young slave in the old house of Donato and Ginevra Nati, which still smelt of the wood and varnish of the *cassone* makers of the past, and in the magnificent palace of the knight Francesco Castellani, still imbued with the exquisite perfumes of the Byzantine emperors and princesses he had welcomed at the Council of Florence.

Caterina passed through all these worlds, retaining the freshness of her skin, the scent of which inflamed the passion of her lover, Piero, in Donato's old house:

> She was like an apparition. The soft step of her bare feet on the stone, the rustle of her long, lightweight maid's clothes that barely concealed her breasts, a radiance, a scent of fresh skin that prevailed over the stale odour of old, weathered documents smelling of mould. (Chap. 10)

The "wild" scent of Caterina's body: this must have been Leonardo's first sensory impression when he was born, the thread that enabled him to rediscover the harmony he had lost in the labyrinth of life.

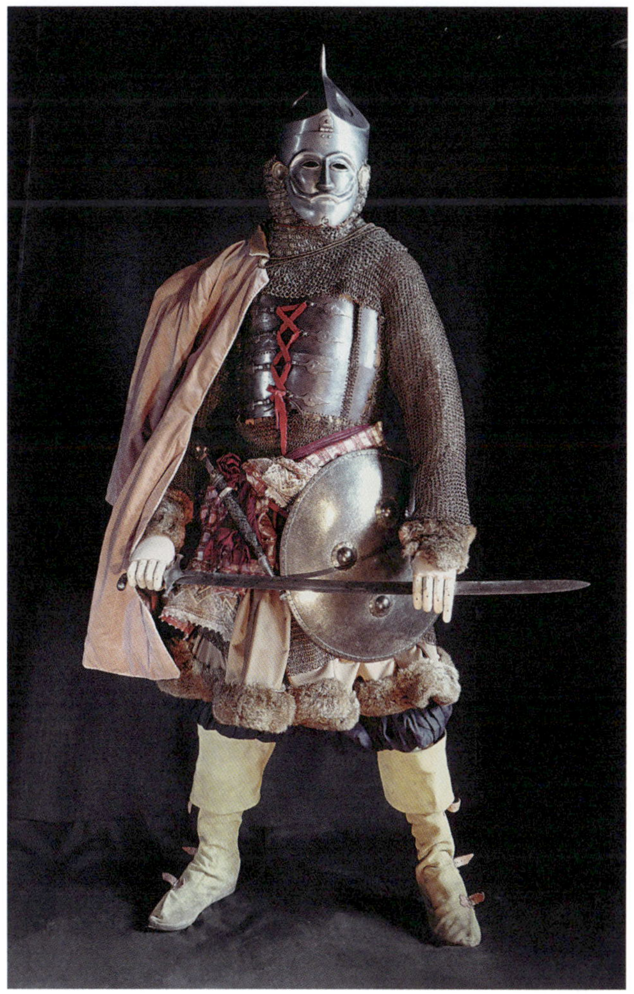

Circassian men's costume, Coll. MERCURIUS More Curious

Bibliography

Čerkesy. Voiny i mastera (Nalchik [Russia]: Kotlyarov Press, 2012).

Abazov Alexey Khasanovich, Ančabadze Ju. D., Kušchabiev Anzor Viktorovich, Paštova Madina Mikhailovna, *Adygi. Adygejcy, Kabardincy, Čerkesy, Šapsugi* (Moscow: 2022).

Vecce Carlo, *Il sorriso di Caterina, la madre di Leonardo* (Florence: Giunti, 2023) (French edition forthcoming: Paris, Seuil, 2024).

Id., *Per Caterina*, "Leonardiana", 1 (2023), pp. 11–48.

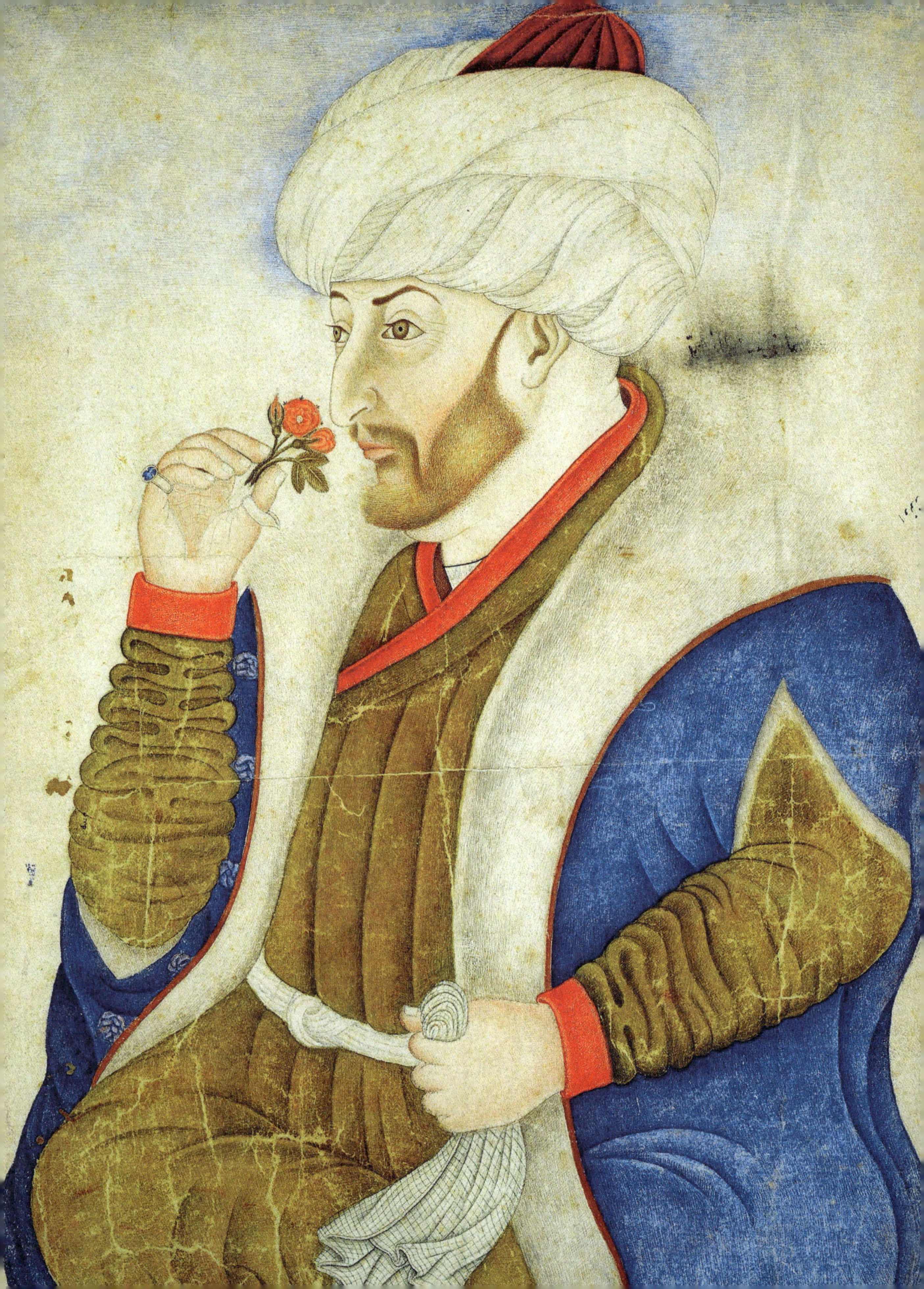

FRAGRANCES IN CONSTANTINOPLE IN THE 15TH CENTURY

Özge Samanci

The spice market (the "Egyptian Bazaar"), where all kinds of spices, perfumes and dried fruit are sold, is a familiar sight in Istanbul today. Shortly before the Ottoman era, the Byzantine city was already a major global trading hub, where spices and aromatics were among the most important and expensive products. A book of regulations for the guilds of retail traders in Constantinople, which dates from the year 900, bears witness to the profusion of perfumes and spices found in the markets. The spice trade featured prominently in the *Book of Eparch*, particularly in the chapter devoted to the *myrepsoi* ("perfumers"). These merchants sold not only perfumes and dyes, but also spices used in food, drink, medicines and incense. They sold pepper, spikenard, cinnamon, aloeswood, ambergris, musk, frankincense, myrrh, balsam, indigo, dyer's herbs, lapis lazuli, fustic, storax and all the different items used in perfumery and dyeing. These spices and aromatics were transported from Trebizond, one of the possible final destinations on the Silk Road at the eastern end of the Black Sea, and above all from the Arab-Muslim markets in the territories under Arab rule. For centuries, spices and perfumes were transported along the same routes as silk.

Perfumes and Scents in Places of Worship

Perfumes and fragrances were used to purify and consecrate places of worship in Constantinople. This age-old practice has been used for thousands of years by many civilisations around the Mediterranean and in the Middle East, and was equally common among the ancient Hebrews, Christians and Muslims; the Byzantine and Ottoman civilisations were no exception. Their use was ubiquitous in late Byzantine religion, whether for daily rites, during monastic hours, or for major ceremonies such as baptisms and funerals. During the liturgy of the Eucharist, Byzantine churches were filled with the smoke of incense, which was diffused both by slowly swinging chain censers and by standing censers placed in front of icons. In the key liturgical texts, particularly those relating to religious services, a detailed description of how incense should be diffused was included to guide the ritual burning of incense and to help understand its significance. Symeon of Thessalonica, one of the great commentators on the late Byzantine world, described incense as "the sweet odour of the Holy Spirit". The "*typikon*", or liturgical rule, listed

LEFT
Nakkaş Sinan Bey, *Portrait of Sultan Mehmet II*, 15th c., Istanbul, Topkapı Palace Manuscripts Collection, inv. H2153, f. 10b

donations of censers and incense to monasteries, as well as information about their use. Myrrh and frankincense were also included in the list of products used for healing. In texts from the late Byzantine period up until the 15th century, frankincense is continually presented as a symbol of divine presence and sacrifice, but also as a substance with medicinal and purifying properties. Censers are frequently depicted in paintings and mosaics, most often in the representation of processions.

The incense used in Byzantine liturgy, in the form of aromatic resin or gum from various species of tree, came in the form of solid, irregular beads. Placed on hot coals at the bottom of an incense burner, it burned slowly, giving off a fragrant smoke. Byzantine censers were generally made of a copper alloy; no trace has been found of more expensive silver models. Benzoin, myrrh and frankincense (also known as "olibanum", depending on its origin) were among the most commonly used fragrances. Myrrh and frankincense are aromatic gum resins, with frankincense being produced specifically from the resin of the *Boswellia sacra* tree. In the 15th century, benzoin was shipped from south-west Anatolia and Syria. Balm of Gilead (*Commiphora opobalsamum*) was also widely used, derived from the bark of a small tree native to Egypt and Palestine.

Like the Byzantines of the late Byzantine period, the Ottomans perfumed places of worship on holy days, as well as graves throughout the year, with an incense called *buhur*. In Islamic civilisation, great importance was attached to perfumes, which were used in both public spaces (mosques) and private spaces (homes, graves). The Ottomans, for example, burned incense in mosques before Friday collective prayers, during the recitation of the Koran, and at religious ceremonies to celebrate the Prophet's birthday, amongst other occasions. The Hadiths and the words and deeds of the Prophet provide a wealth of information on the use of perfume by Muslims, particularly on a daily basis for personal hygiene, to perfume their clothes and to complement religious rites. Furthermore, perfume was used as a distinguishing feature to differentiate between good and evil: in the Koran, paradise is described as a sweet-smelling place.

In the 15th century, the Ottomans used animal-based products, resins and exotic woods for their incense. Unlike the Byzantines, they preferred composite fragrances to perfume religious spaces. Ottoman tradition, for example, frequently combined musk, a secretion from the anal glands of the Siberian deer, with *buhur*. Repeatedly mentioned in Hadiths, musk was considered one of the Prophet's favourite fragrances. Calambac (aloeswood) and ambergris are other fragrances that were often combined to make incense. Ambergris, which is an intestinal concretion of the sperm whale (*Physeter macrocephalus*), was prized as greatly as musk for its marine, earthy scent. Calambac, a very dense resinous wood found in India and South-East Asia, with a strong aromatic scent, had the same medicinal properties as incense. Like sandalwood, it was used as a raw material for furniture and prayer beads (*tesbih*). Both woods gave off a heavy, sweet smell when burnt. Finally, camphor, a solid aromatic substance extracted from the camphor tree, was another fragrance included in the preparation of *buhur*. In the 15th century, musk, amber and red sandalwood were among the spices and aromatics purchased for the imperial palace. The Ottomans imported these materials from the Indian Ocean region and shipped them to Istanbul along with many other aromatic spices.

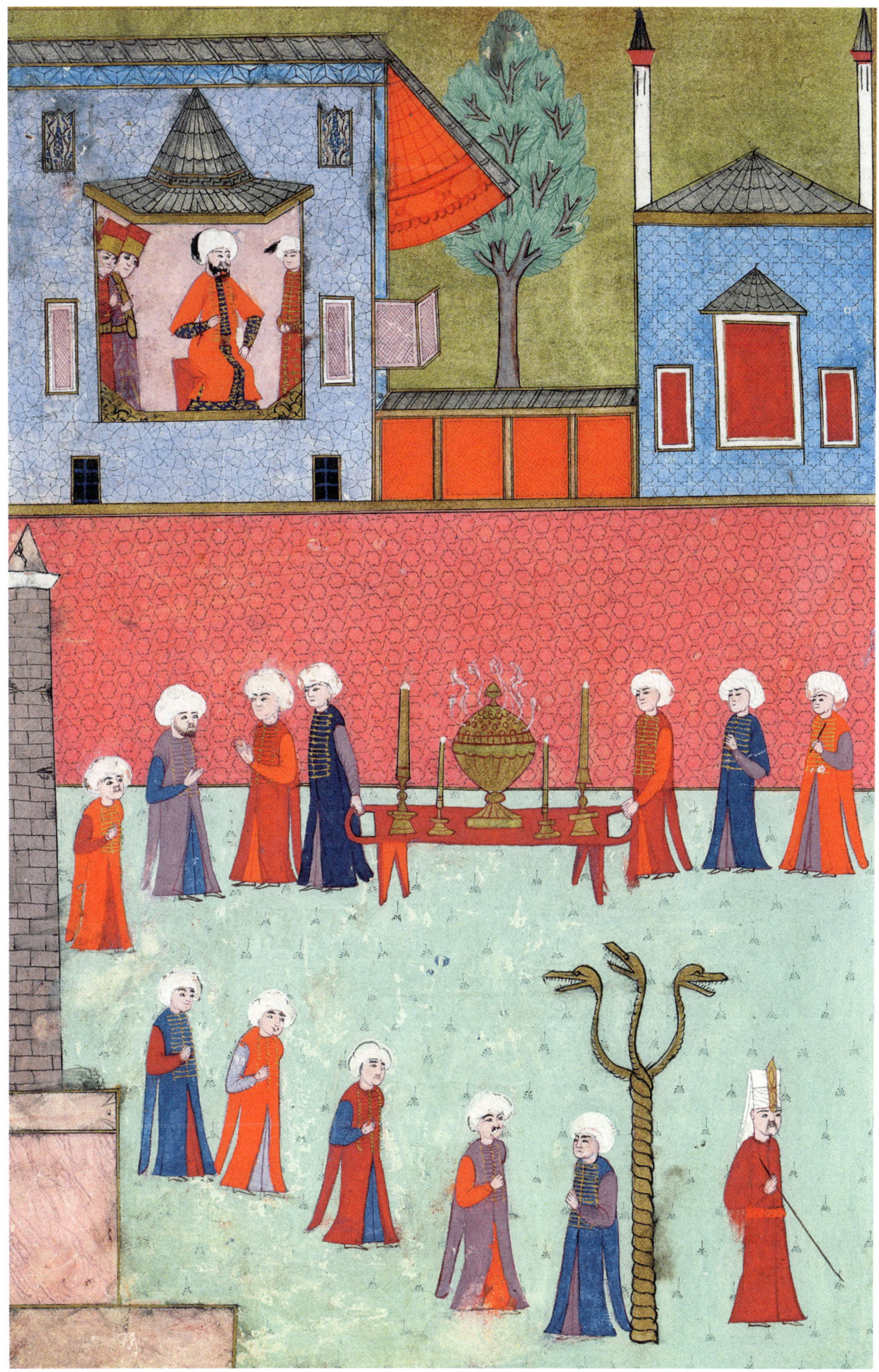

Nakkaş Osman, *Procession of the Guild of Buhurcus in Surname-i Hümayun*, ca. 1582, Istanbul, Topkapı Palace Manuscripts Collection, inv H.1344, f. 112b-13a

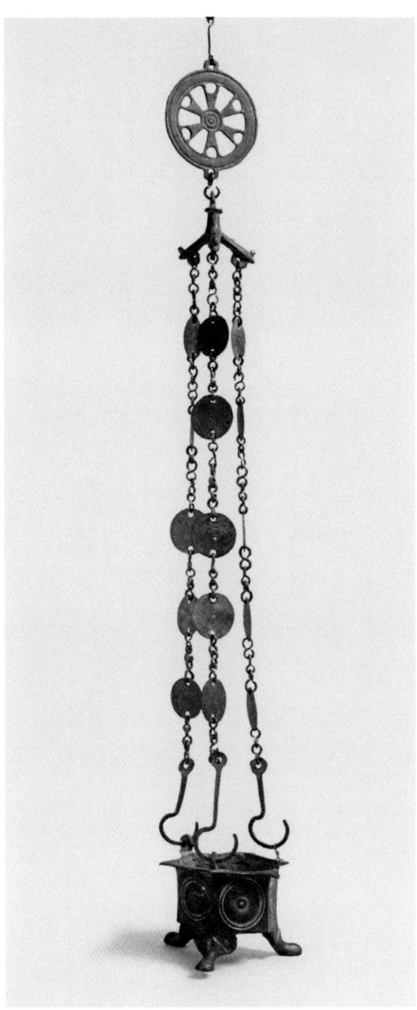

Censer, 6th c., Constantinople, Byzantium (?), cast copper alloy, 77.5 × 10.9 cm, New York, Metropolitan Museum of Art, donated by the Estate of Lawrence J. Majewski, 1999

Calambac and ambergris could be burnt pure in small pieces after being placed on embers at the bottom of the censer, or they could be mixed with an additive, such as coal dust, sawdust or other types of resin. The result was then moulded into sticks, round pellets and so on. The censer, known as a *buhurdan*, meant to burn the incense pellets, could be used in three different ways: suspended, fixed or mobile. In Ottoman culture, roses were another favourite material in the preparation of incense. Rose water was often used in religious ceremonies, as it was linked to the belief that the Prophet Mohammed himself naturally smelt of roses. Recipes for incense were varied. Those used in the Ottoman palace were prepared in the imperial confectionery (*helvahane*). The recipe for the Prophet's incense, for example, incorporated materials as diverse as ambergris, benzoin, calambac, mastic, saffron, hyacinth, myrtle leaves, camphor, bitter orange

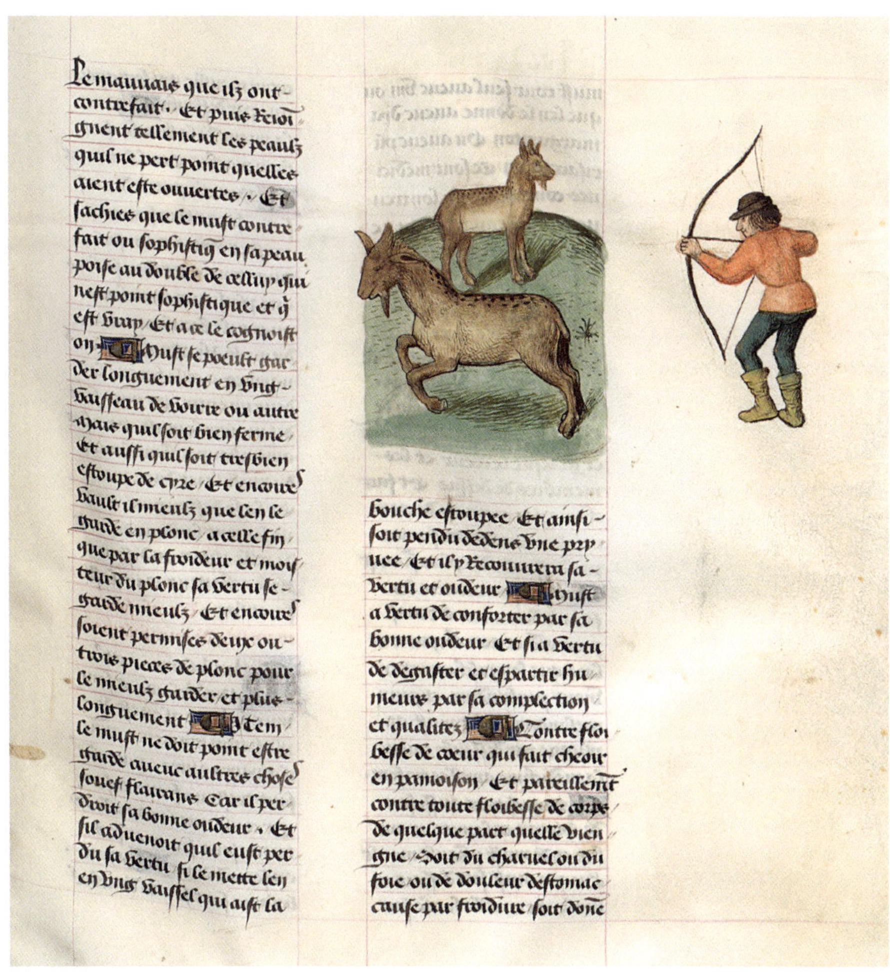

Matthaeus Platearius, *The Book of Simple Medicines, also known as a herbal, in alphabetical order*, 1401–1500, Ms Fr 9136, f. 189, Paris, Bibliothèque nationale de France

peel, musk, sugar and willow charcoal.

Perfumes in Daily Life

In Byzantine times, rosemary was one of the spices used to perfume the streets of Constantinople. Along with myrtle and ivy, it was used to decorate the imperial dining room. Mixing perfumes and making aromas were an integral part of Byzantine imperial culture. The Byzantine emperor's cabinet contained various incense and scented materials, such as musk, ambergris, dry aloeswood, cinnamon, mastic, sugar and saffron. Roses, prized for their "divine" scent, were used to prepare crowns and crosses to be presented to the emperor, and their water was used in cooking, for example, to prepare flavoured wine.

In the Ottoman era, rosewater and incense were essential components of ceremonies – banquets or meetings – held in the palace. After meals, on days when the Divan (the Ottoman sultan's council) was meeting, a servant would offer rose water to the guests to wash their hands, while another would perfume the room with incense, usually composed of aloes, rose water and

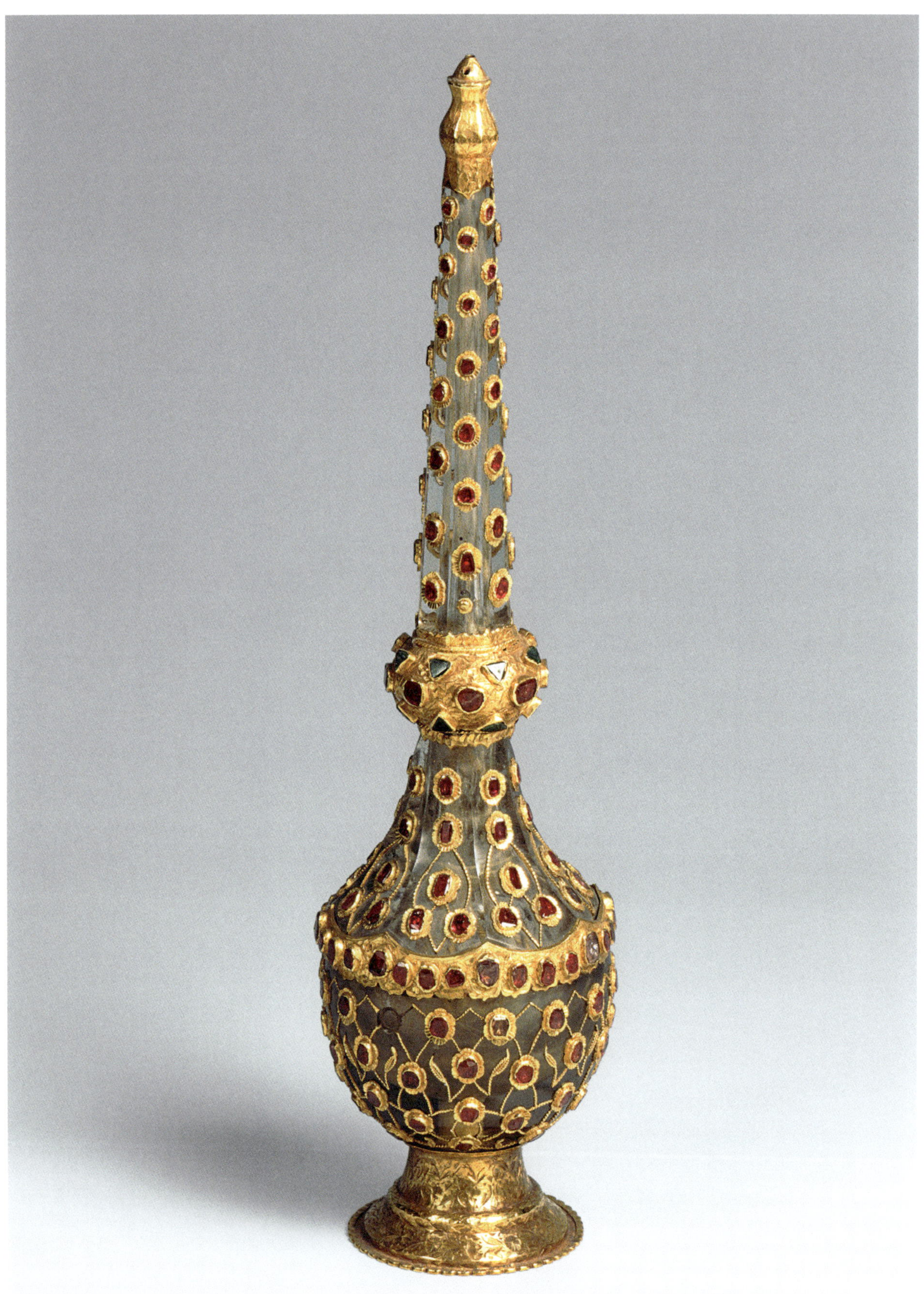

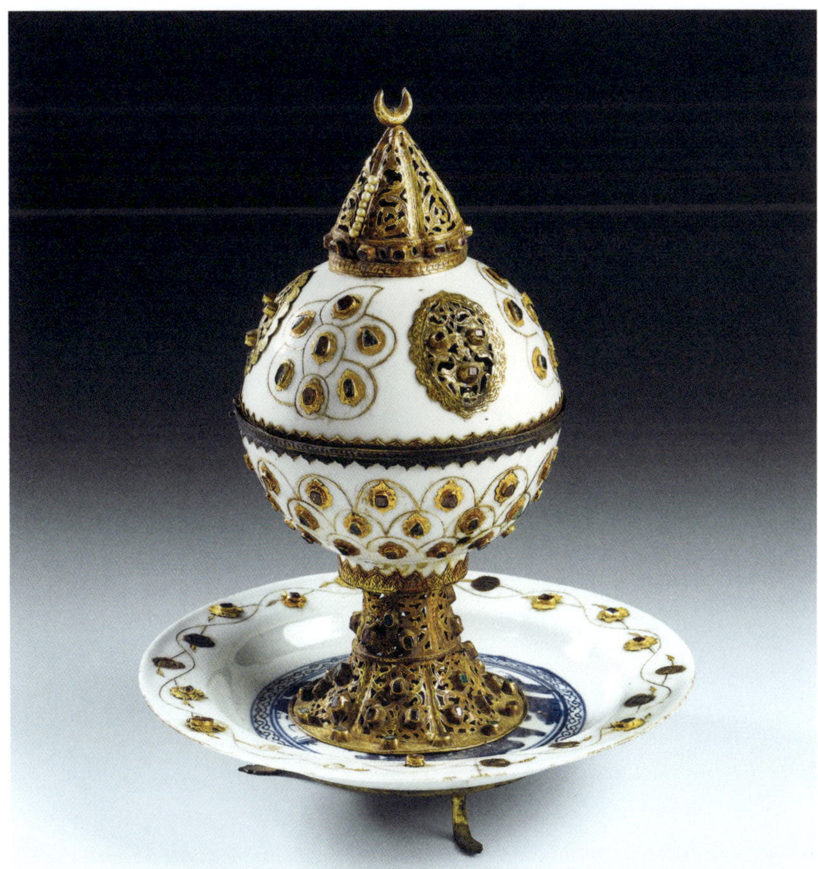

Censer decorated with precious stones, Istanbul, Topkapı Palace Chinese and Japanese Porcelains Collection, inv. 15/2771

ambergris. It was also customary to burn incense in the sultan's harem after the meal.

The distillation of rose water, like the burning of incense, became an indispensable tradition in Ottoman palace culture. Because of the significance given to perfumes in Islamic culture, sultans placed great importance on them as a means of demonstrating their power. A classic example is when Mehmet II, known as Mehmet the Conqueror, after taking Constantinople in 1453, had Hagia Sophia reopened for worship after having it completely cleaned with rose water. Under the Ottoman Empire, no fewer than forty servants were assigned to the ceremony of offering rose water and incense, and when musk and ambergris arrived in Istanbul, the sultan took precedence over everyone else in their purchase. These two facts clearly illustrate the importance of perfumes in reflecting the magnificence of Ottoman power.

Ottoman incense burners were usually made in the shape of pine cones, poppy-seed pods or similar fruits. Incense burners designed on a single-footed base and placed on a wide table were covered by a lid with a grid or perforations to allow the smoke to escape. The lid, generally pointed or dome-shaped, had a long handle on the side.

LEFT
Rose water sprinkler
16th c., Istanbul, Topkapı Palace Treasury Collection, inv. 2/7

The Topkapı and Edirne palaces were renowned for their rose gardens. On the south side of the Topkapı palace, along the banks of the Sea of Marmara, there were large gardens filled with roses and a variety of flowers – the "Gülhane gardens" (from *gül*, Turkish for "rose"). Rose water was poured into precious sprinklers called *gülabdan*, and was frequently used by the women of the court as an ingredient, particularly to add to a perfume that had already been prepared using ambergris, aloe vera, rose oil and powdered pearls. Rose water was also used in cooking, as a sweetener or for its fragrance, in the same way as other flavours. According to the 15th-century culinary manuscript written by the physician Şirvani, rose water, musk and hyacinths were among the fragrant aromatics found in a number of recipes, particularly sweet ones. Finally, rose water mixed with orange blossom water could also be used to flavour drinks made using fruit, flowers or spices.

Bibliography

Dalby Andrew, *Flavours of Byzantium* (London: Prospects Books, 2003).

Ergin Nina, "The Fragrance of the Divine: Ottoman Incense Burners and Their Context", *Art Bulletin*, College Art Association, vol. XCVI, no. 1 (March 2014).

Gedük Serkan, "Osmanlı Saray Kültüründe Buhur ve Gül Suyu Geleneği", *Topkapı Sarayı Müzesi Yıllık-6*, 124 (2013).

Hedrick Tera Lee, Ergin Nina, "A Shared Culture of Heavenly Fragrance: A Comparison of Late Byzantine and Ottoman Incense Burners and Censing Practices in Religious Contexts", *Dumbarton Oaks Papers*, vol. 69 (2015), pp. 331–54.

Uzun Beyza, *Ottoman Olfactory Traditions in a Palatial Space: Incense Burners in the Topkapı Palace*. Unpublished Master's Thesis, Anatolian Civilizations and Cultural Heritage Management, Koç University, 2015.

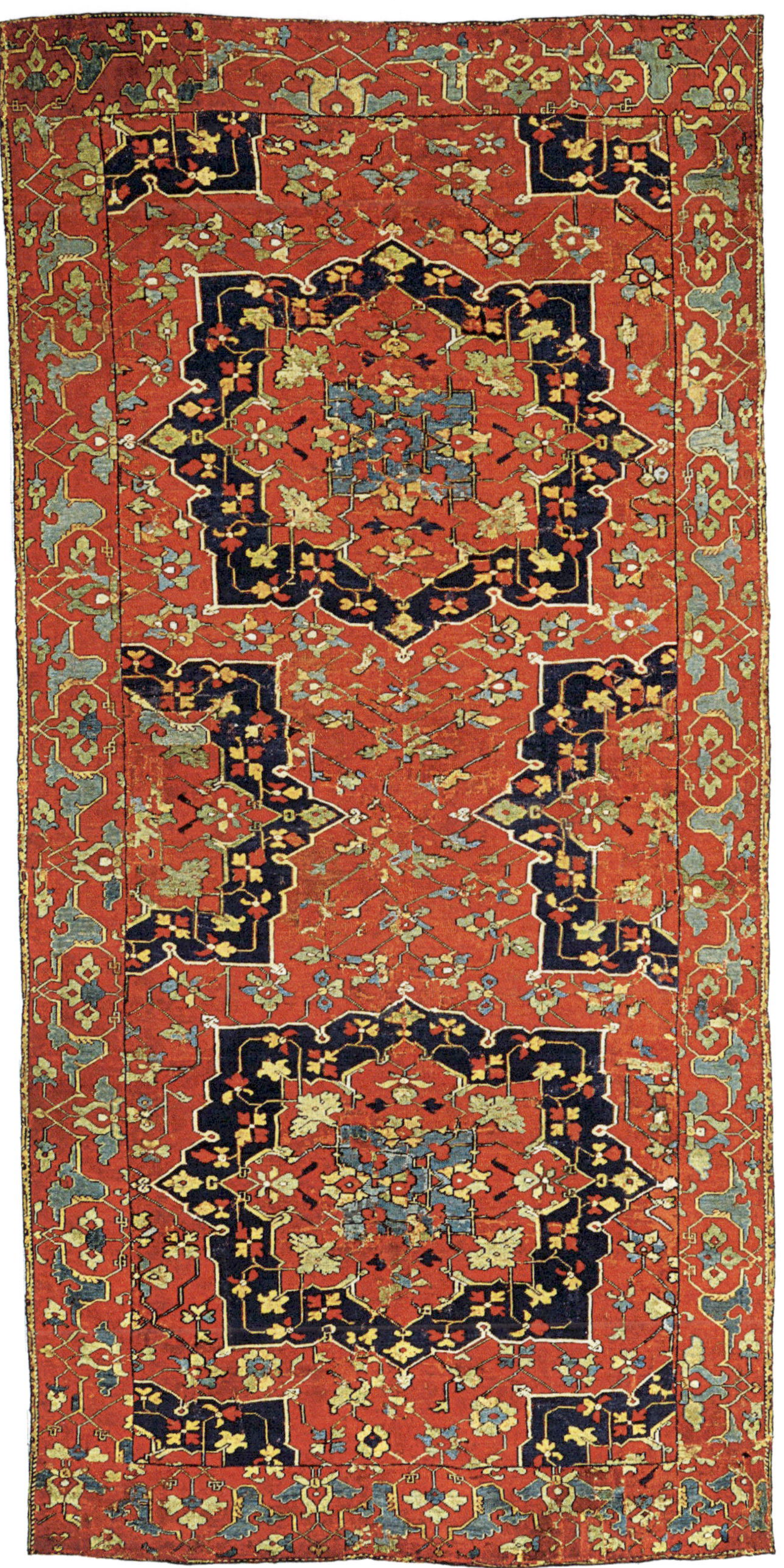

Star Ushak carpet from West Anatolia, 15th c., wool, 297 × 148 cm, Milan, Galleria Moshe Tabibnia, inv. 124326

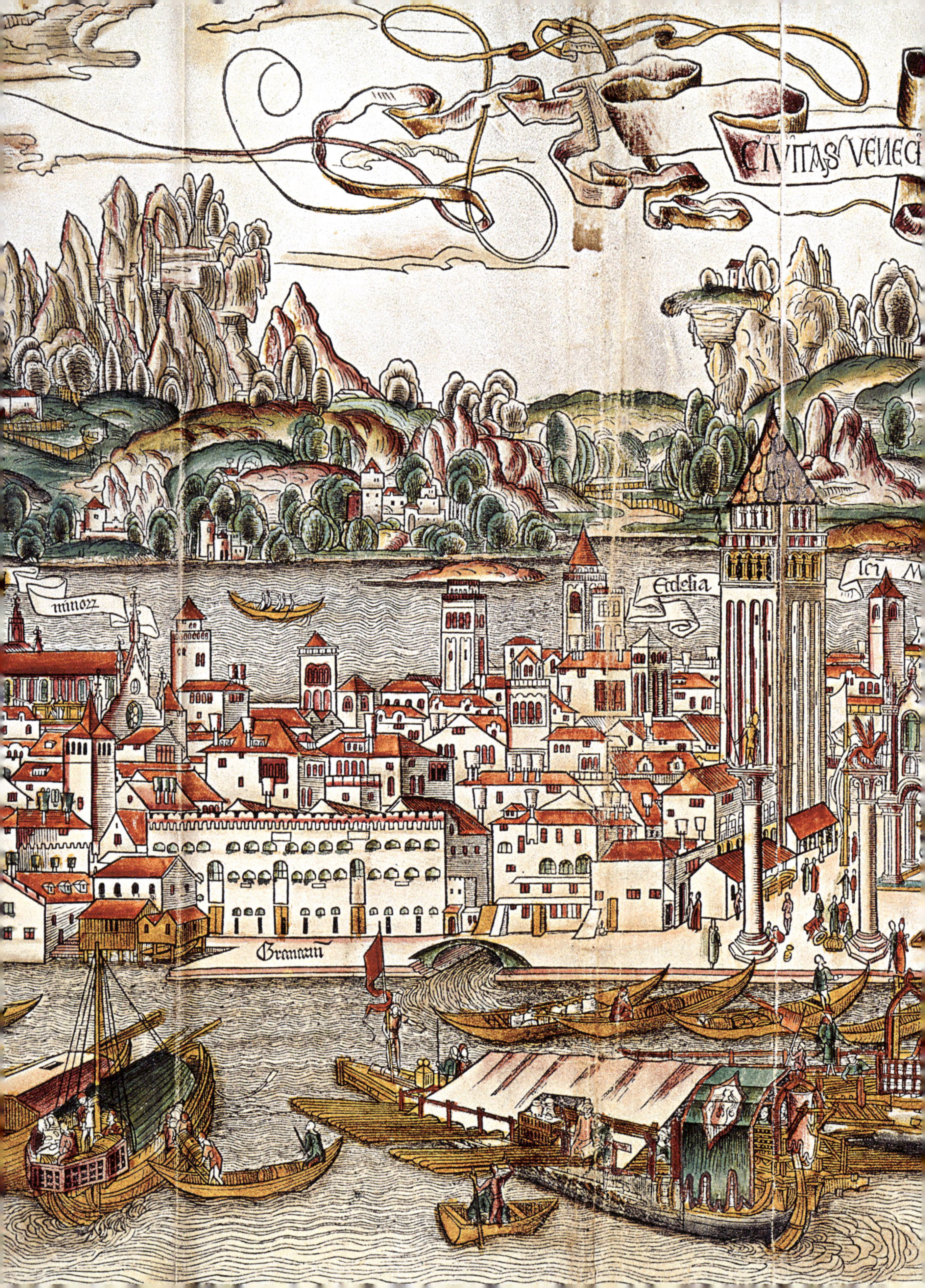
CIVITAS VENECI
minor
Ecclesia
Granaii

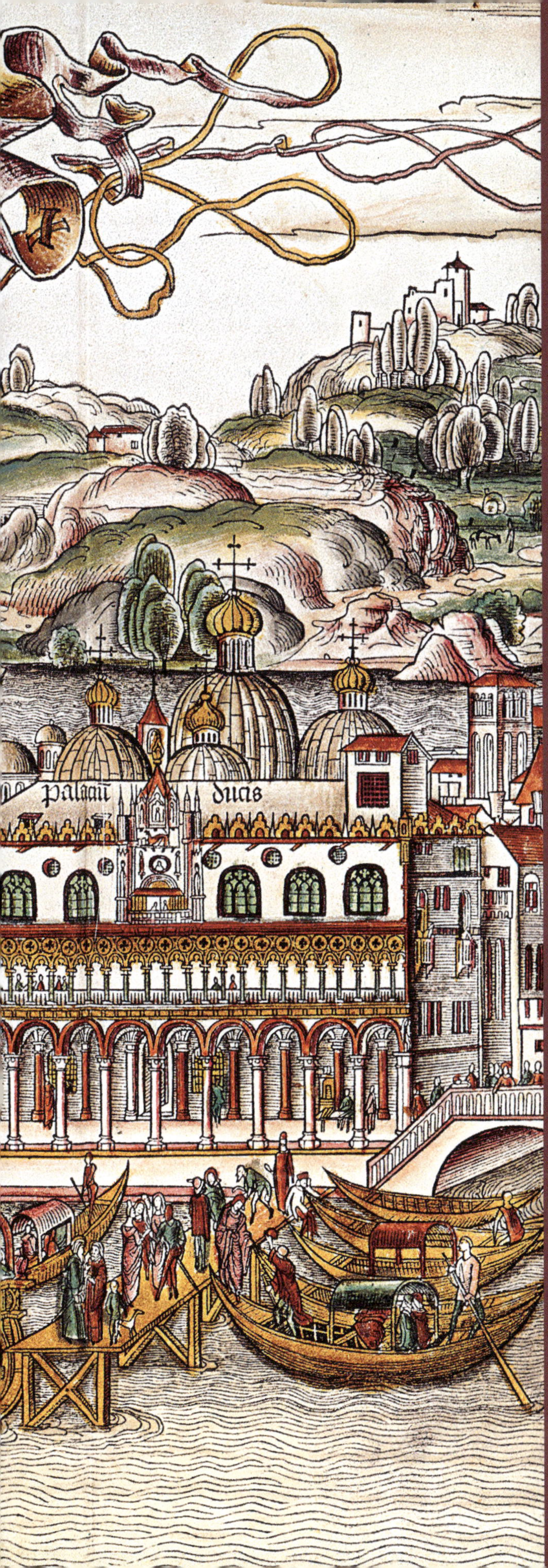

Venice, Gateway to the Orient

Chapter II

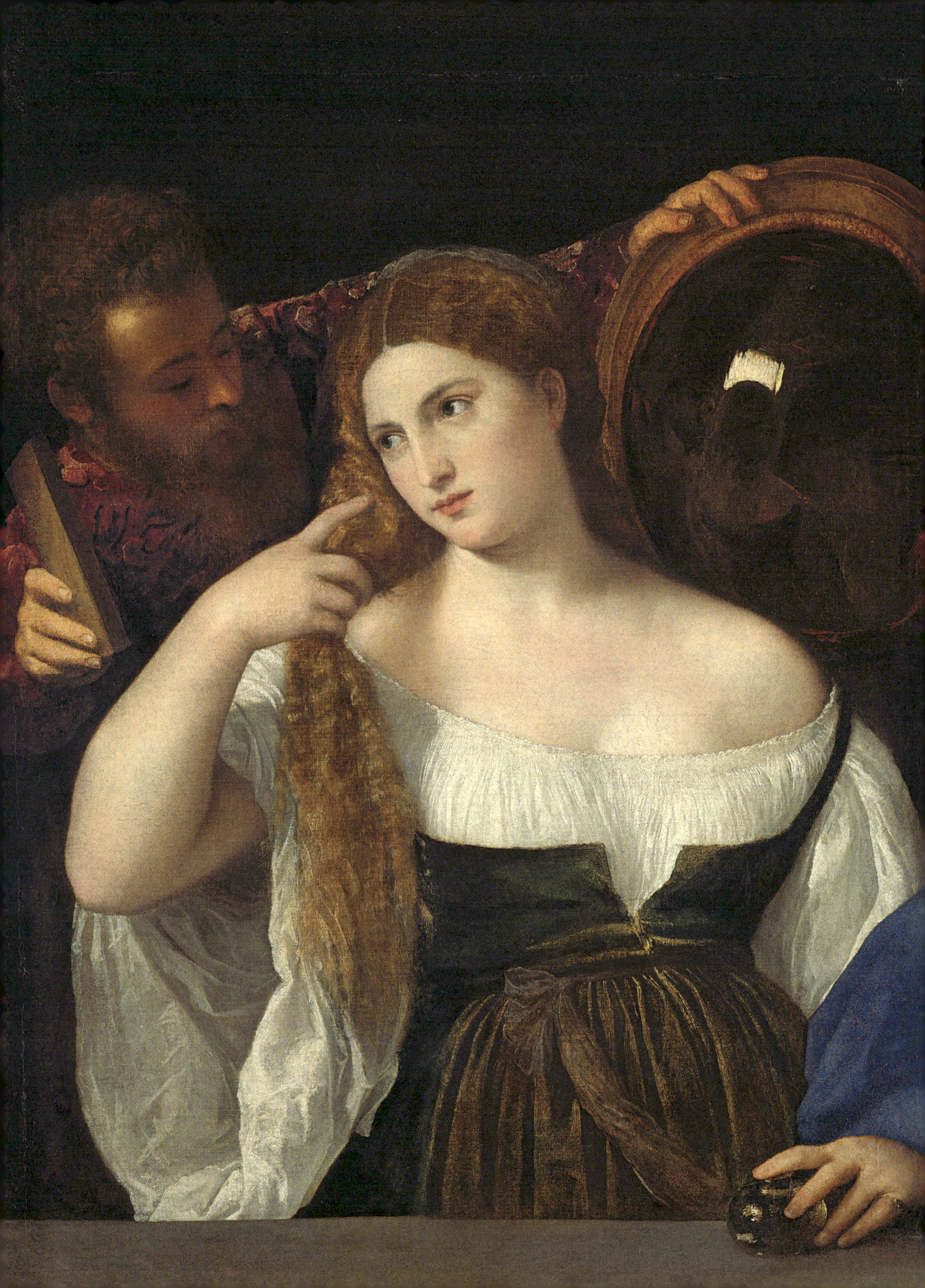

PERFUME IN VENICE IN THE 15TH AND 16TH CENTURIES

Anna Messinis

Venice's role in the understanding and distribution of perfumes is reflected in its trade in precious raw materials from the Orient, in the recipe books and treatises on cosmetics and perfumery that were produced by Venetian printing works in the 16th century, and in the existence of specialised workshops in the city. Venetians set up a powerful trading network that supplied the Serenissima and exported to Europe the raw materials of Oriental origin that were essential for making perfumes; in particular, materials derived from animals, which played a major role in perfumery in the late Middle Ages and early modern period.

Many of the substances used in perfumery can be found in the trade manuals of the 14th century, and had already received attention from Marco Polo in his *Il Milione*, which, for example, describes the extraction of ambergris from the body of a whale, and gives fairly precise information about musk, both in terms of the musk deer from which it derives and the methods used to extract it.

This information can be found in the *tariffe*, texts that provided merchants with rules and practical ideas for juggling goods, duties, weights and measures, as in the Alexandrian *tariffe* (Sopracasa, 2013), drawn up at the turn of the 15th and 16th centuries, that combined customs information with notes on the characteristics and properties of products. For example, the annotation on musk is curious: "it has a powerful odour and a bitterness in the mouth and if it is of good quality it will pass into your brain and fill you with desire" (Sopracasa, 2013, p. 584).

Musk, ambergris, civet, camphor, ladanum, aloeswood, storax, benzoin, incense, sugared almonds, cloves, nutmeg and sandalwood arrived in Venice from Constantinople, Damascus, Aleppo and Alexandria. From there, these goods were transported to Milan, Genoa, Ferrara, Bologna, Florence, Rome and the Kingdom of Naples: this is the overview of trade movements offered by Bartolomeo Paxi's *"Tariffa" of Weights and Measures* of 1503, the first such work to be published in Venice.

These precious goods, which were difficult to procure, received particular attention from merchants. The account book of the Venetian patrician Giacomo Badoer records the daily transactions carried out during his stay in Constantinople from 1436 to 1440. He makes several references to musk and civet, which he bought to order from other Venetian merchants, bartering them for

PREVIOUS PAGE
Bernhard de Breydenbach (author)
Illustrations in *Opusculum sanctorum peregrinationum ad spulcrum Christi venerandum*, plate 1, central part, view of Venice 1486, woodcut, 106.5 × 23.5 cm, Paris, Bibliothèque nationale de France, BNF RCC3926

LEFT
Fig. 1. Titian, *Portrait of a Woman at her Toilet*, oil on canvas, 99 × 76 cm, Paris, musée du Louvre, inv. 755

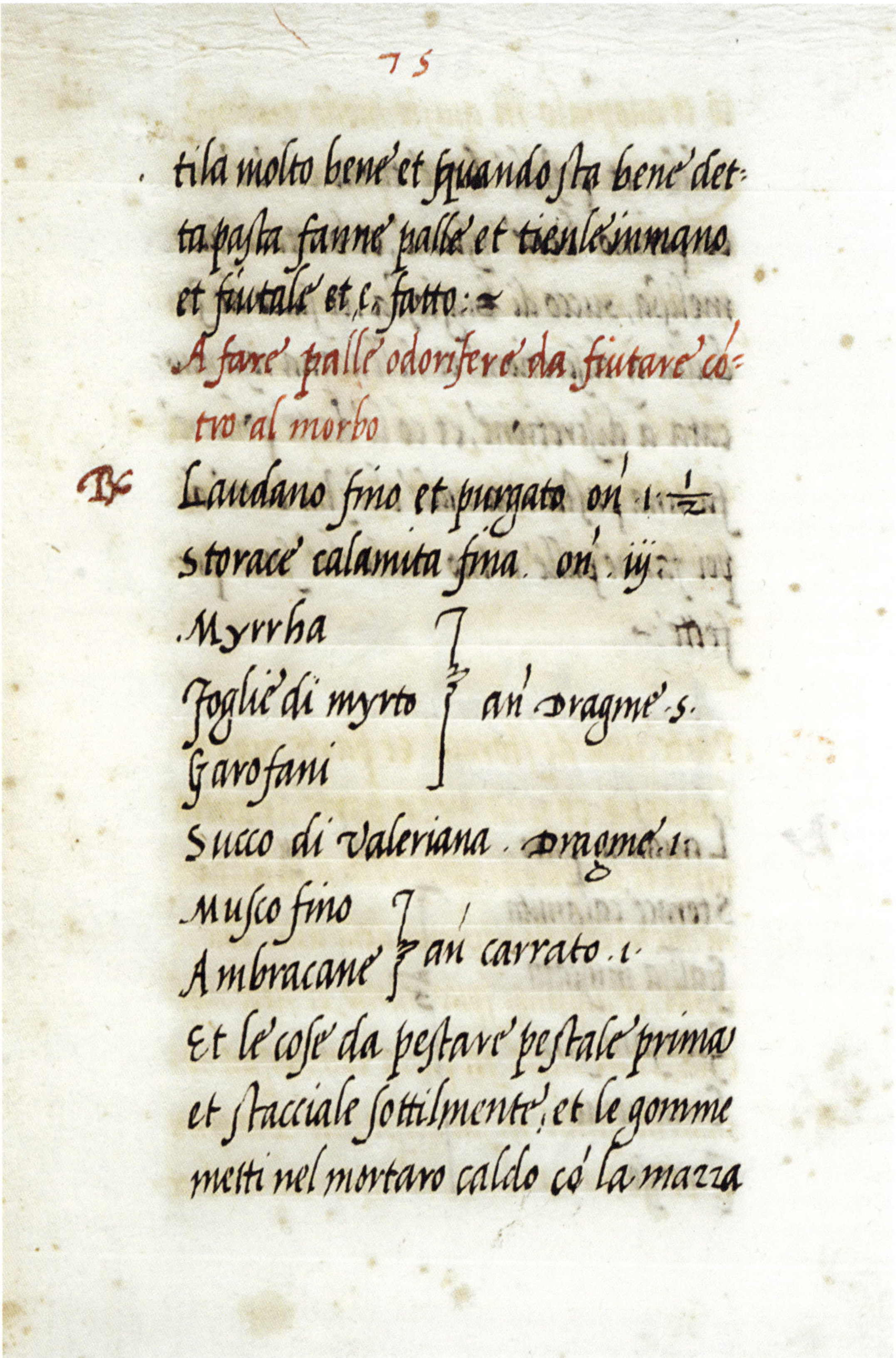

75

tila molto bene et quando sta bene det-
ta pasta fanne palle et tienle in mano
et fiutale et è fatto:

A fare palle odorifere da fiutare co-
tro al morbo

℞ Laudano fino et purgato on. 1 ½
Storace calamita fina. on. iij.
Myrrha
Foglie di myrto } an. dragme .s.
Garofani
Succo di valeriana. dragme 1
Musco fino
Ambracane } an. carrato .1.
Et le cose da pestare pestale prima
et stacciale sottilmente, et le gomme
metti nel mortaro caldo cō la mazza

Fig. 2. *Ricettario o libro dei segreti galanti*, MS. It. III, 9 (=5221), c. 75r "A far palle odorifere", early 16th c.
Venice, Biblioteca Nazionale Marciana

valuable fabrics. Giacomo Badoer had his own trusted supplier of musk and civet, and usually delivered the precious cargo directly to the ship's captain. In fact, musk was worth slightly less than gold (in Constantinople, one gram of musk was worth 0.8 grams of gold), while civet was worth half as much. A century later, the merchant Andrea Berengo, who ran a trade in goods between Syria, Cyprus and Venice from Aleppo, devoted the same attention to buying and transporting ambergris, chypre powder, perfumed waters, "eau de naffe" (distilled from orange blossom) and, above all, musk deer bladders, which were shipped as quickly as possible, even if the quantities were insufficient to meet demand. Pressure from buyers, including some very famous figures, was very strong. In Venice, Isabella d'Este bought musk, amber, civet, benzoin, rosewater and musk water through her agent, the musical instrument maker Lorenzo Gusnasco from Pavia, who was also approached by Ludovico Sforza (Lorenzo was also the author of the letter of 13 March 1500 in which he informed Isabella of Leonardo's presence in Venice, and of the fact that he had seen a portrait of the Marchioness of Mantua herself) [fig. 1].

To explore the world of the preparation of waters, oils, pastes, powders, cosmetics and scented soaps, one must look at the recipe books. At the beginning of the 16th century, an anonymous manuscript was discovered, the hitherto unpublished *Ricettario o Libro dei Segreti Galanti* [fig. 2]. Of the two hundred recipes it contains, thirty-six are devoted to scented waters made mainly from the distillation of flowers, in particular lavender and orange blossom, preferably combined with musk. The recipe book opens with the preparation of a "celestial water" made from an enormous number of ingredients: a wide variety of spices, herbs, flowers and dried fruit, as well as orange

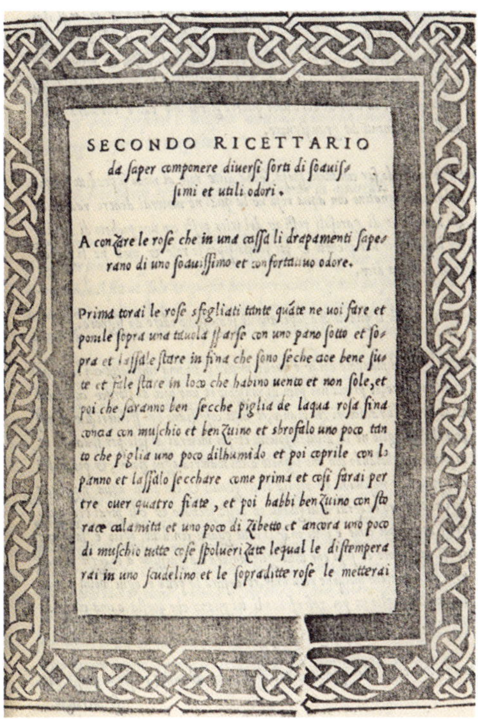

SECONDO RICETTARIO
da saper componere diversi sorti di soauis-
simi et utili odori.

A conzare le rose che in una cassa li drapamenti sape-
rano di uno soauissimo et confortativo odore.

Prima torai le rose sfegliati tante quãte ne uoi fare et
ponile sopra una tauola sparse con uno pano sotto et sopra et lassale stare in fina che sono seche ace bene su-
te et fale stare in loco che habino uento et non sole, et
poi che saranno ben secche piglia de laqua rosa fina
conca con muschio et benzuino et sbrofalo uno poco tan
to che piglia uno poco dilhumido et poi coprile con lo
panno et lassalo secchare come prima et cosi farai per
tre ouer quatro fiate, et poi habbi benzuino con sto
race calamita et uno poco di Zibetto et ancora uno poco
di muschio tutte cose spoluerizate lequal le distempera
rai in uno scudelino et le sopraditte rose le metterai

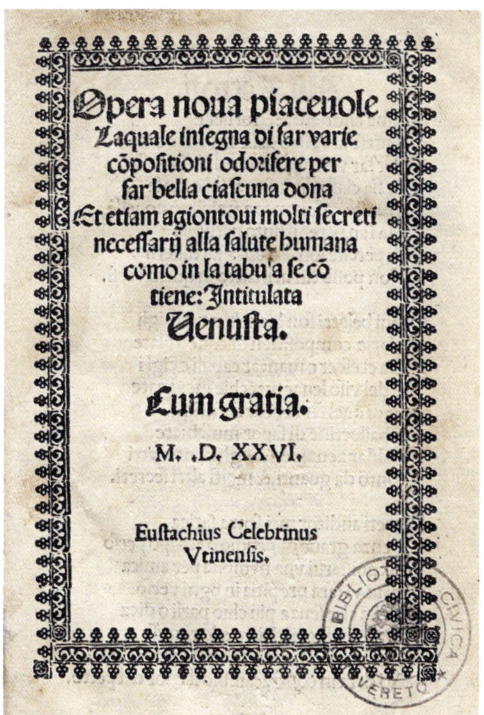

Opera noua piaceuole
Laquale insegna di far varie
cõpositioni odorifere per
far bella ciascuna dona
Et etiam agiontoui molti secreti
necessarij alla salute humana
como in la tabula se cõ
tiene: Intitulata
Venusta.

Cum gratia.

M. .D. XXVI.

Eustachius Celebrinus
Vtinensis.

Fig. 3. *Opera nuoua intitolata Dificio di ricette* [...], f. 20r, 1525, Venice, Biblioteca della Fondazione Giorgio Cini

Fig. 4. Eustachio Celebrino, *Opera nova piacevole la quale insegna di far varie compositioni odorifere per far bella ciascuna dona et etiam agiontovi molti secreti necessarii alla salute humana como in la tabula se contiene intitulata Venusta*, 1526, Rovereto, Archivi Storici, Biblioteca Civica "Girolamo Tartarotti", r-Ar IV op 21

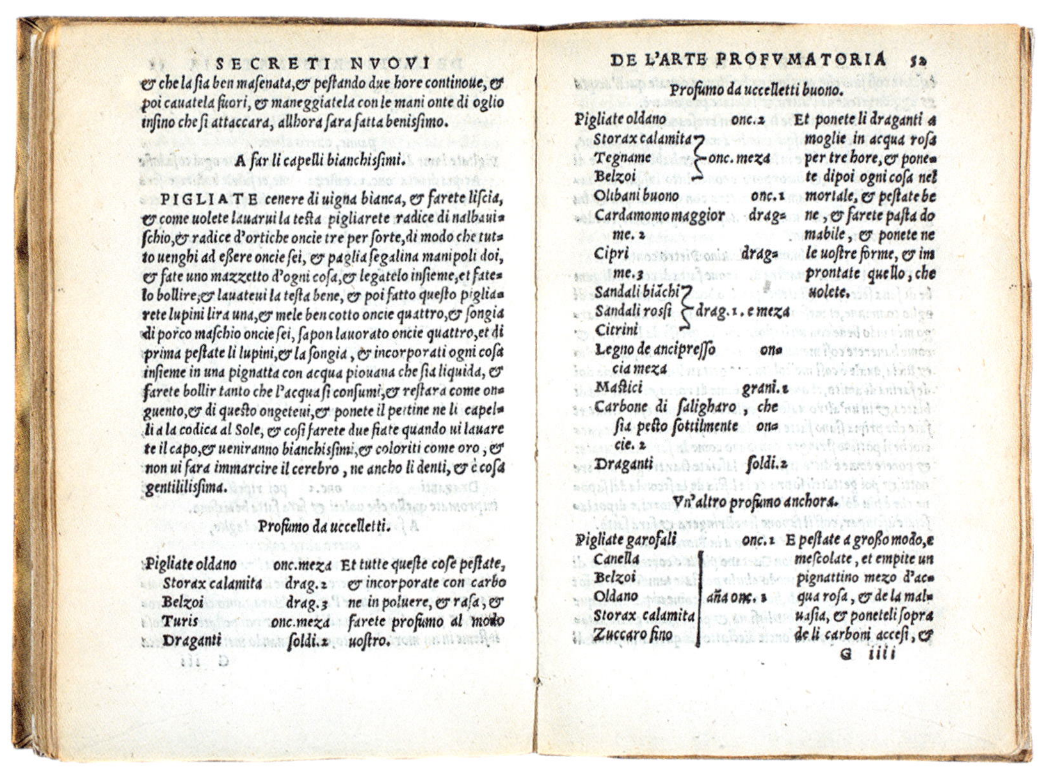

SECRETI NVOVI

& che la sia ben masenata, & pestando due hore continoue, & poi cauatela fuori, & maneggiatela con le mani onte di oglio insino che si attaccara, allhora sara fatta benissimo.

A far li capelli bianchissimi.

PIGLIATE cenere di uigna bianca, & farete liscia, & come uolete lauarui la testa pigliarete radice di nalbauischio, & radice d'ortiche oncie tre per sorte, di modo che tutto uenghi ad essere oncie sei, & paglia segalina manipoli doi, & fate uno mazzetto d'ogni cosa, & legatelo insieme, et fatelo bollire, & lauateui la testa bene, & poi fatto questo pigliarete lupini lira una, & mele ben cotto oncie quattro, & songia di porco maschio oncie sei, sapon lauorato oncie quattro, et di prima pestate li lupini, & la songia, & incorporati ogni cosa insieme in una pignatta con acqua piouana che sia liquida, & farete bollir tanto che l'acqua si consumi, & restara come onguento, & di questo ongeteui, & ponete il pettine ne li capelli a la codica al Sole, & cosi farete due fiate quando ui lauarete il capo, & ueniranno bianchissimi, & coloriti come oro, & non ui fara immarcire il cerebro, ne ancho li denti, & è cosa gentililissima.

Profumo da uccelletti.

Pigliate oldano onc. meza
Storax calamita drag. 2
Belzoi drag. 3
Turis onc. meza
Draganti soldi. 2

Et tutte queste cose pestate, & incorporate con carbone in poluere, & rasa, & farete profumo al modo uostro.

DE L'ARTE PROFVMATORIA 52

Profumo da uccelletti buono.

Pigliate oldano onc. 2
Storax calamita, Tegname, Belzoi onc. meza
Olibani buono onc. 1
Cardamomo maggior dragme. 2
Cipri dragme. 3
Sandali biāchi, Sandali rossi, Citrini drag. 1. e meza
Legno de ancipresso oncia meza
Mastici grani. 2
Carbone di saligharo, che sia pesto sottilmente oncie. 2
Draganti soldi. 2

Et ponete li draganti a moglie in acqua rosa per tre hore, & ponete dipoi ogni cosa nel mortale, & pestate bene, & farete pasta domabile, & ponete ne le uostre forme, & improntate quello, che uolete.

Vn'altro profumo anchora.

Pigliate garofali onc. 1
Canella, Belzoi, Oldano, Storax calamita, Zuccaro fino añaonc. 1

E pestate a grosso modo, e mescolate, et empite un pignattino mezo d'acqua rosa, & de la maluasia, & poneteli sopra de li carboni accesi, &

G iiii

Fig. 5. Giovanventura Rosetti, *Notandissimi secreti de l'arte profumatoria*, 1555, printed text, 16 × 11 cm
Paris, bibliothèque Sainte-Geneviève, inv. 8 T 1692 INV 4483 FA, f. 51v-52r

peel, aloe vera, mastic and incense, all of which are capable of making the skin radiant and fragrant, as well as having multiple healing qualities. It should be noted that distillation and the use of *eau de vigne* (grapevine water) are frequently mentioned in the recipe book. In some cases, there are also precise instructions on the quantities of ingredients to be used. There is no shortage of oils and soaps, pastes and powders to burn to scent rooms, such as "Damascus perfume" made from musk, civet, benzoin, aloeswood, storax and "whale amber" (an unusual but effective term to avoid confusion with amber, which is a fossil resin of plant origin), and "sweet-smelling balls whose fragrance was breathed in to avoid catching the plague". Perfumes were believed to protect against certain diseases, particularly the plague, a belief that had developed from the 14th century and was reinforced throughout the 16th century. Among the many texts on this subject is the *Consilium Clarissimi Doctoris Domini Petri de Tausignano pro Peste Evitanda*, written in 1398 by the physician Pietro Curialti and published in Venice in Johannes de Ketham's *Fasciculus medicinae* in 1491.

There are many published recipe books for cosmetics and perfumes, not least of which is the anonymous *Opera nuova* entitled *Dificio di ricette*, which was first printed in 1525 [fig. 3]. The second of the three volumes that make up this little book of a few dozen pages is dedicated to formulations for obtaining various kinds of pleasant and beneficial smells. It was a great success between 1525 and 1535, and was reprinted in Venice almost every year by two different printers. A similar pamphlet by Eustachio Celebrino appeared in Venice in 1526 under the delightful title: *Opera nova piacevole la quale insegna di far varie compositioni odorifere per far bella ciascuna*

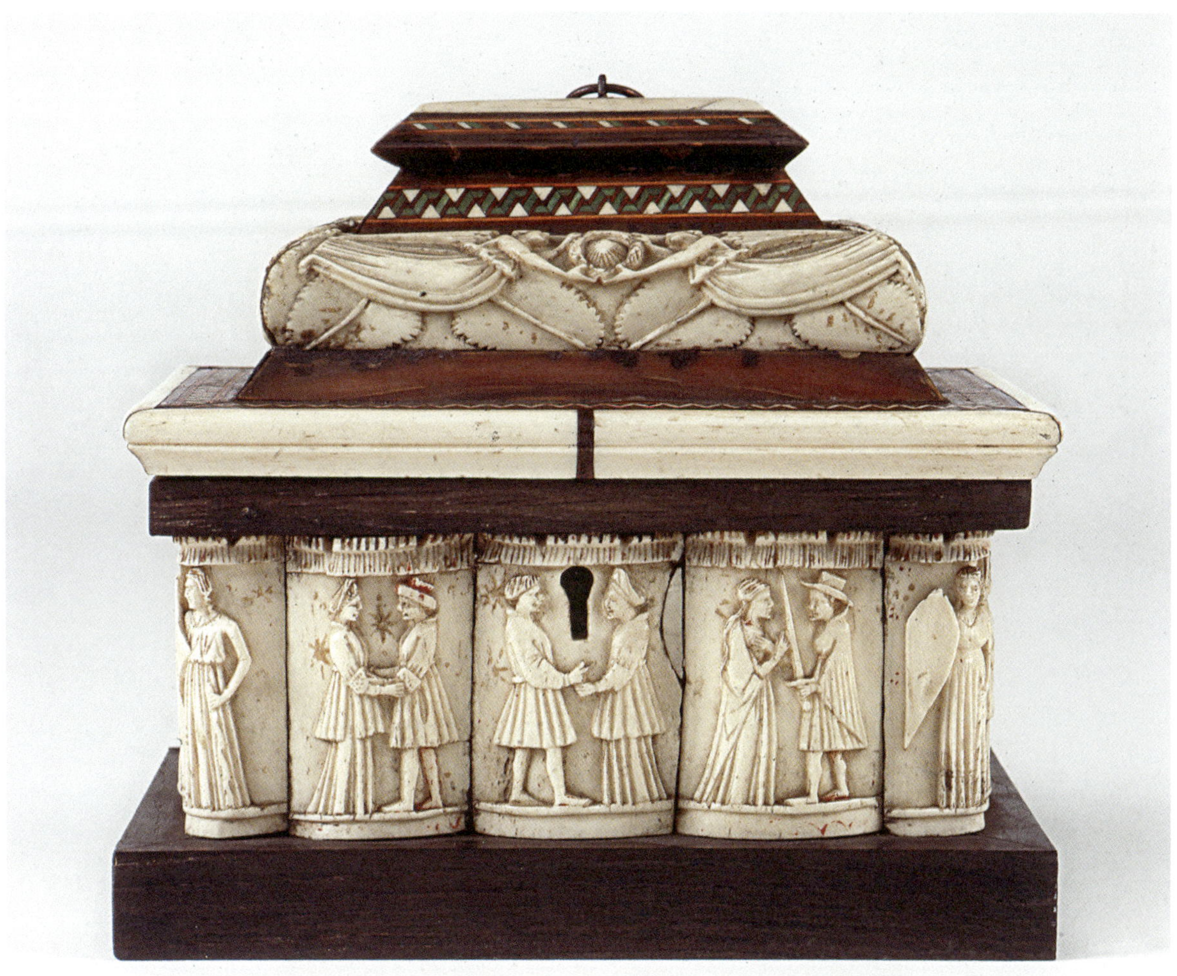

Balthazar Embriachi's workshop, ivory casket, early 16th c., 17 × 20 cm, Pavia, Musei Civici del Castello Visconteo, AM 28

dona et etiam agiontovi molti secreti necessarii alla salute humana como in la tabula se contiene intitulata Venusta [fig. 4].

Far more important was the book dedicated specifically to perfumes and cosmetics, the *Notandissimi secreti de l'arte profumatoria* by the Venetian, Giovanventura Rosetti [fig. 5], published in Venice in 1555, but written before 1549, the year of the author's death.

The 330 recipes include solid, powdered and liquid preparations used to perfume people, rooms and objects, linen and clothing, especially gloves. Animal substances played an important role, with musk appearing in over a hundred recipes, civet in forty-six, and amber in thirty-six. Resins were important, particularly benzoin, which appeared in around sixty recipes. Lastly, flowers such as Damask rose, orange blossom and jasmine are frequently mentioned. The dedication of the work, "To virtuous women who delight in the art of perfumery", suggests that perfumery was first and foremost an amateur and domestic practice, but by listing the instruments needed for the trade – mortars, alembics, cookers, scales and glass containers of various shapes – the author also shows that the art of the perfumer was well developed in Venice.

In the same years, the production and sale of perfumes became an explicit facet of Venetian

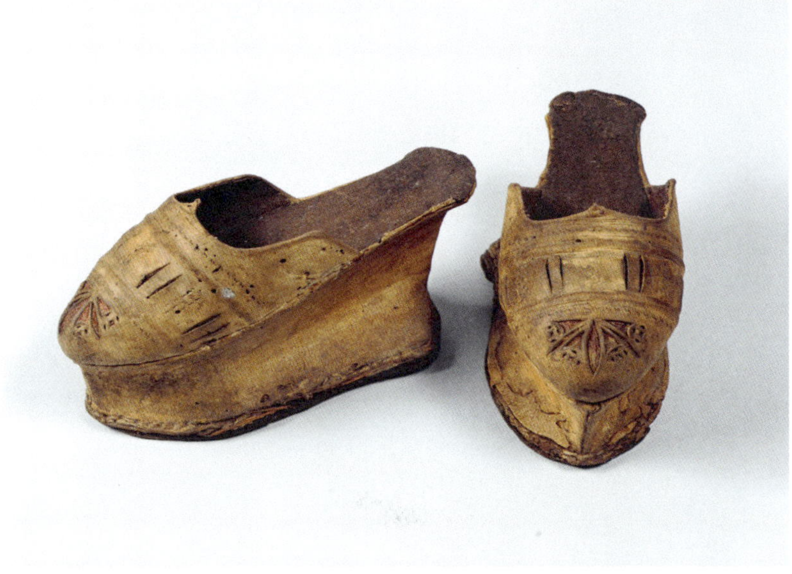

Pianelle, Venetian workmanship, 16th c., wood and leather, 10 × 21 cm
Florence, Museo Stefano Bardini, inv. MCF-MB 1922-812

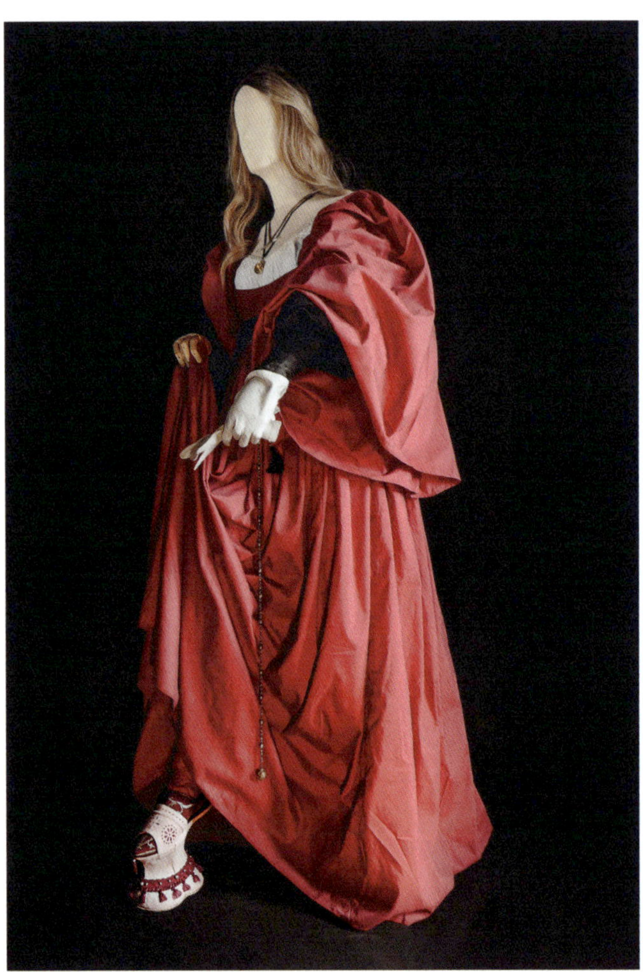

Venetian woman's costume after a work by Titian Coll. MERCURIUS More Curious

arts. The "*muschieri*", who were both glove-makers and perfumers and who did not constitute an independent guild but were part of the "*marzeri*" (mercers) guild, demanded the exclusive right to sell products belonging to "[their] art of perfuming" (Archivio di Stato di Venezia, Arti, busta 312, Mariegola, chap. 228, c. 127). The first surviving archival source that gives us an overall picture of the *muschieri* dates from 1568: it states that there were twenty-four shops concentrated in the central area of Venice, between the Rialto Bridge and St Mark's Square, all of which sold "items pertaining to perfumery", while only nine of them also sold gloves (ASVe, Milizia da mar, busta 446, "Libro de Inquisicion II", cc. 117-195).

Some workshops are described in post-mortem inventories, where one finds amber and musk, also in phials; fragrant waters and oils; benzoin; storax calamita; tragacanth gum; alembics; mortars; scales; all of which were the raw materials and equipment cited by Rosetti in his *Notandissimi secreti*, proving that his descriptions were consistent with the activities of Venetian workshops.

BIBLIOGRAPHY

Badoer Giacomo, *Le Livre de comptes de Giacomo Badoer*, Umberto Dorini and Tommaso Bertelé (eds.) (Rome: Libreria dello Stato, 1956).

Berengo Andrea, *Lettres d'un marchand vénitien Andrea Berengo* (1553-1556), presented by Ugo Tucci, *Bibliothèque de l'École des Chartes* (Paris: S.E.V.P.E.N., 1957), pp. 234–36.

Brown Clifford M., with the collaboration of Anna Maria Lorenzoni, *Isabella d'Este and Lorenzo da Pavia. Documents for the History of Art and Culture in Renaissance Mantua* (Geneva: Librairie Droz, 1982), p. 13, and *passim*.

Brunello Franco, *Marco Polo e le merci dell'Oriente* (Vicenza: Neri Pozza Editore, 1986).

Id., *Cosmetici e profumi del passato*, Vicenza, Associazione Artigiani della Provincia, 1989.

Messinis Anna, *Storia del profumo a Venezia* (Venice: Lineadacqua, 2017).

Sopracasa Alessio, *Venezia e l'Egitto alla fine del Medioevo : le tariffe di Alessandria* (Alexandria: CEAlex, 2013).

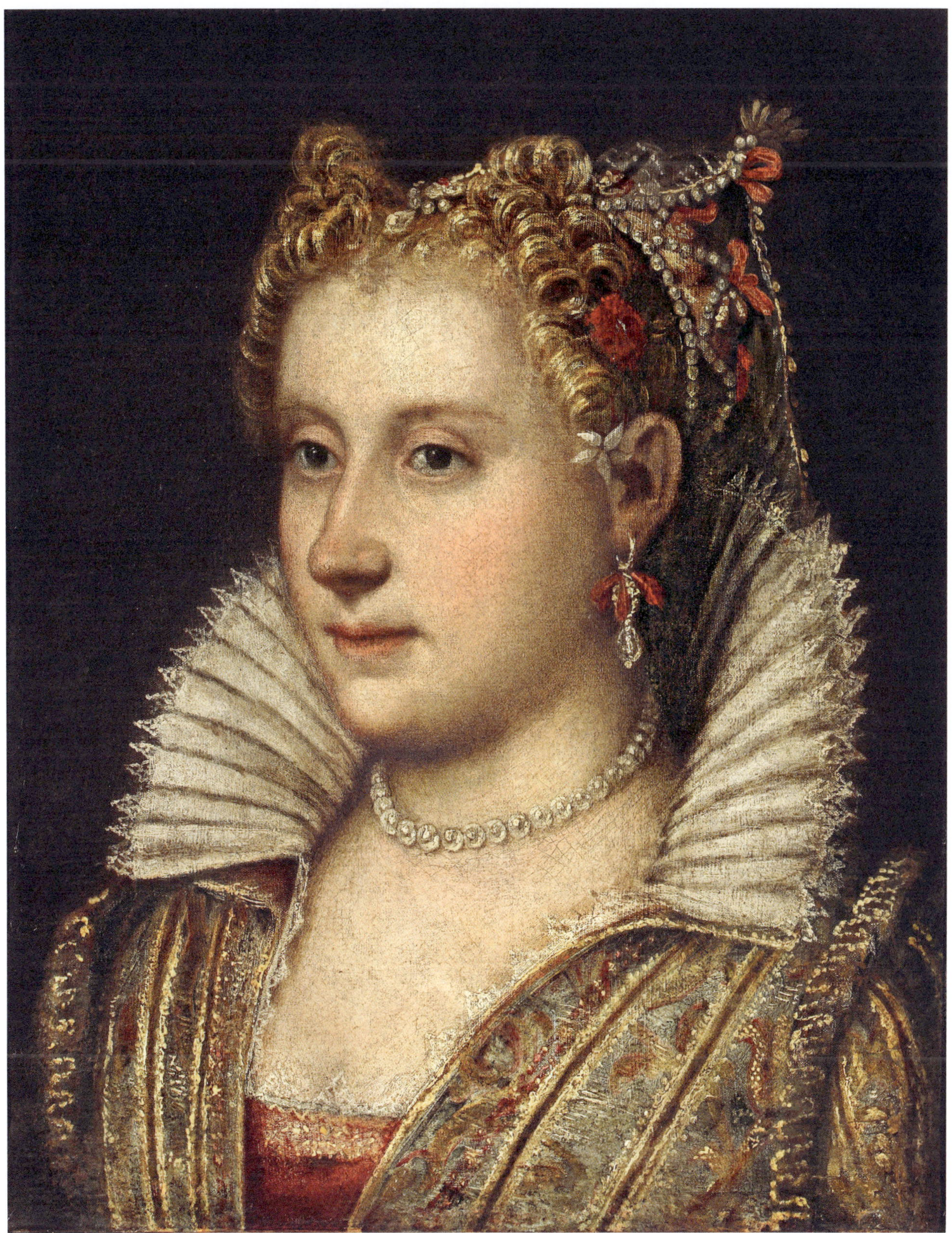

Veronese school, *Portrait of a Lady*, 16th c., oil on canvas, 95 × 80 cm, Pavia, Musei Civici del Castello Visconteo, inv. p.95

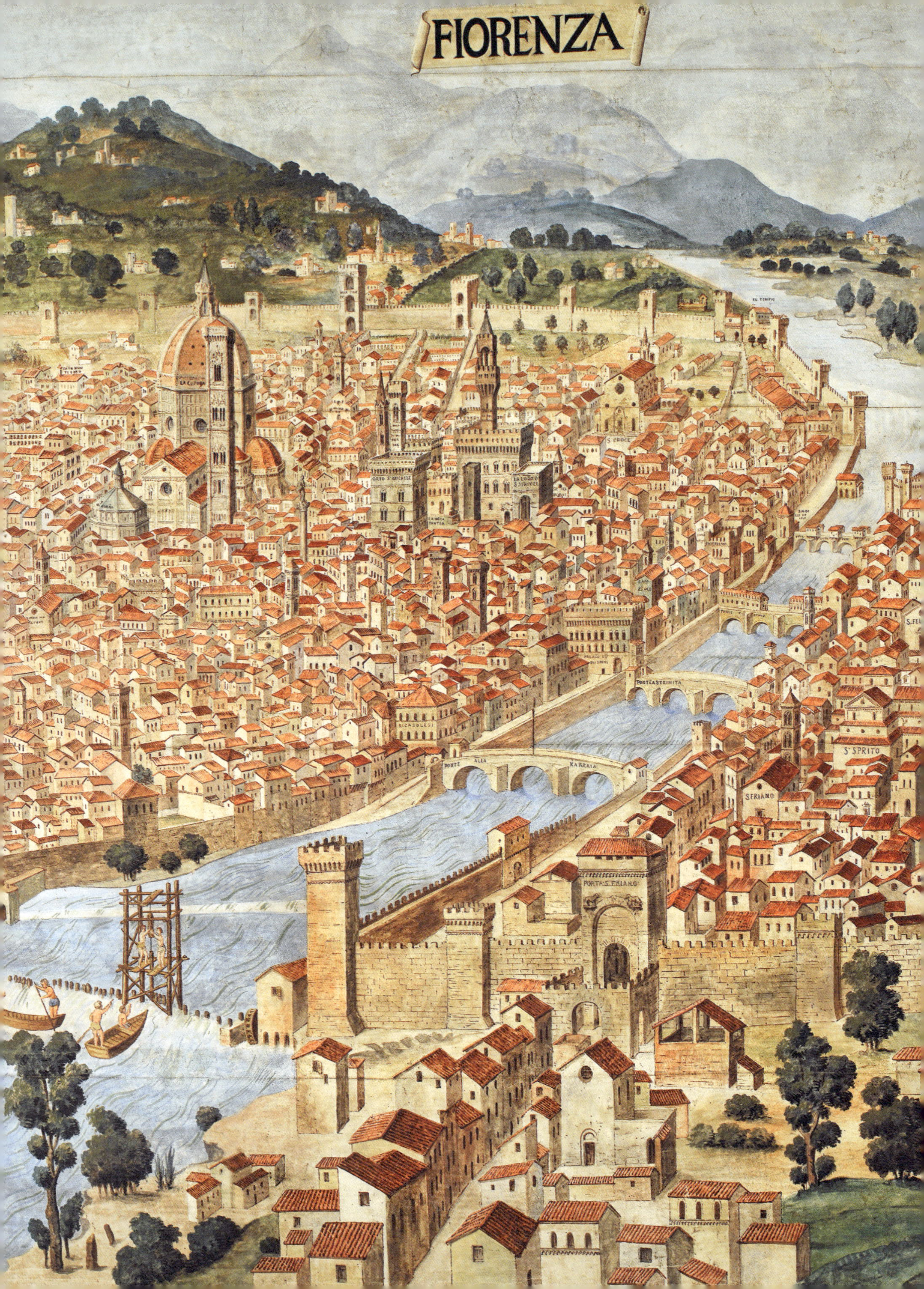
FIORENZA
PONTE ALLA KARRAIA
PORTA S. FRIANO
S. SPIRITO
SERIANO

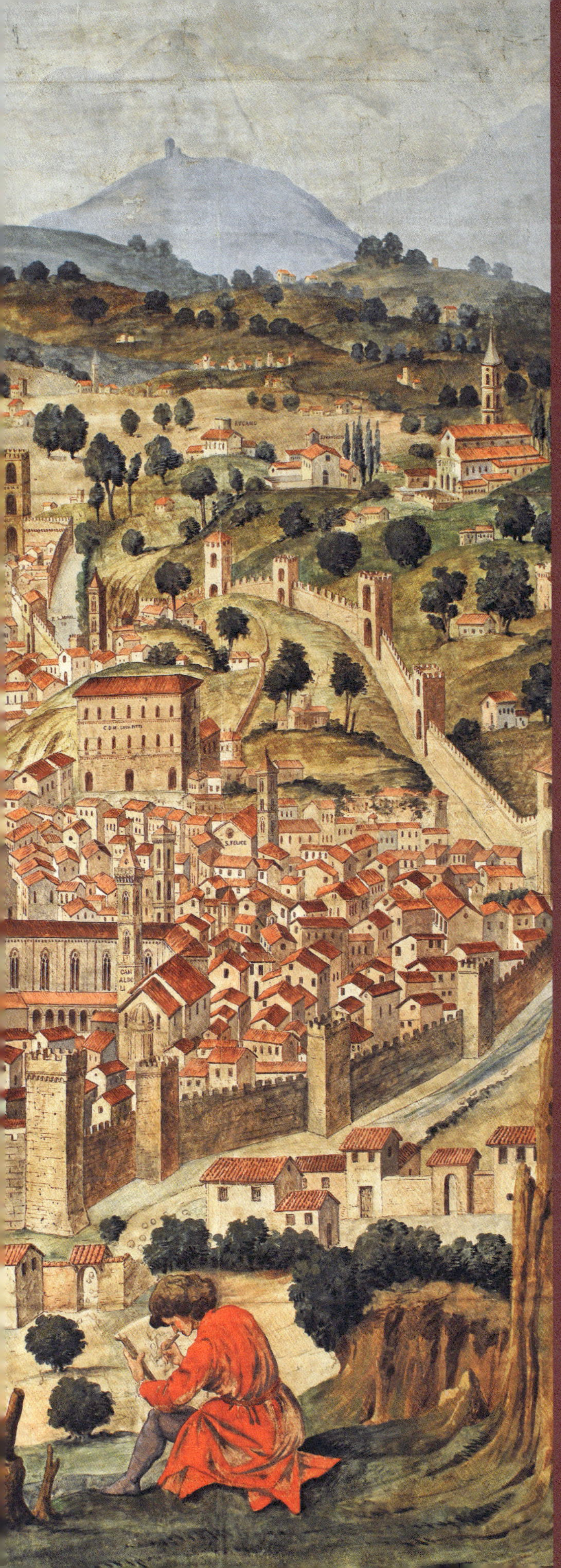

Vinci and Florence, Fragrances of Childhood

Chapter III

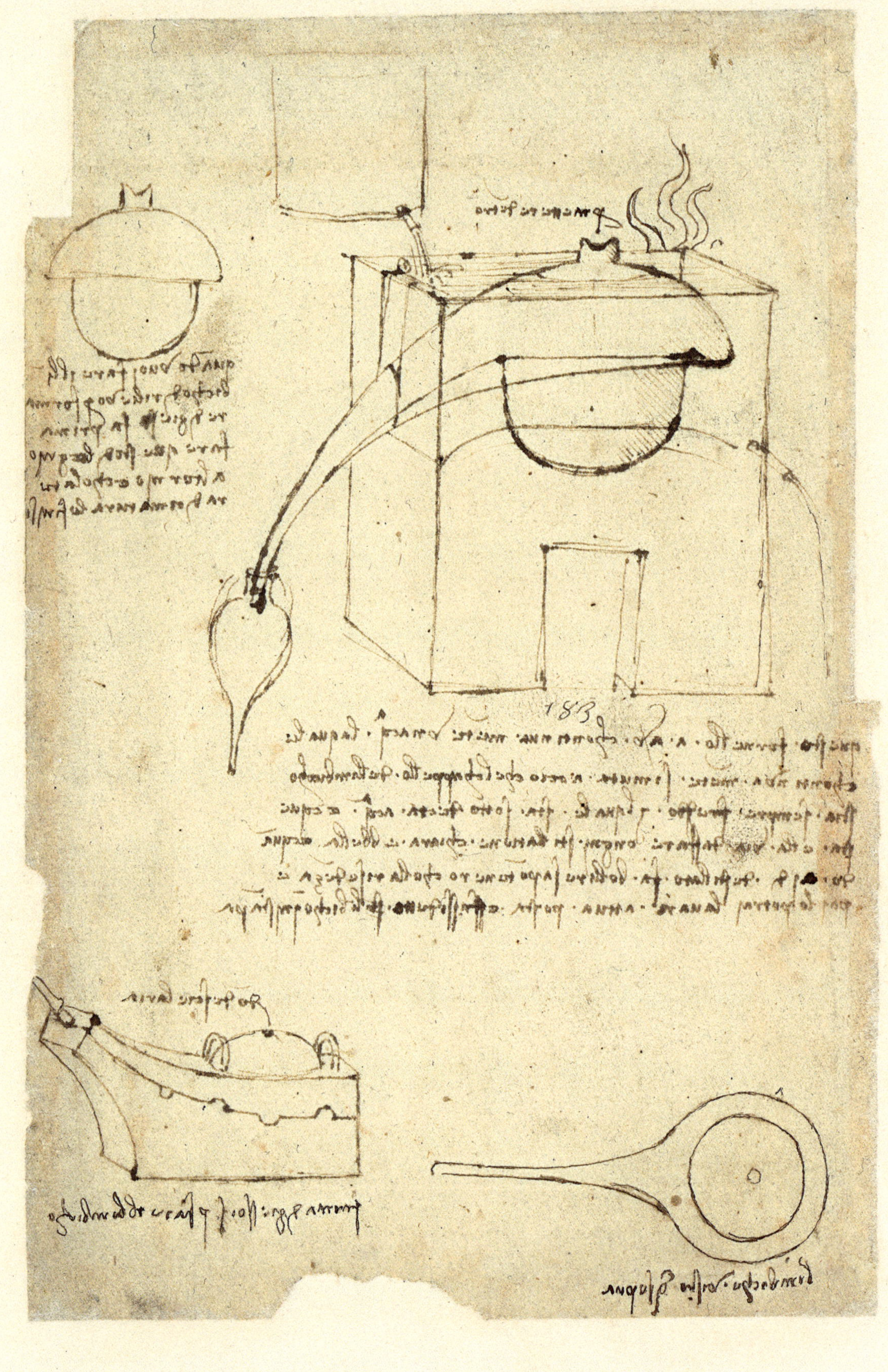

LEONARDO DA VINCI'S ALEMBIC

ALEXANDER NEUWAHL, ANDREA BERNARDONI

Distillation is a technique for separating substances that has been used since ancient times. The term distillation, which literally means 'drop-by-drop separation', was once used to refer to all known separation processes such as filtration, crystallisation and oil extraction. Later, as techniques evolved and were refined, the term came to refer more specifically to the thermal processes of separation by evaporation and subsequent condensation. Distillation takes advantage of the different temperatures at which substances pass from the liquid phase to the gas phase to progressively separate the more volatile components of a mixture from the less volatile ones. Distillation was used early on in the manufacture of pharmaceuticals, cosmetics and alcoholic beverages.

Although more efficient and precise devices have been developed over the centuries, the traditional instrument used for distillation is the alembic, a special vessel (the Arabic word *al ambiq* comes from the Greek *ambix*, meaning glass) capable of collecting and then condensing the vapours that separate from a suitably heated mixture. An alembic is made up of two parts: the "cucurbit" or cauldron, which contains the mixture to be distilled, and the "head" or "cap", which is attached to the cucurbit and collects the vapours, then conveys the distillate to the receiving vessel through the "nose", an outlet tube that acts as a condenser. A distillation device similar to the alembic is the retort, in which the cap and the cucurbit are joined to form a single vessel.

The first description and schematic drawings of alembics are found in a Byzantine manuscript by Zosimos of Panopolis (3rd century), which gives an overview of the alchemist's tools, including single- and triple-ended alembics. According to the manuscript, the idea of using alembics, which were made of copper at the time, came from Mary the Jewess, a probably legendary figure who is sometimes referred to as the sister of Moses or the companion of Hermes Trismegistus, and who has remained in common parlance via the name of the heating technique known as "bain-marie".

PREVIOUS PAGE
Attributed to Francesco di Lorenzo Rosselli
View of Florence, or of the Catena, ca. 1471–82, woodcut, Florence, Palazzo Vecchio

LEFT
Fig. 1. Leonardo da Vinci
Codice Atlantico (*Codex Atlanticus*), f. 216r
"Note sul vento, sulla pioggia e sul moto dell'acqua che scende dai monti", ca. 1485, Milan, Veneranda Biblioteca Ambrosiana – Pinacoteca

The technique of distillation came to the West from the Arab and Greek-Byzantine worlds during the centuries of the Latin Middle Ages, spreading mainly in Benedictine and Franciscan monasteries and convents. Here, different types of alembics were used for the production of galenic preparations, perfumed essences and solvents for the arts, as well as for alcohol distillation and alchemical research. Many testimonies have come down to us from doctors, such as Michael Scot, and from alchemical monks, such as Jean de Roquetaillade, who, in his treatise on Quintessence, describes about 150 distillation processes for isolating this substance, and Paul of Taranto (known as Pseudo-Geber), who, in his highly successful *Summa perfectionis magisterii*, describes processes and installations for metallurgical alchemy. None of these manuscripts are accompanied by drawings illustrating the equipment used or its operation: it was not until the 15th century that Leonardo da Vinci was the first to depict this type of apparatus in detail.

As far as the materials used to make alembics are concerned, the information becomes less clear the further back in time we go. The oldest glass artefacts known today, probably used in alchemical medicine, come from the archaeological excavations at Pompeii; others from the late Roman period have been found in Egypt. The techniques of working glass by moulding or blowing have been known since ancient times and, for the medieval period, there is an important testimony in Michele Savonarola's *Trattato Dell'acqua Ardente*, according to which modern (at that time) alchemists used glass alembics. Despite a certain diffusion of these apparatuses in the workshops of alchemists and artisans, the first explicit testimony, after Savonarola, of the use of glass alembics is a note by Leonardo on folio 3r of manuscript E: "Let this be proved by the smoke that is produced in the enclosed space, as can be seen in the glass vessels..."

Folio 216r of the *Codex Atlanticus* [fig. 1] shows a refrigerated distillation system using a vessel built around the lid of the still, from which the now hot water is drained and continuously replenished from an external reservoir. Again, this is the oldest known evidence of the construction of an alembic. The folio contains drawings and notes relating to the construction of the alembic, which Leonardo intended to make using the moulding technique. In the top left-hand corner, the model of the body of the alembic, to be made in wood on a lathe, is drawn. On the same page, at the bottom, is the mould, made of plaster. The technique seems to be very refined, since the mould – as the cutting line with the alignment teeth and the handles at the top seem to indicate – seems to have been designed for serial casting, as Vannoccio Biringuccio described in *De la pirotechnia* some forty-five years later. The material used may have been glass, as suggested by the above-mentioned note on folio 3r of manuscript E. The moulding of glass in the thin thicknesses required for an alembic could probably be achieved by blowing, i.e. without the use of a mould core. Ladislao Reti has in the past proposed an alternative hypothesis involving the use of a metal alloy such as bronze or brass. However, it cannot be ruled out that Leonardo was thinking in terms of actual glass casting, a technique that he discusses in folio 10v of manuscript B for making a bell: "you will make the burner used in the manner of bombards and when the glass is melted, pour it into the flaming mould".

Folio 989r of *Codex Atlanticus* [fig. 2] shows a distillation system similar to the previous one; here the cooling device is separated from the heating device, so that part of the vessel containing the distillate vapours remains in contact with the ambient air. This creates an intermediate temperature zone between the hot part of the burner and the cold part of the vessel, in order to limit the thermal shock that might have caused the glass of the alembic to crack.

On several pages of his codices, Leonardo proposes innovative solutions for the construction and operation of alembics, particularly with regard to cooling systems. Until the end of the 15th century, this process was carried out by placing wet pieces of cloth on the alembic; Leonardo's drawings are therefore once again the oldest evidence of real condensation systems. Of particular importance are the two drawings contained in the respective fragments that make up folio 1114r of *Codex Atlanticus* [fig. 3]. The first shows a system similar to that of folio 216r of *Codex Atlanticus*. Next to it, in the same fragment, is a drawing of an alembic in vertical section, in which, at the base of the alembic cap, the condensate collecting channel is highlighted, which conveys the liquid obtained to the twisted tube through which it flows out.

In the second fragment that makes up the folio, another alembic is drawn, which seems to be an evolution of the previous one. To solve the problem of vapour condensation, Leonardo abandoned the idea of an external basin and thought of creating a cavity around the surface of the alembic itself, into which the cooling water could flow. The complex morphology of this alembic seems to rule out the possibility of it being made of glass; as Ladislao Reti has pointed

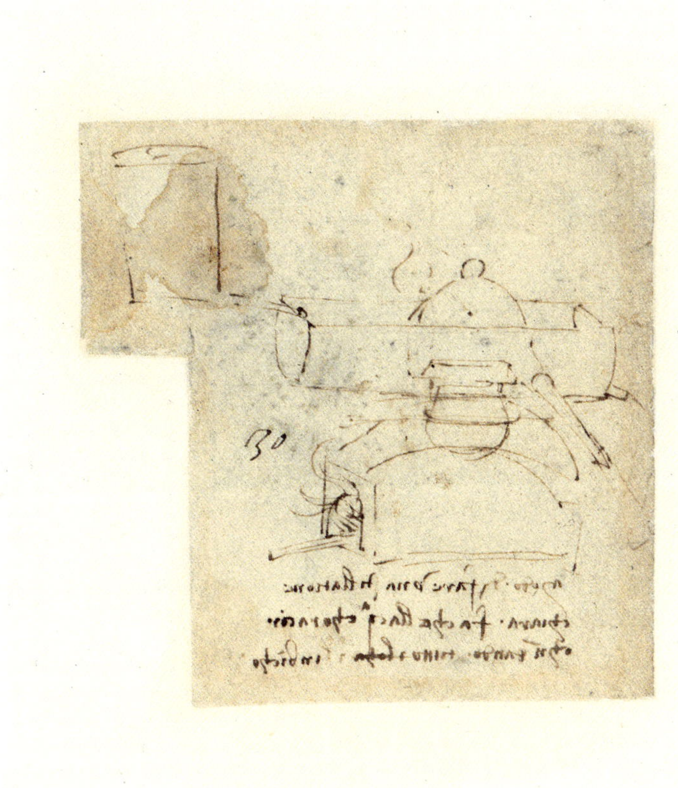

Fig. 2. Leonardo da Vinci, *Codice Atlantico* (*Codex Atlanticus*), "Alambico", f. 989r, ca. 1487 Milan, Veneranda Biblioteca Ambrosiana – Pinacoteca

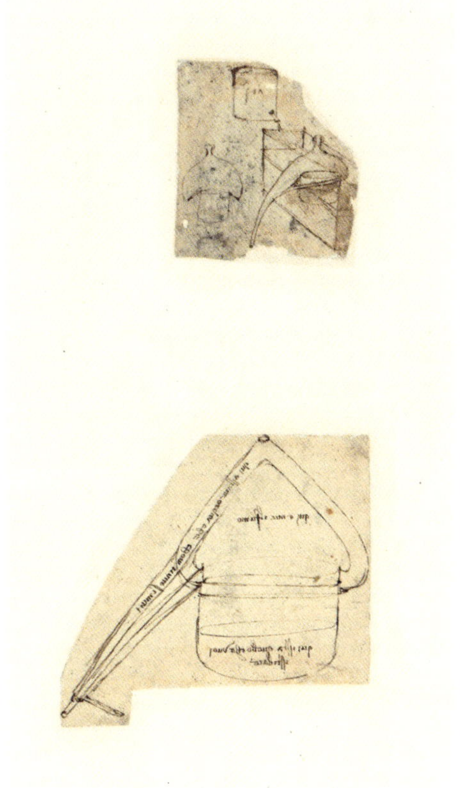

Fig. 3. Leonardo da Vinci, *Codice Atlantico* (*Codex Atlanticus*), "Alambico", f. 1114r, between 1479 and 1490, Milan, Veneranda biblioteca Ambrosiana – Pinacoteca

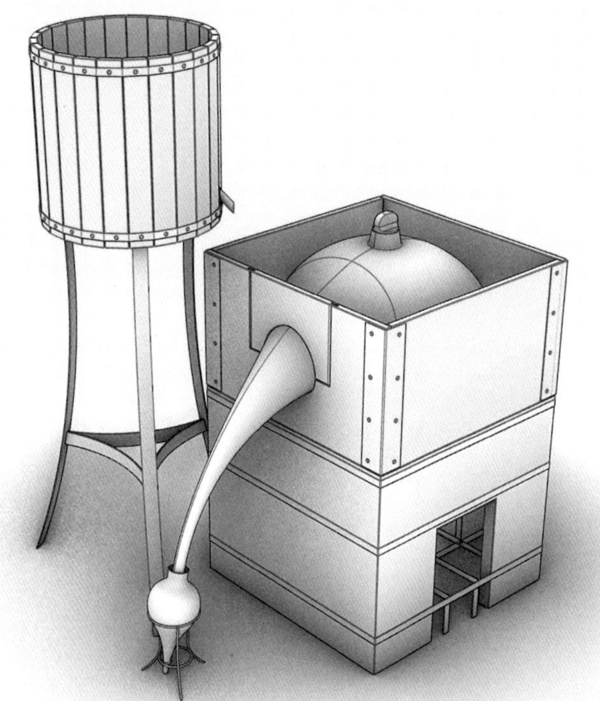

Fig. 4. Alexander Neuwahl, reconstruction of an alembic designed by Leonardo da Vinci

out, a soldered copper version is more likely. According to the date traditionally attributed to the folio, 1479, this alembic belonged to the early Florentine period; it would therefore predate the models with refrigerated bowls designed between 1485 and 1489. In this chronological hypothesis, the models with refrigeration in the bowl could represent the alternative, more concrete solution adopted by Leonardo when he realised the impossibility of making the more sophisticated model with the cavity in glass [fig. 4, fig. 5].

At the time, the technique of distillation, based on the physical phenomenon of the transition from liquid to gas to liquid, was not only important for art, but was also the focus of speculation in the field of natural philosophy. In folio 3v of the *Leicester Codex*, Leonardo, following the microcosm-macrocosm analogy that so often led him to reflect on the most diverse subjects, compares the mountains to natural alembics that, by condensing vapours and smoke from the hot bowels of the earth, produce the water springs in high mountains and the metalliferous veins. In folio 28r of the *Leicester Codex*, Leonardo proposes another striking analogy, this time between the alembic and artillery. The functioning of both is based on a change in the state of matter that generates movement and force: for Leonardo, in the case of artillery, it is the phenomenon of condensation that causes the vapours of the explosion to thicken and thus propel the projectile. These are bizarre ideas that Leonardo himself did not hesitate to abandon in order to put phenomena into the right perspective, for example, by identifying the origin of rivers in the melting of glaciers and rain in high mountains.

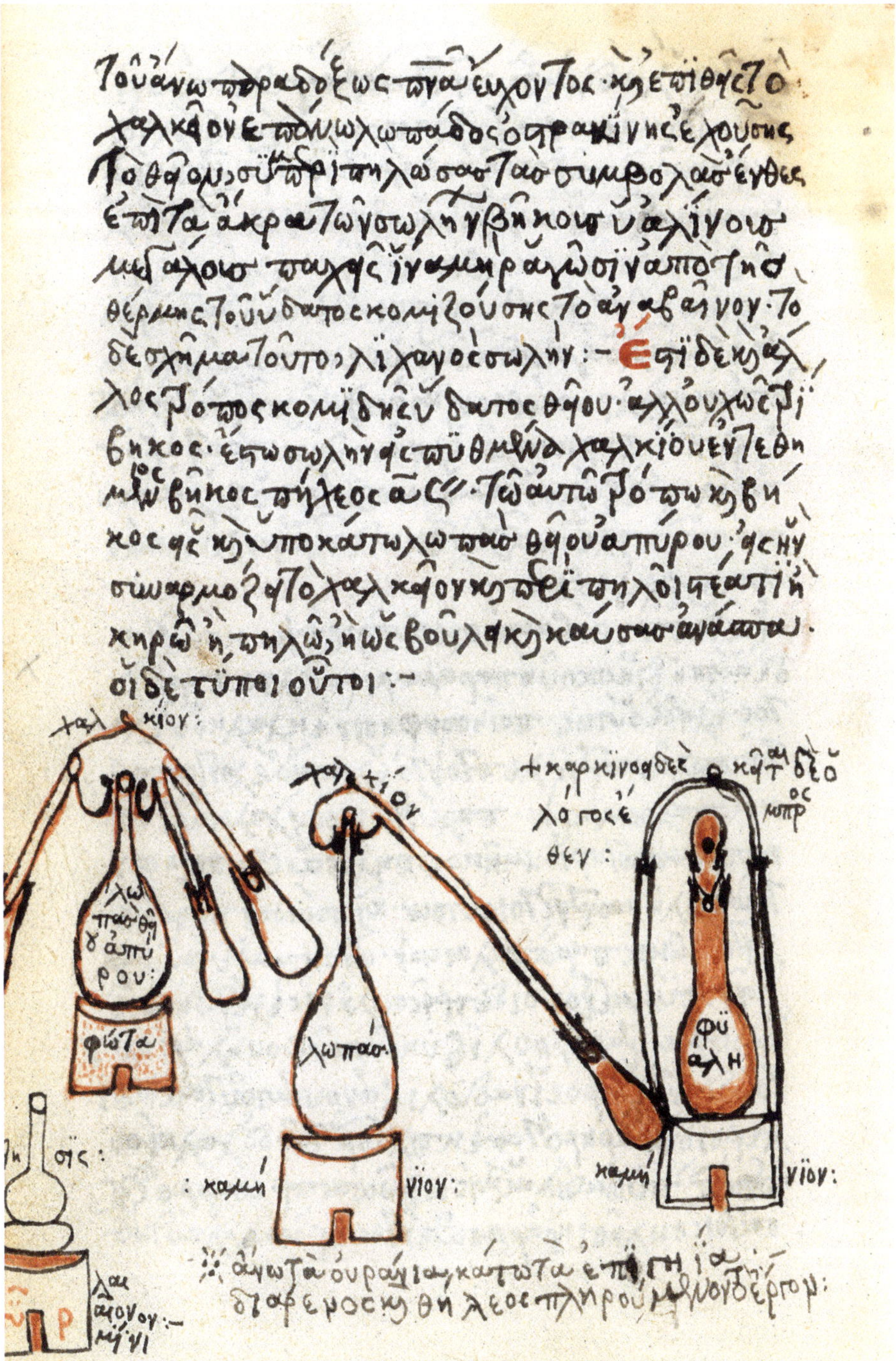

Fig. 5. *Treatise on Alchemy*, 15th c., Bibliothèque nationale de France, Grec 2327, f. 81v

Bibliography

Beretta Marco, *The Alchemy of Glass: Counterfeit, Imitation and Transmutation in Ancient Glassmaking* (Sagamore Beach: Science History Publication, 2009).

Bernardoni Andrea, "Leonardo and the Chemical Arts", in *Nuncius*, vol. 27, no. 1 (2012) pp. 11–55.

Id., *Esplosioni, Fusioni e Trasmutazioni: Il Monumento a Francesco Sforza e le Arti Chimiche in Leonardo: disegni di Leonardo dal Codice Atlantico* (Novara: De Agostini, 2013).

Berthelot Marcellin, "La découverte de l'alcool et la distillation", in *Science et Morale* (Paris: Calmann-Lévy, 1896), pp. 352–80.

Reti Ladislao, *Le arti chimiche di Leonardo da Vinci* (Milan: Soc. an. editrice di chimica [1952], reprinted in *La chimica e l'industria*, anno 34 [Nov.-Dec. 1952]).

Saffrey Henri-Dominique (ed.), *Proclus. Théologie platonicienne*, tome IV (Paris: Les Belles Lettres, 1981).

Zosimos of Panopolis, *Mémoires authentiques / Zosime de Panopolis*, trans. Michèle Mertens, published in *Les Alchimistes Grecs* (Paris: Les Belles Lettres, 1981).

A Work of Art, a Vision: Leonardo da Vinci's Alembic

The traditional chemico-alchemical furnace, known as a tower furnace or perpetual (self-powered) furnace, is a large device consisting of a central container that continuously feeds coal into the burner, alongside which are two heating chambers for the alembics (also known as retorts). This drawing is the earliest graphic evidence of this heating system, which had many uses in the Renaissance, from metallurgy to medicinal chemistry and cosmetics. The description accompanying the drawing states that it is a cooker for distilling *aqua fortis*, an acid mainly used for engraving metals in metallurgy, and from the 16th century onwards to prepare copper plates in printing works. Alembics are used in perfume production to prepare essential oils and alcohol.

Andrea Bernardoni

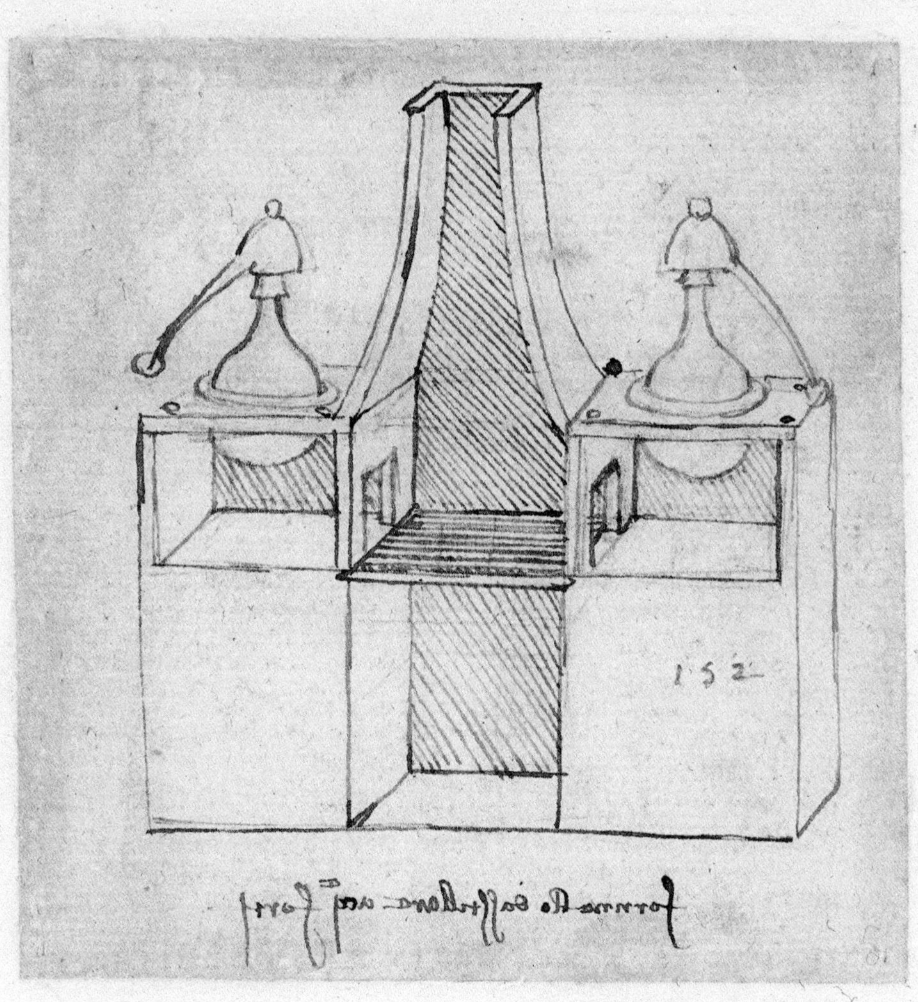

Leonardo da Vinci, *Codex Atlanticus*, fol. 912r, *Study of a Tower Furnace for the Distillation of Aqua Fortis*, 1479–80, 11.9 × 11.6 cm, Milan, Veneranda Biblioteca Ambrosiana – Pinacoteca

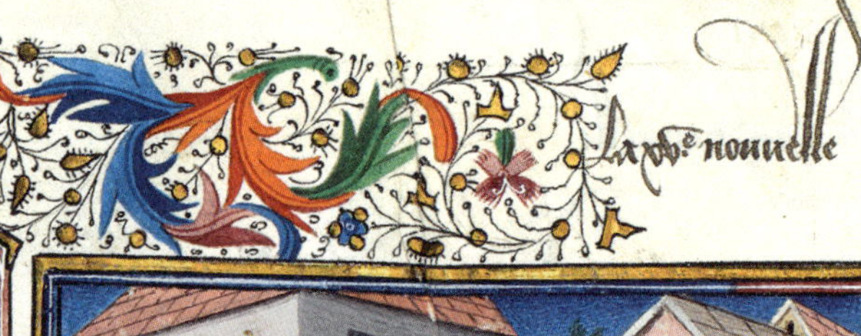

La xve nouvelle

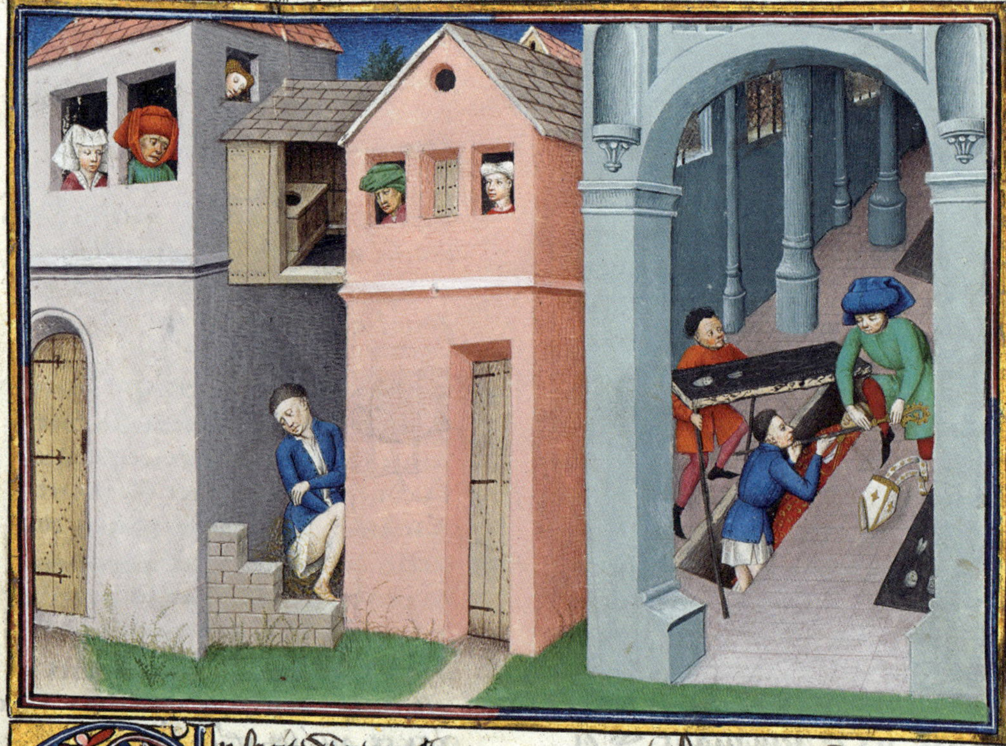

En la cite de perouse come autrefois jay oy dire fu ung juene homme appelle andreuce pierre courratier de chevaulx. Cestui oy dire que en la cite de naples estoit grant marchie de chevaulx. Sy mist andreuce en sa bource cinq cens florins dor / il qui autrefois navoit este hors de perouse avec autres marchans ala a naples. Quant il fu illec venu en ung dimenche au soir / et a heure de vespres / il fu informez de par son oste comment et aquel pris se vendoient chevaulx. Celle au lundi matin mena au marchie andreuce / illec vit mains chevaulx / et aucuns dilz lui pleurent et essaia en acheter aucuns. Le juenne andreuce qui avec les vendeurs ne povoit acorder du pris daucun cheval / afin que il monstrast que il vouloit acheter aucuns chevaulx il comme rude et pou cauteleux par maintes fois en la presence des alans et des venans par le marchie monstra sa bourse quil avoit plaine de florins. Et tandis que andreuce estoit en ces traities et que il monstroit sa bourse / avint que une tres belle jouvencelle sicilianne qui sestoit disposee a complaire a chascun homme pour assez petit pris passa par empres andreuce sans ce que il la veist / la jouvencelle qui sa bourse vit elle dist en son cuer soudaine-ment. Qui est cellui ou celle

THE OLFACTORY THRESHOLDS OF DISGUST IN THE TIME OF LEONARDO DA VINCI

Pascal Brioist

As historians Alain Corbin and Georges Vigarello have shown, the notions of what is clean and what is dirty are social and historical constructs in much the same way as the olfactory thresholds of what is pleasant and what is repellent. However, we must shake off the prejudices that lead us to believe that the 15th century was a time of stench, when people readily tolerated dirt, washed little and used perfumes to hide their bad smells. Nothing could be further from the truth. On the one hand, both men and women bathed, particularly in high society, but not exclusively. Public steam baths still existed in towns, a remnant of the Roman thermal baths, even if they were mistrusted after the major outbreaks of the Black Death; large houses also had wooden tubs and towns like Siena were renowned for their thermal baths. It was not until much later, in the 16th century, that a mistrust of water, which "opens the pores of the skin and exposes it to miasmas", took hold (Vigarello, 2014).

However, urban hygiene remained a concern in the great Italian cities that had suffered from the plague. But in this case, what were the levels Leonardo da Vinci set for his perception of what was tolerable and intolerable? This question can only be answered by examining his texts or contextual sources for clues.

The Stench of the cities

We might start with the towns where Leonardo lived: what was their relationship with hygiene and what were the smells in the streets? There are several types of documentation that can help us answer these questions: legal statutes preserved by such cities as Bologna, and pictorial and literary sources.

Around 1400, in a dialogue with the humanist Leonardo Bruni, Coluccio Salutati, Chancellor of the Florentine Republic, praised Florence in the following terms: "In its magnificence, Florence surpasses most cities of today, but in terms of cleanliness, it surpasses even those of yesteryear... for neither Rome, nor Athens, nor Syracuse were, I think, so clean and well kept." Salutati, concerned about hygiene, also declared in a medical treatise that the smell of urine and excre-

LEFT
The Decameron
(Andreuccio da Perugia falling into a "*chiasso*")
Italian manuscript 5070-B, reserve collection, f. 54v
Paris, Bibliothèque nationale de France

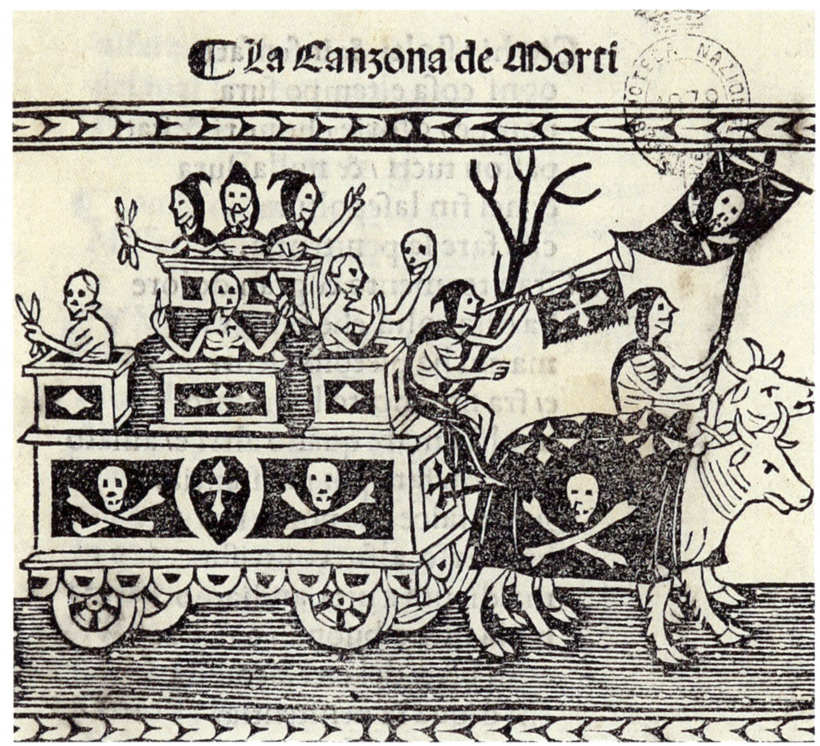

Fig. 1. *La Canzona de' morti*, Palatino E.6.6.154.I/15, f. 1r, Florence, Biblioteca Nazionale Centrale

ment was repulsive. In his *Panegyric to the City of Florence*, Bruni went even further, setting his native city above those cities "so repulsive that the excrement produced during the night is thrown out into the street in plain view of passers-by, who might easily slip in it." In his opinion, there could be no beauty in the most prosperous cities without cleanliness.

So was Florence spared from bad smells? It is hard to believe, but the main cobbled streets were probably equipped with underground systems for draining the "blackwater" that flowed down from the houses. Some palaces also had cesspits that were regularly emptied and cleaned by servants. However, this did not prevent the streets from being contaminated by horse and ox dung, or even certain areas (such as the Ponte Vecchio), where animals were slaughtered, from smelling of faeces and blood before they were cleaned with water from the Arno. The carcasses were also thrown into the river. In general, such places were kept out of the way (in Venice, for example, this was done on the island of Giudecca), which simply meant that cleanliness was reserved for the most public places, such as Piazza della Signoria (where the cages that held seventeen lions must have smelt of wild animals!) or Piazza Santissima Annunziata. The suburbs – such as the area around the Stinche prison in Via Ghibellina, which housed Verrocchio's studio – were less fortunate.

Florentines also played on the contrast between putrid and sweet smells for amusement. For example, during the Carnival in 1513, a float of the dead – with men in robes and cowls singing songs of penitence and actors disguised as skeletons – performed a parody of the Savonarolian processions [fig. 1]. The cart pulled by oxen carried carrion, the stench of which was then dispelled by salutary perfumes.

In Milan, people also knew how to keep the streets clean, a much easier task since the city

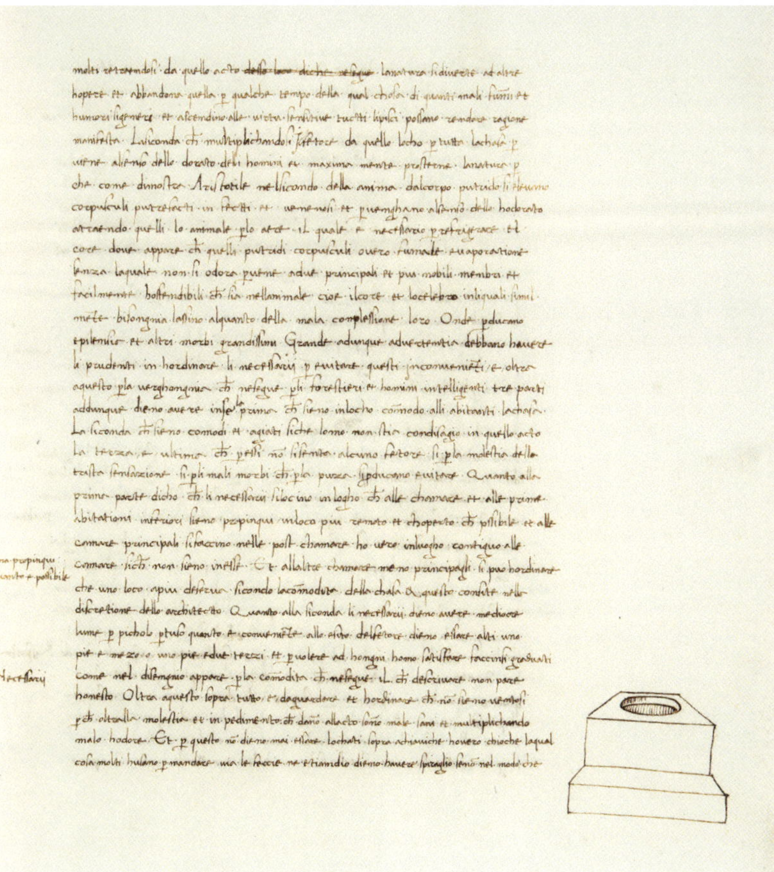

Fig. 2. *Trattato di architettura ingegneria e arte militare*, 2nd half of the 15th c.
Florence, Biblioteca Nazionale Centrale, II.I.141, f. 14r: toilet designed by Francesco di Giorgio Martini

was criss-crossed by canals capable of evacuating wastewater. In his 1465 treatise on architecture, a Florentine architect by the name of Antonio Averlino, known as "Filarete", even proposed the creation of a formidable "Sforzinda" (city of the Sforzas) divided into sectors by sixteen avenues lined with canals leading to the central square where the cathedral stood. In 1485, however, the city was hit by a terrible plague, the spread of which Leonardo attributed to miasmas emanating from the corpses. In 1492, a hospital was built to isolate the sick, and Leonardo – in his plans for an ideal city, which he drew up in 1485 – sought to rid the city of foul odours.

In his view, they were the result of overcrowded and insufficiently ventilated cities. His advice was to think of urban planning in terms of flows, to open up wide avenues with arcades and to combine streets and canals: "You will disperse so great a concourse of people who, herding together like goats one upon the back of another filling every part with their stench, sow the seeds of pestilence and death." (*Codex Atlanticus*, folio 184v)

In another codex, he advocated an even more precise configuration:

> The privies, stables, and noisome places are emptied by underground passages situated at a distance of three hundred braccia from one arch to the rest, each passage receiving light through openings in the street above, and at every arch there should be a spiral staircase... At the first turn there should be a door of entry into the privies, and this staircase should enable one to descend from the high-level to the low-level road. (manuscript B of the Institut de France, folio 16r)

In the suburban villa he designed for Charles d'Amboise in 1509, which was never built, Leonardo also envisaged the odours of the garden as an important element of the multi-sensory paradise he intended to build for his patron:

> By means of a mill I shall be able at any time to produce a current of air; in the summer I shall make the water spring up fresh and bubbling, and flow along in the space between the tables which will be arranged thus. The channel may be half a braccio wide, and there should be vessels there with wines, always of the freshest. Other water should flow through the garden moistening the orange and citron trees according to their needs. Overhead we must construct a very fine net of copper which will cover over the garden and shut in beneath it many different kinds of birds. So you will have perpetual music together with the scents of the blossoms of the citrons and the lemons. (*Codex Atlanticus*, folio 732v.b)

Later, in his project for Romorantin, he took up the idea of using flowing water to evacuate the household sludge:

> The main underground channel does not receive turbid waters, but that water runs in the ditches outside the town with four mills at the entrance and four at the outlet; and this may be done by damming the water above Romorantin. (*Codex Arundel*, folio 270r)

Domestic odours

On a domestic level, it was also necessary to eliminate foul odours. It was simply not acceptable to allow a house to become impregnated with the stench of defecation, and Leonardo's contemporaries wrote quite openly on the subject. Filarete, in his *Treatise on Architecture*, envisaged plans for public latrines, and Leon Battista Alberti also raised the issue in *On the Art of Building*. Francesco di Giorgio Martini, an engineer whose *Trattati di Architettura Ingegneria e Arte Militare* (II.I.141, folio 14r BNCF) Leonardo read, designed a seat with a hole in it [fig. 2]. For sanitary reasons, he recommended that latrines in houses should be easily accessible and kept in a place that keeps odours at bay. He also gave the measurements for a cesspit, which should be pyramidal in shape and lined with sand. Such a pit (referred to as a *chiasso* in Boccaccio's *Decameron* [fig. 3]) had to be emptied regularly by the servants. In Palazzo Vecchio, Florence's Gonfalonier (Standard Bearer), Piero Soderini, had a lavatory with a chair made of chestnut wood with a hole in it and frescoed walls. The Palazzo Davanzatti was equipped with this type of lavatory as early as the 14th century. Leonardo was no stranger to the subject, as he twice recommended that care be taken in their creation for the palazzo project in Romorantin:

> Let all the privies have ventilation [by shafts] in the thickness of the walls, so as to exhale by the roofs... The privies must be numerous and going one into the other in order that the stench may not penetrate into the dwellings; and all their doors must shut off themselves with counterpoises. (*Codex Atlanticus*, folio 209r)

Leonardo mentioned a bathroom only once, in 1499, when he designed a mixer tap for a palatial bathtub: "For the bath of the duchess Isabella; a Spring. Made for the stove or bath of the duchess Isabella; it is in this position because the screw does not turn with its socket." (*Codex Atlanticus*, folio 289r)

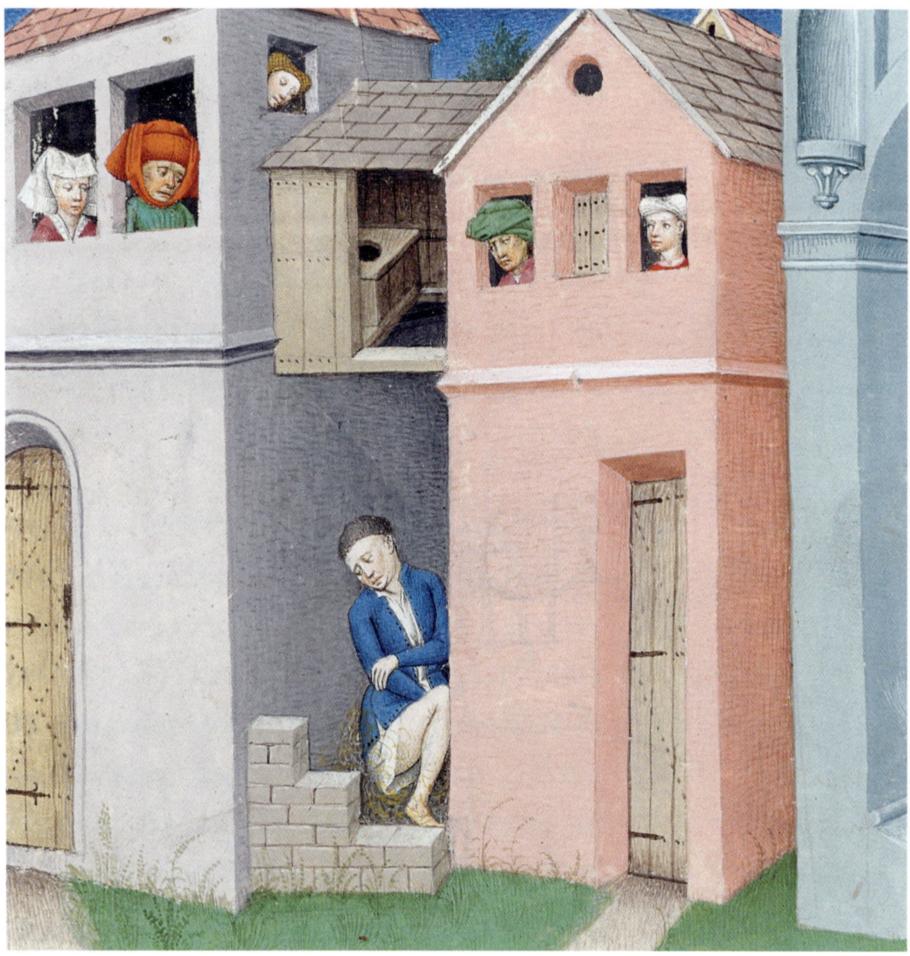

Fig. 3. Detail from *The Decameron* (Andreuccio da Perugia falling into a "*chiasso*"), Italian manuscript 5070-B, reserve collection, f. 54v, Paris, Bibliothèque nationale de France

The grand palaces were in fact equipped with stone bathrooms. A fine example of these can still be seen in the Montefeltro household in Urbino. Although Leonardo did not describe his own ablution facilities, in common with his contemporaries, he was certainly not averse to washing his hands when he sat down to dinner: "Take some rose water and wash your hands in it, then take a lavender flower and rub it with your palms, and you will achieve the desired effect." (*Codex Atlanticus*, folio 807r)

The preoccupation with odours haunted the artist even in the workshop, where the scent of walnut oil, which he associated with sadness in a strange synaesthesia, had to be addressed:

> Take the rank oil and put ten pints into a jar and make a mark on the jar at the height of the oil; then add to it a pint of vinegar and make it boil till the oil has sunk to the level of the mark and thus you will be certain that the oil is returned to its original quantity and the vinegar will have gone off in vapour, carrying with it the evil smell. (manuscript K of the Institut de France, folio 32v)

The stables, on which Leonardo worked in Milan [fig. 4], Vigevano, Florence and Romorantin,

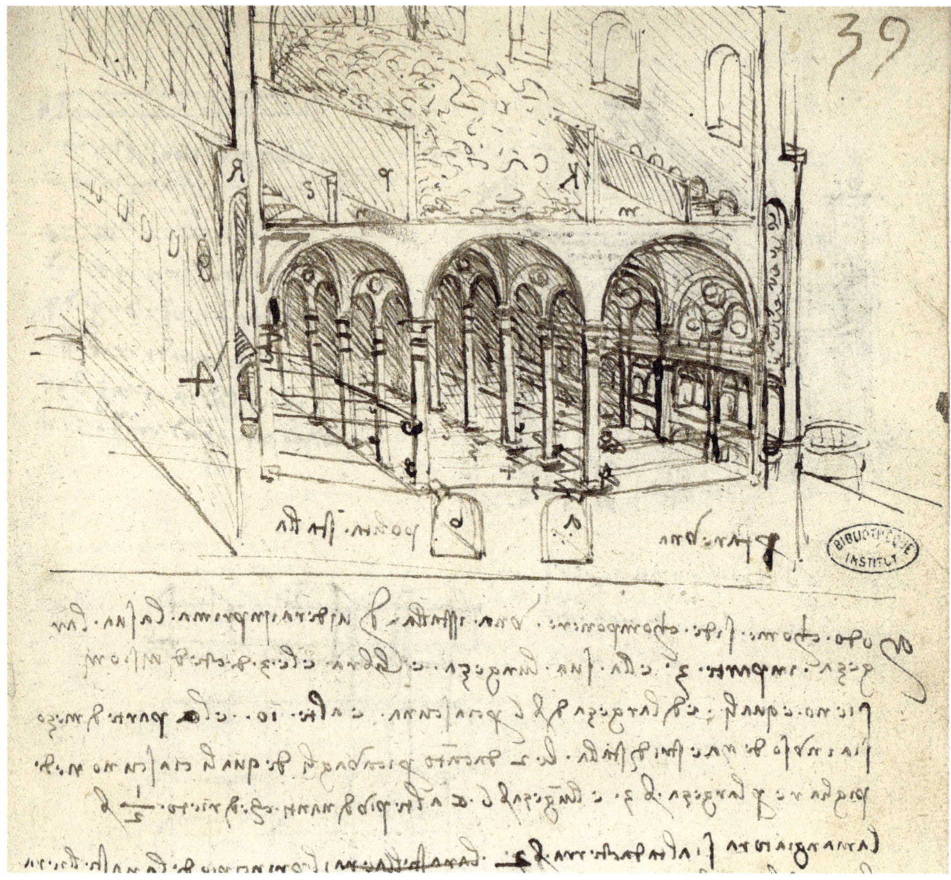

Fig. 4. Leonardo da Vinci, *Stables for Milan*, ca. 1485, manuscript B, Ms 2173, f. 39r, Paris, Institut de France

also warranted being impeccably maintained in the eyes of the Tuscan, with underground conduits to drain away the liquid manure, and devices to keep the stalls clean and dry:

> Now, in order to attain to what I promise, that is to make this place, contrary to the general custom, clean and neat: as to the upper part of the stable, i.e. where the hay is, that part must have at its outer end a window six braccia high and six broad, through which by simple means the hay is brought up to the loft, as is shown by the machine. (manuscript B, folio 39r)

The Cesspool of the Human Body

For Leonardo, it was clear that foul odours come from the corruption of organic matter, which gives rise to unbreathable gases. In a fable about wine, he contrasts the nobility of the alcoholic drink with the stench of the human body:

> Wine: What am I about, that I should rejoice, and not perceive that I am now near to my death and shall leave my golden abode in this cup to enter into the foul and fetid caverns of the human body, and to be transmuted from a fragrant and delicious liquor into a foul and base one. Nay, and as though so much evil as this were not enough, I must for a long time lie in hideous receptacles, together with other fetid and corrupt matter, cast out from human intestines. (*Codex Atlanticus*, folio 188r)

Who better than Leonardo, who claimed to have dissected nearly thirty corpses [fig. 5] and had witnessed scenes of extreme violence in war, to recognise the foul odours of corpses, both living and dead? He therefore anticipated the repugnance of a student at his anatomical demonstrations:

> But though possessed of an interest in the subject (anatomical demonstration) you may perhaps be impeded by your stomach, or if this does not restrain you then perhaps by the fear of passing the night hours in the company of these corpses, quartered and flayed, and horrible to behold... (Windsor, RL 19070v)

If one takes a closer look at the master's anatomical writings, it becomes clear that he considered food to be the primary source of corruption:

> This stench enlarges the intestines and penetrates into all the interstices and swells and puffs out the bodies in the shape of casks; and if you should say that this stench arose from the heat in the bodies, this would not be found to be the case with inflated bodies which are covered with snow, and the power of the stench is much more active and multiplies much more than does that of the heat. (Windsor, RL 19054r)

Other passages even explain the process of digestion and its fetid production:

> By the ramification of the vein of the chyle in the mesentery, nourishment is drawn from the corruption of the food in the intestines, and in the last instance it returns by the final ramifications of the artery to these intestines where this blood, being afterwards dead, is corrupted and acquires the same stench as comes from the faeces. (Windsor, RL 19020r)

Elsewhere, Leonardo compares the stench of excrement with that of corpses:

> Of the two thick veins which go from the liver to the spleen, which come from the larger veins of the spine, I think that these collect the superfluous blood, which being every day evacuated by the mesenteric veins is deposited in the bowels, causing the same stench when it has reached there that arises from the dead in the sepulchres, and that is the stench of excrement. (Windsor, RL 19051v)

Yet he viewed these symptoms with detachment, as did the physicians he read, such as Bartolomeo Montagna (*Tractatus de Urinarum Iudiciis*, 1487), who used the smell and colour of urine to identify their patients' illnesses.

Leonardo was convinced of the power of smells. He found justification for this in the mythology of his day, when he wrote about the weasel: "This beast finding the lair of the basilisk kills it with the smell of its urine, and this smell, indeed, often kills the weasel itself" (manuscript H, folio 24v). He even imagined weapons that would use foul odours to dispatch enemies, like the explosive he called the "*stocladle*":

> If you wish to make use of it on a galley, make the rockets of paste-board, and fill the space between each with pitch mixed with powdered sulphur; and this will serve three purposes: first it will do harm

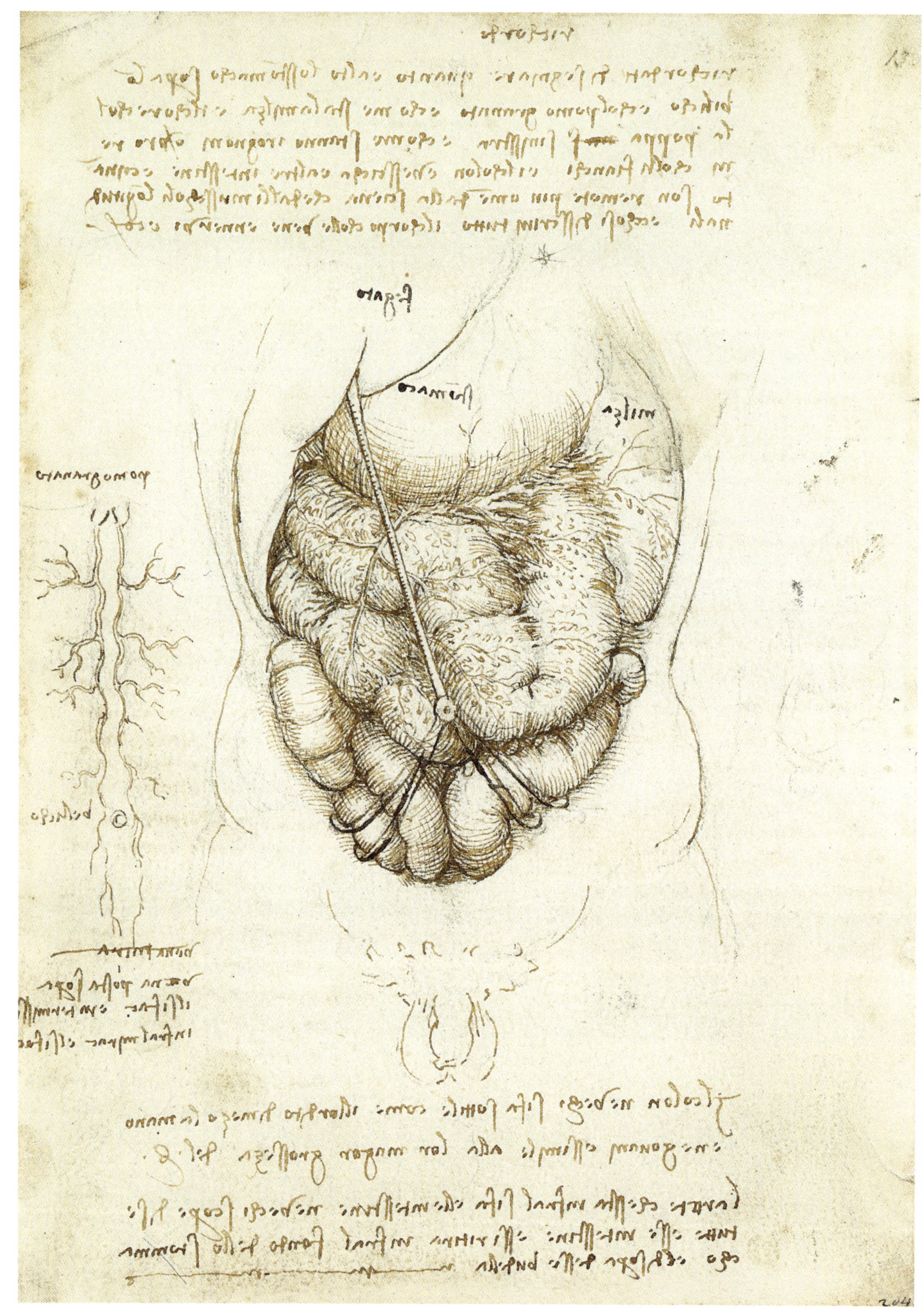

Fig. 5. Leonardo da Vinci, *Abdomen*, ca. 1508, pen and ink over black chalk, 19.2 × 14.1 cm, Windsor, Royal Collection Trust, RL 19039v

with the rockets, second it will kindle a fire there which cannot be put out, and will burn the wood, and [third] no one will be able to approach it because of the great stench. (manuscript B, folio 80v)

Or this one called a "Fragilica":

> A ball half a foot across, filled with small barrels made of paper and crammed with pepper, sulphur and of "*cono corsico*" (?). And whoever might smell it will swoon.

He even dreamt of being able to measure the range of a smell, just as elsewhere he measures the range of a sound:

> What will they say of the musk which always keeps a great quantity of its surrounding atmosphere charged with odour, and which when carried miles will permeate a thousand miles with that perfume without diminution of itself? (*Codex Atlanticus*, folio 729 v)

Both bad and good smells inspired the Tuscan scholar to think in ways that complemented and echoed each other.

Bibliography

Biow Douglas, *The Culture of Cleanliness in Renaissance Italy* (Ithaca: Cornell University Press, 2006).

Boisseuil Didier, "Espaces et pratiques du bain au Moyen Âge", *Médiévales*, Presses universitaires de Vincennes (2002), 21 (n° 43), pp. 5–11.

Corbin Alain, *Le Miasme et la Jonquille – L'odorat et l'imaginaire social (xviiie-xixe siècles)* (Paris: Flammarion, coll. « Champs histoire », 1982).

Cowan Alexander and Steward Jill (eds), *The City and the Senses: Urban Culture since 1500* (Aldershot: Ashgate, 2007).

Prizer William F., "Reading Carnival: The Creation of a Florentine Carnival Song", *Early Music History*, vol. 23 (Cambridge: Cambridge University Press, 2004), pp. 185–252.

Stevens Crawshaw Jane L., *Cleaning Up Renaissance Italy. Environmental Ideals and Urban Practice in Genoa and Venice* (Oxford: Oxford University Press, 2023).

Vigarello Georges, *Le Propre et le Sale. L'hygiène du corps depuis le Moyen Âge* (Paris: Points, Seuil, 2014 [re-ed.]).

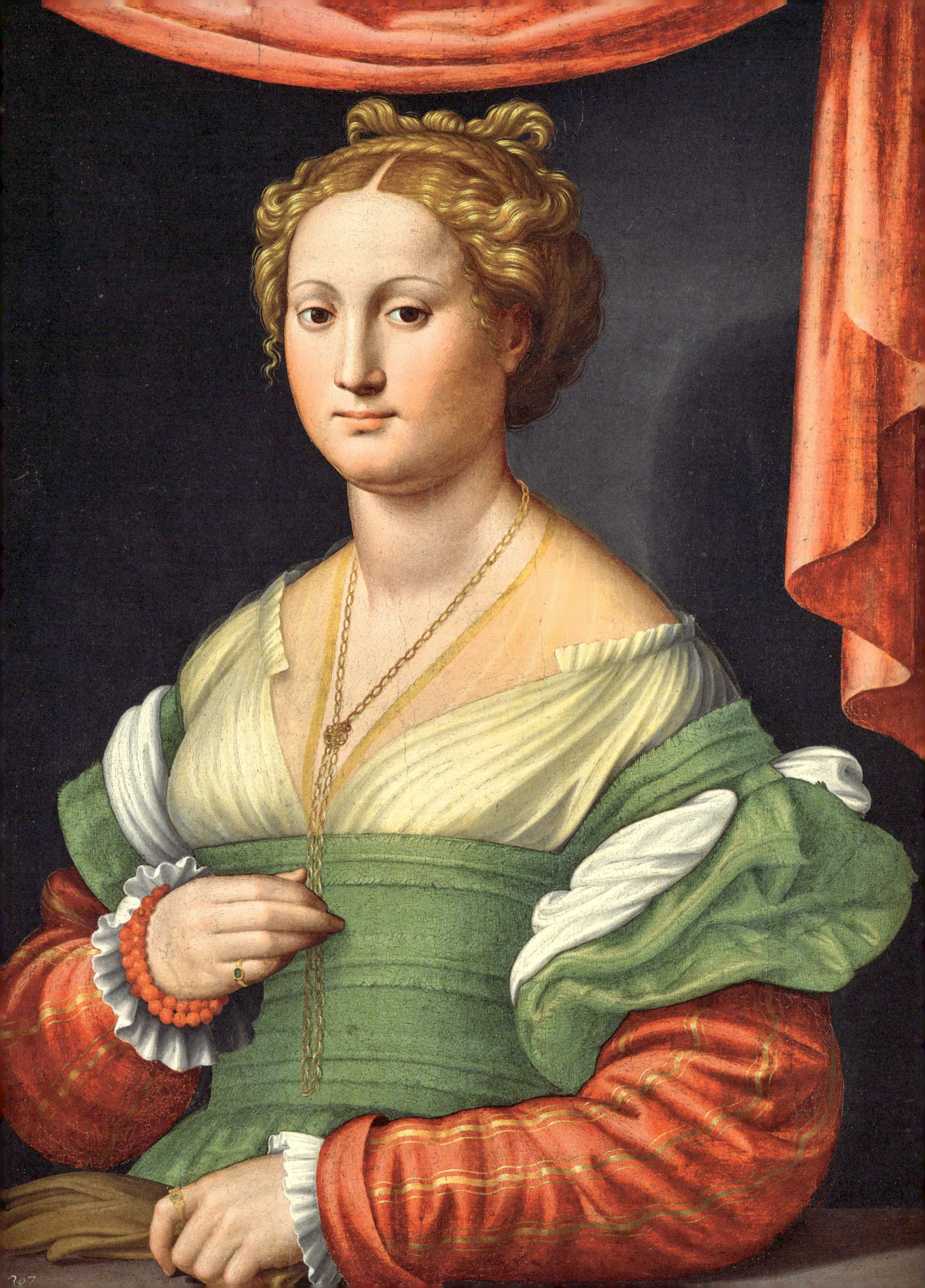

WHAT DID THE YOUNG LEONARDO HEAR?

JESSE RODIN AND LORENZO TUNESI

Three bell strikes resound in the darkness. Emanating from the campanile of the Badia Fiorentina, a church just off the central Piazza della Signoria, these early morning sounds are familiar to all Florentines. As the day breaks, the city's largest bell, the Leone (lion), rings out six times from the tower of the Palazzo della Signoria. As it tolls, yet another bell begins to peal just 200 metres north, in the Palazzo del Podestà (known today as the Bargello), and then, with hardly an interruption, the People's Bell (*del Popolo*) chimes, again from the Palazzo della Signoria [fig. 1].

As we learn from the statutes of the Florentine Republic, on most mornings these were the first sounds people heard. Florence's bells not only marked the beginning and end of liturgical celebrations in churches and monasteries, but also helped organise the city's daily routine. At around 9am, the Badia bells rang again, and were joined for thirty minutes by those of the cathedral (Santa Maria del Fiore) to call the people to High Mass. Meanwhile the Montalina bell tolled from the top of the tower in the Palazzo del Podestà to herald the start of the day's tribunals. Around midday, bells and trumpets announced that members of the city's executive council (the *priori*) were about to take lunch; at dusk these same bells and trumpets signalled the start of their dinner (ATKINSON, 2016, pp. 69–120). For ordinary citizens, church bells marked the end of the working day by ringing out a well-known *Ave Maria* melody: this was the time to close up shops, recite a prayer, and go home. At dusk, three peals of the Montalina and the Leone marked the official end of the day. Then the taverns closed and the city fell silent.

The young Leonardo's daily life was punctuated by these communal, attention-grabbing sounds. This essay strives to reconstruct some of Leonardo's early sonic experiences by describing the sounds and musical performances he heard or might have heard, above all in Florence's streets. Between 1469 and 1472 he served as an apprentice at Andrea del Verrocchio's workshop on what is now the Via de' Macci. As was customary at the time, Leonardo probably lived with the other apprentices in Verrocchio's house. In the course of his daily routine, his ears became attuned to the civic sounds that marked the beginning of work hours, his lunch break, and the moment he put away his canvases and brushes at the end of the day.

Walking around town, Leonardo doubtless bumped into and chatted with passers-by, amid

LEFT
Francucci Innocenzo, also known as Innocenzo da Imola, *Portrait of a Woman* (thought to be Vannozza Cattanei), 16th c.
Oil on wood, 97.5 × 77 cm
Rome, Galleria Borghese, inv. 416

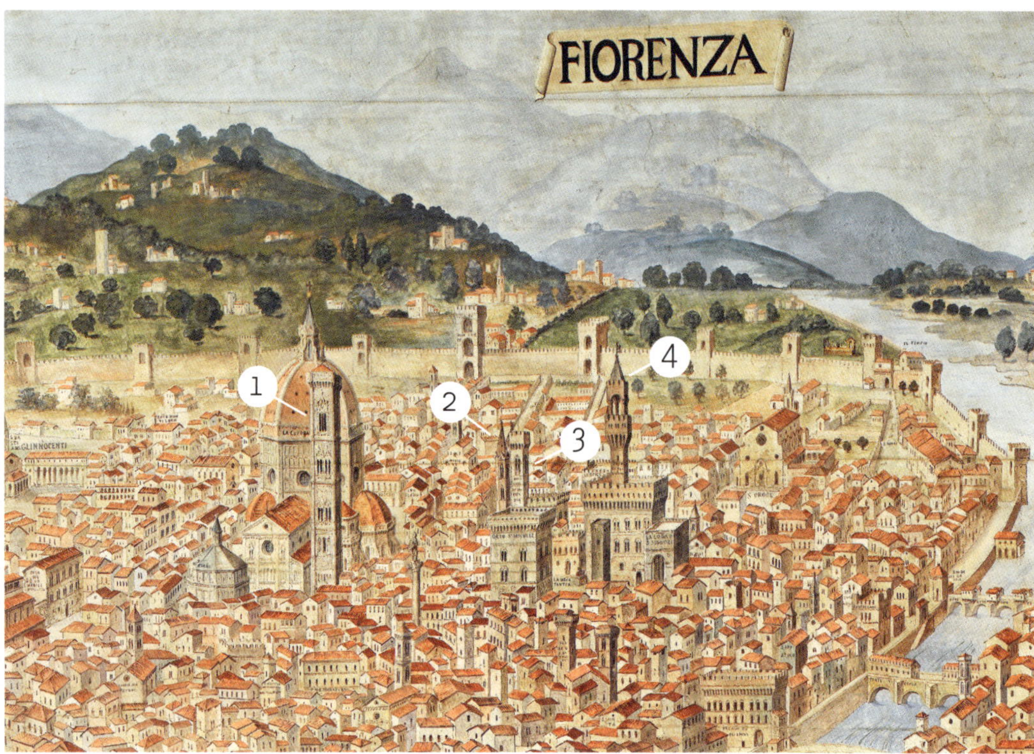

1. The Cathedral
2. The Badia Fiorentina
3. The Leone / the Popolo
4. The Montalina

Fig. 1. Attributed to Francesco di Lorenzo Rosselli, *View of Florence, or of the Catena* (detail), ca. 1471–82, woodcut, Florence, Palazzo Vecchio

a din of street noises and undecipherable conversations. An especially important venue for conversation, gossip included, was the Piazza della Signoria, the epicentre of Florence's communal life. This public square was frequented by city criers making announcements and by storytellers and minstrels entertaining local crowds with humorous tales, nursery rhymes, and sayings in the Florentine vernacular (Atkinson, 2016, pp. 152–81). In a world with neither motorised vehicles nor digital screens, this cacophony of urban sounds, especially those with entertainment value, must have captured people's attention far more than streets noises do today, even those in the background. Indeed, navigating the city's social and political life meant listening to official proclamations, gossiping about the latest news, and laughing at off-colour verses recited by street performers.

The Feast of Saint John the Baptist

Holidays and festivals animated the city, helping to forge Florence's identity while being a source of civic pride to its citizens. Two Florentine feasts are exceptionally well documented: the celebration of the city's patron saint and Carnival time.

Held at the start of the summer, the feast of Saint John the Baptist was grandiose. Detailed chronicles spanning circa 1340–1480 make it plain that by the time Leonardo was a youth, the feast had expanded considerably in scope. By the mid-15th century, this was a day when commercial activities were suspended and workshops closed, including Verrocchio's. In 1454, Florence's archbishop, Antonino Pierozzi, lengthened the feast to fill not two days, but four (21–24 June).

On the morning of the 22nd, members of the merchants' guild of Calimala organised a grand procession of the *edifici*, decorated wagons on which actors staged scenes from the Bible; in the evening all of the city councillors paraded in the streets. The following morning, to the uninterrupted tolling of the city's bells, the city's full complement of clergy processed along a precise itinerary that began and ended at the cathedral (Ventrone, 2011, pp. 49–76).

Watching perhaps from the street, Leonardo's attention would have been caught by the sound of trumpets and *pifferi* heralding the procession's arrival intermingled with the city bells – their sounds would have gradually receded at the approach of the *laudesi*, semi-professional singers performing devotional hymns in Latin and Italian. Leonardo could have heard the *laudesi* singing in unison during the refrains, and in relatively simple two- or three-voice polyphony during the verses. If he stayed out all day, he would have seen the evening procession of the *priori*, who paraded through the streets accompanied by the city's sixteen heraldic banners (gonfalons), each blazoned with a coat of arms of one of the city's districts. On the last morning of the feast, Leonardo probably made directly for Piazza della Signoria, where the city's judges and representatives had gathered, bearing offerings and wooden candles, to pledge their allegiance to the *priori*. Later in the day Leonardo would have joined his friends at the city walls. There they would have watched as the horse-keepers (*barberi*) used their bodies to stop the horses at the end of the *palio de' barberi*, a centuries-old, riderless race that brought the celebration to a close. The winner was greeted with trumpet blasts and a cheering crowd [fig. 2].

Carnival - and the Song of the "Perfume-Makers"

Lorenzo de' Medici, who assumed de facto leadership of Florence after his father's death in 1469, totally redesigned the city's carnival celebrations. Traditionally, Florence's aristocratic families had celebrated the carnival season by organising jousts (*armeggerie*) and courtly and knightly dances. Lorenzo progressively excluded the Florentine nobility from the festivities, meanwhile inaugurating new celebrations in which groups of masked and costumed young people (*brigate di giovani*) mimicked the artisan class. Between 1474 and 1478, the jousts that had taken place in the Piazza Santa Croce were gradually replaced by carnival songs (*canti carnascialeschi*) and *mascherate*, that is, contests of wit featuring songs that became gradually lewder and filled with double-entendres (Orvieto, 1992, pp. 103–24; and Macey, 1998, pp. 32–58).

The Piazza Santa Croce was close to Verrocchio's workshop. During carnival Leonardo would have seen crowds of people in the square cheering and chatting noisily, youngsters running through the streets shouting and laughing, and peddlers selling waffles with almonds and honey (*confortini*) from baskets, the smell of which would have filled the air [fig. 3].

Everyone would have suddenly turned to look as a masked group dressed as peddlers and carrying small vases and bottles paraded into the square, singing a song exalting the quality of their product. From the first lines, listeners would have understood that this was the song of the perfume-makers (*Canto dei profumi*) – not real perfume-makers, but a fictional guild conjured up solely for the sake of parody. The song survives in the Florentine manuscript *Banco Rari* 230 with an attribution to no-one less than Lorenzo himself [fig. 4].

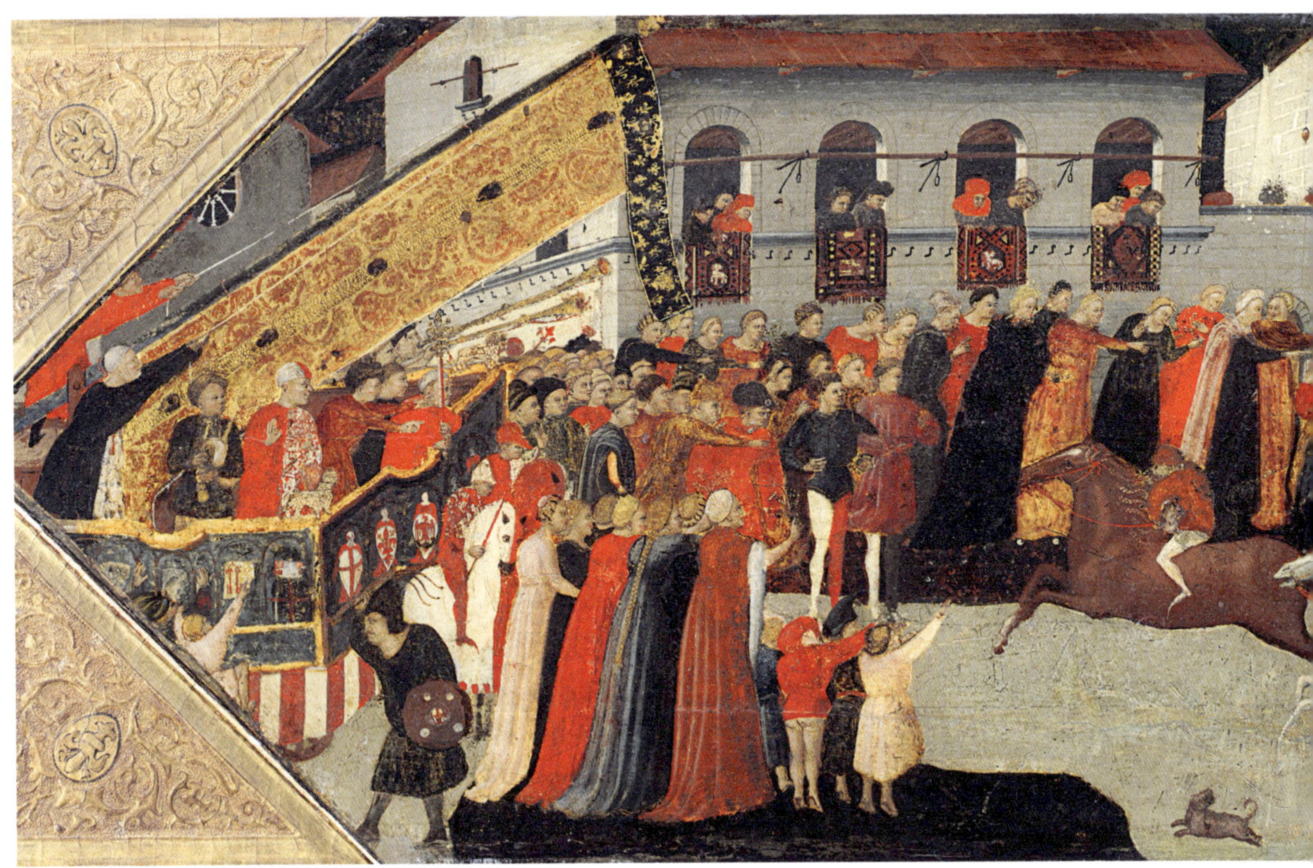

Fig. 2. Giovanni Francesco Toscani, *Panel from a Cassone: The Race of the Palio in the Streets of Florence*, 1418, tempera and gold on wood, 42.1 × 139.5 cm Cleveland, Cleveland Museum of Art, Holden Collection 1916.801

Like most carnival songs, the text of *Canto dei profumi* is relatively simple: seven eight-line stanzas (octonaries) plus a four-line refrain, all governed by eight-syllable lines and a regular rhyme scheme. The song's fictional perfume-makers repeatedly evoke smells and fragrances – but innuendo and double-entendre make plain that the real aim has nothing to do with beauty products. On the surface, the text can be understood to describe the perfumers approaching the women of Florence and promoting their rare products: small vases containing fragrant ointments made of mulberry, orange, and sap. But even the opening stanza offers a clue to its true message: "But we have already fallen in love / With the ladies of Florence" (lines 3 and 4). As the song proceeds, the real intentions of the perfume-makers become clear, as they offer the ladies their "long-necked bottles", "oils" and "foamy" soaps that, if rubbed properly, "heal every pain" while changing the minds of those ladies who refuse love. The young Leonardo would surely have understood the jokes – and been riveted to every word.

The music is no less attention grabbing. For one thing, the composer makes the words audible through syllabic writing and by relating the voices mostly homorhythmically, that is, with all three voices singing the same syllables at the same time. For another, individual phrases tend to begin with simple declamatory rhythms before introducing more rousing dotted rhythms, then even livelier syncopation. Phrase by phrase, excitement builds as the voices are heard increasingly individually in rhythm, in order to avoid all cadence. A contrasting passage is created in each

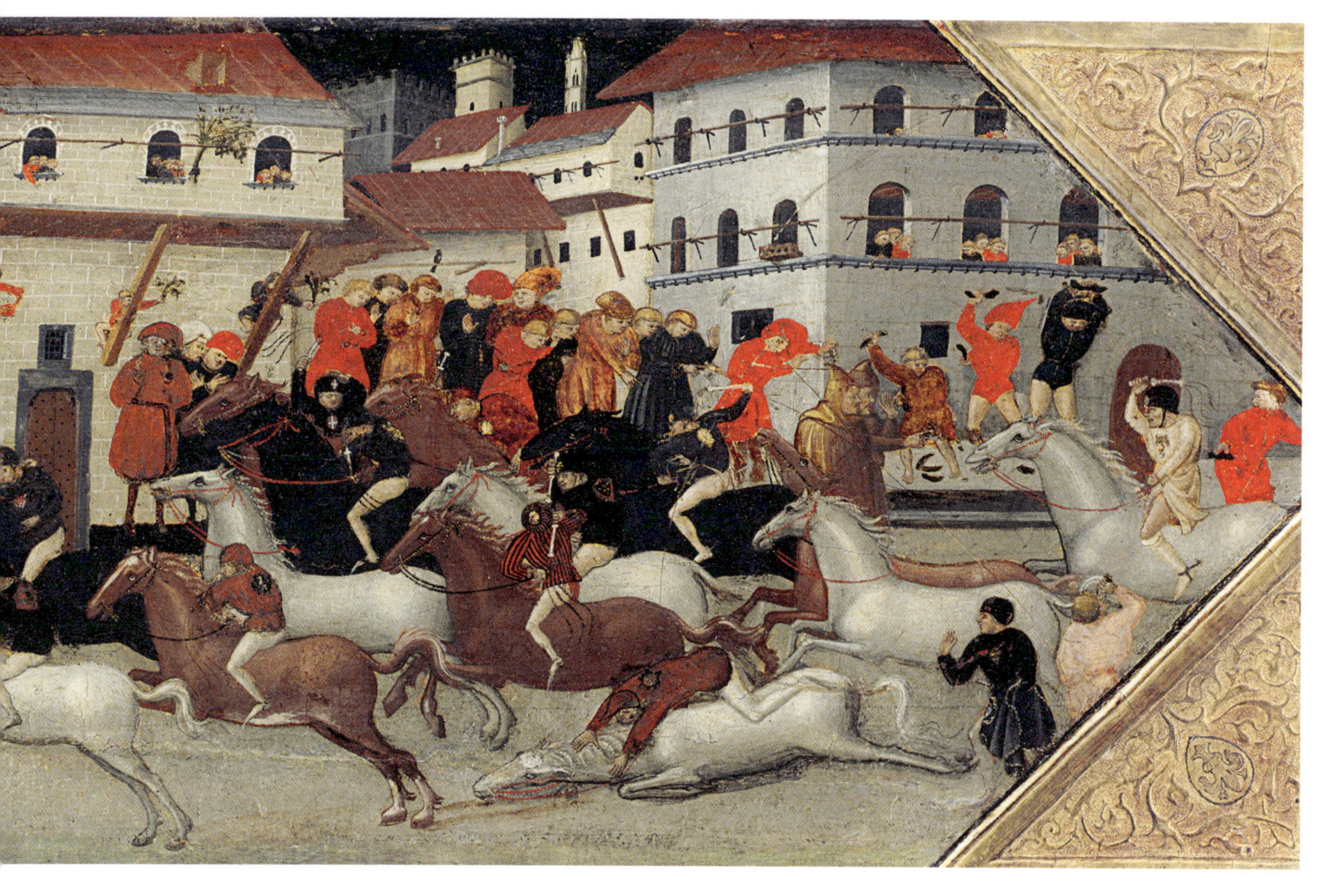

stanza by lines 5 and 6 being set in triple metre.

Would Leonardo have noticed, let alone cared about, these musical details? We cannot be sure, even if from later in his life we have evidence of his musical interests, not least the creation of new instruments (Carpiceci, 1978, pp. 3–46). Extrapolating from what we know about Leonardo more generally, it is hard to resist the idea that he paid attention not only to the racy text, but also to the song's simple yet effective music and neatly balanced phrases. Who knows – he may even have joined one of the *brigate*, donned a costume of his own design, and sung.

But now the day's celebrations are over and the square is emptying fast. The late winter sun is already setting and the bells are ringing. Like his fellow Florentines, Leonardo is headed home. A few dedicated revellers are still in the taverns, drinking their last cup of wine – but the innkeeper is shouting that it's time to leave so he can close up for the night. And he's right: the *Ave Maria* has already rung and the Leone bell has just struck for the last time.

Canzone per andare in maſchera p carneſciale facte da piu perſone.

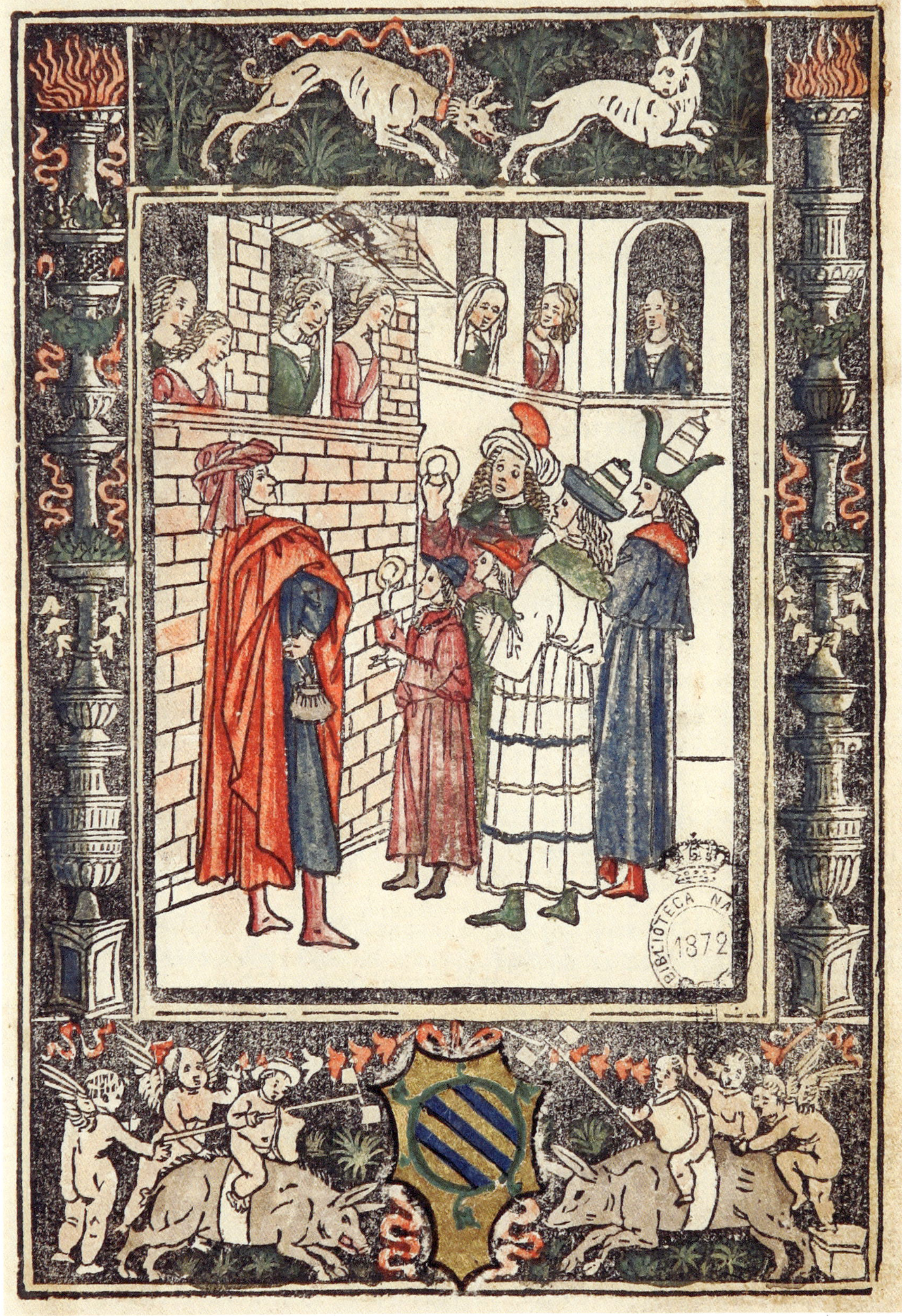

Bibliography

Atkinson Niall, *The Noisy Renaissance: Sound, Architecture, and Florentine Urban Life* (University Park, PA: The Pennsylvania State University Press, 2016).
Carpiceci Mauro, "I Meccanismi musicali di Leonardo" in *Raccolta Vinciana*, XXII (1987), pp. 3–46.
Macey Patrick Paul, *Bonfire Songs: Savonarola's Musical Legacy* (Oxford: Clarendon Press, 1998).
Orvieto Paolo, "Carnevale e feste fiorentine del tempo di Lorenzo de' Medici" in *Lorenzo il Magnifico e il suo tempo*, Garfagnini Gian Carlo (ed.) (Florence: Olschi, 1992), pp. 103–24.
Ventrone Paola, "La festa di San Giovanni: Costruzione di un'identità civica fra rituale e spettacolo (secoli xiv-xvi)", *Annali di Storia di Firenze*, vol. II (2007), pp. 49–76.

LEFT
Fig. 3. Bartolomeo di Libri *Canto dei Confortini de Canzona per andar in maschera x carnasciale facte da diverse persone*, 1515, Florence, Biblioteca Nazionale Centrale, Pal. E 6.5.47

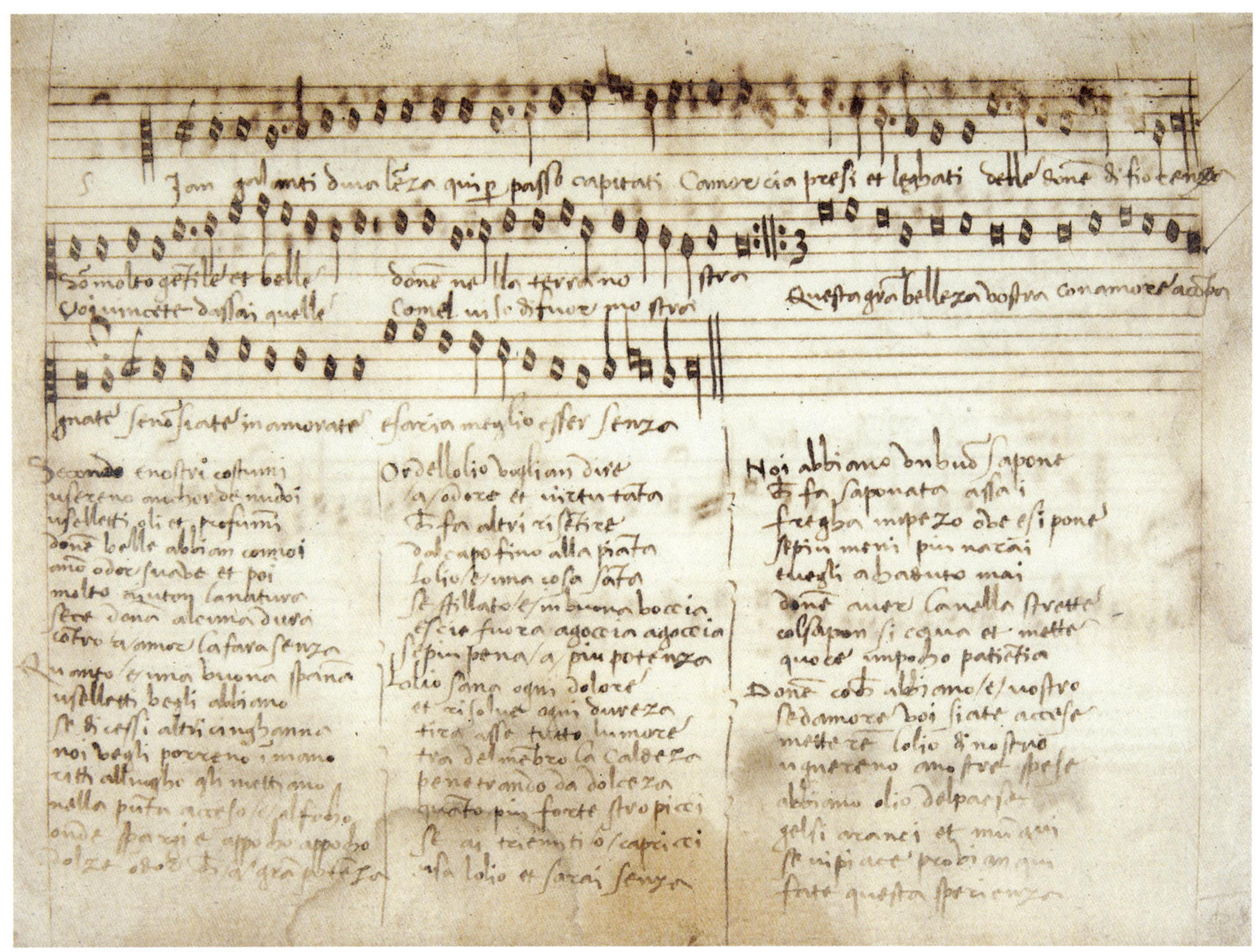

Fig. 4. Collection of musical songs (Song of the Perfumers), 16th c., manuscript, 33.5 × 26 cm, Florence, Biblioteca Nazionale Centrale, Banco Rari 230, inv. 230

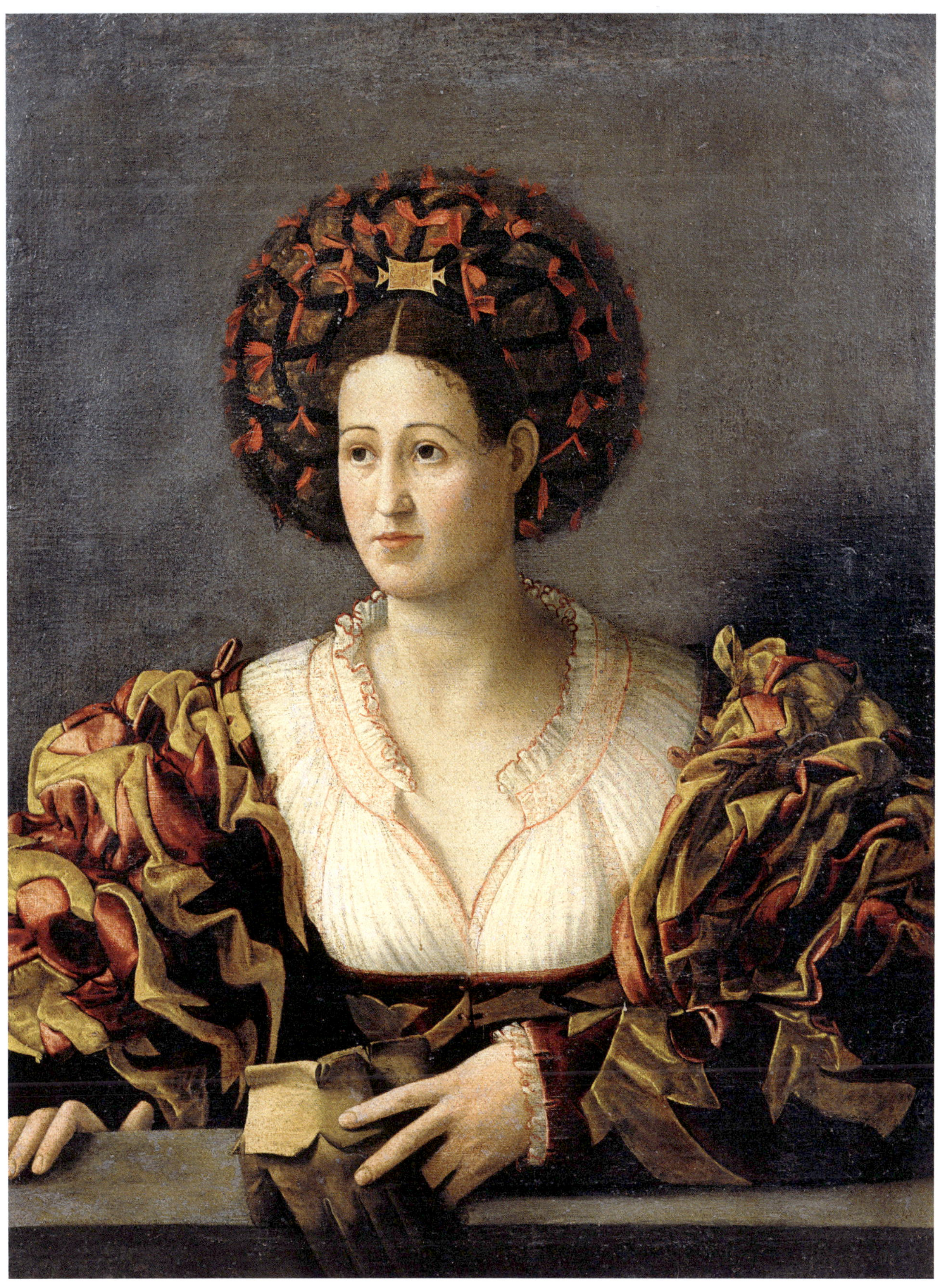

Paolo Morando, also known as Cavazzola, *Portrait of a Woman*, 16th c., oil on canvas, 74.2 × 96.4 cm, Bergamo, Accademia Carrara, inv. 58MR 00036

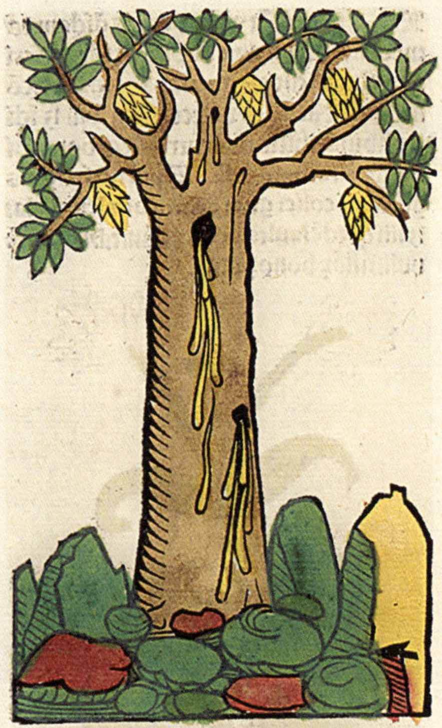

Ca.cccc xcj.

Vernix latine. arabice sandaros vel baratin vel gressa vel sandaraca. grece gium. Serap. li. aggre. cap. sandros. i. vernix: et est gūmi ca. et sic. complexionis est in. ij. gradu. Et idem auctor. Habix. Ca. est et sic. sz caliditas est pauca: est enim simile karabe: sed non ita dur. et in eo parum est amaritudinis et affert a terris cristianorum. Paulus caplo. de vernice. Vernix est gummi cuiusdā arboris que in cristianorum ptibus nascit quae arbor iuniperus vocat. vnde ab eo tpe estiuo qdam gūmositas egredit quae actōe caloris exiccat et induratur. et dr vernix. quae cū colligit est albi coloris: et cū antiqt est subcitrini. et cū plus antiquat est ruffi coloris qcūqz sit. dūmō sit lucida et clara eligenda ē. Et dr etiā vnix qddā qd pficit ex oleo seis lini et vnice. et inde illiniunt vel psolidant colores ad picturā. hz ān vnit vtutē pglutinādi ex viscositate sua. et clarificādi: et pfuādi qd satis ptz. Nā pictores sup alios colores pfuāt.

Operationes.

A Sera. Vernix autem quod est gūmi absqz confectione valet contra fluxum sanguinis ex naribus si puluis eius confectus cum albumine oui tempibus et fronti supponatur. contra vomitum colericum fiat ex puluere eius emplastr et olibano et albumine oui et stomacho supponat.

B Idem etiam fiat contra dissinteriā addito aceto et supponat pectini. puluis etiam eius in ouo sorbili datus valet contra vomitum colericū vel dissinteriā. valz etiam puluis contra interiorem et exteriorem solutōem.

C Serap. predicto li. et cap. Vernix confert catarro quando fit fumigatō cum ea. et desiccat vlcera. et abscindit sanguinem menstruū:

D Et idem auc. Medigoras. De ppetate eius et cōfert catarro. et desiccat fistulas: et est sicca et calida i. ij. gradu. euellit supfluitates flegmaticas. quae sunt in stomacho et intestinis:

E Et occidit lūbricos et ascarides. et confert fluxibilitati neruorum quae accidit a frigiditate et humiditate et repletōe

F Et idem auct. Habix. Qñ fit suffumigatio cum eo pfert catarro capitis: et quā do pulverizatur sup vlcera desiccat ea:

G Et idem auct. Atabari. Sādaraca est similis karabe in vtute sua. et cōfert fumigatō eius corize et desiccat fistulas: et cōfert sputo sanguinis et emoroidibus. Et est gummi citrini coloris simile karabe. et est in eo parum amaritudinis. et affert a terris cristianorum. et virtus eius est similis vtuti karabe.

H Et qñ fit cū ea fumigatio pfert fistulis. et qñ accipit ex sādaraca et oleo rosarum et linit cum eo cōfert scissuris quae fiunt in mēbris et manibus et pedibus. et si nō inuenis: pone loco eius pōdus tercie ptis plus pondē ipius de karabe qd dixit Galienus esse gummi baur romane.

I Ubi sciendū quod illud vocabulū sandaraca aliter intelligit in libris arabū. et aliter in li. grecorum. nā arabes p sandaraca intelligūt vnicē. sicut iā dcm ē. sz greci p sādaraca intendūt qndā lapidē rubeū. Vñ Pli. Sādaraca affertur a pōto et Capodocia et Sicilia. et est lapis ignei coloris.

THE SCENT OF OIL AND RESIN IN LEONARDO'S WORKSHOP

MARJOLIJN BOL

To humans, some of the stronger scents come from different types of oils, including drying oils, essential oils, and the resinous exudations from plants. The scents of many oils and resins are so striking that they have a long and global history in perfume production, continuing to the present day. In Leonardo's world, oils and resins played an important role in the many practices he was interested in. They are profusely documented in his notebooks and materially testified to in the artworks he left behind. From walnut oil to turpentine and from camphor to juniper resin, Leonardo's working space must have been perpetually perfumed by the scent of resins and oils.

Leonardo is perhaps best-known for using oils and resins as part of his painterly practice. He was renowned – and to a degree infamous – for his experiments with these materials in the art of mural painting. These experiments did not guarantee long-term stability and some of Leonardo's works degraded so quickly that his contemporaries remarked upon it (FARAGO, 1994). Leonardo's notebooks suggest that he was particularly interested in using walnut oil as a binder for his pigments and as an ingredient for varnish, the final coating applied to his work. Analysis of the grinding binders he used shows that, in addition to linseed oil, Leonardo did indeed employ walnut oil in his paint (KEITH *et al.*, 2011). In the notebooks that today make up the *Codex Atlanticus*, Leonardo documents his interest in the properties, clarity, and purity of walnut oil (folios 18v and 304v). He writes that all oils contained in fruits or seeds are very clear by nature but that they become yellow if you do not know how to extract them. The clarity and non-yellowing of oil was important to Leonardo because he did not want his grinding binder to impart a yellow hue to the precious pigments he was using. A yellow oil could make blue pigments look green, or make white pigments appear yellow. Leonardo continues that such discolorations in walnut oil come from the small skin, or husk that surrounds the nut. If the husk is crushed with the nut, it will become part of the oil after extraction. This husk then tinges the paint, thus changing its colour. For Leonardo, it was therefore essential to remove the husks before extracting the oil from the walnuts. To achieve this, the nuts are soaked in water so that the rinds can be more easily removed. Practical reconstructions of Leonardo's recommendations show that it is a rather painstaking process to remove the rinds from each nut and that it would have likely

LEFT
Fig. 1 Jakob Meydenbach
Ortus sanitatis, 1491
Cambridge, Cambridge University Library, Inc.3.A.1.8[37], f. 232v

taken quite some time for a large volume of them. Once they are cleaned of their rinds, the nuts are soaked in water which is refreshed until it stays clear. The nuts are then left until they have completely disintegrated – in effect they are left to rot. Upon decomposition of the walnuts, the oil contained in them rises to the surface (oil being lighter than water) and can then be siphoned off as per Leonardo's instructions. The practice of decomposing walnuts in water to obtain oil would not have resulted in the most pleasant of smells. But what is interesting here is that Leonardo believed that using the process of decomposition to separate the nut's oil component would result in a purer end-product.

In addition to the unpleasant smell associated with walnut oil extraction, Leonardo also provides various notes about how to deal with oils that smell bad, typically because they have gone rancid. Drying oils, such as walnut oil, slowly go rancid upon exposure to heat and oxygen. An oil gone rancid is recognisable by its distinctly unpleasant smell, which in the case of walnut oil goes from a mildly nutty scent to a bitter and sour smell, by some even described as reminiscent of "paint thinner". Leonardo records a note about how to clean a foul-smelling oil, the scent of which he describes as "sad" (*tristo odore*), by boiling it with vinegar (manuscript A, Institut de France, folio 20r). In several other recipes in his notebooks, Leonardo reveals that he was similarly concerned with the scent and taste of oil. In one of these notes, on the same folio of the *Codex Atlanticus* mentioned above, Leonardo describes how to add a bit of camphor to walnut oil to make the oil taste good and to prevent it from thickening.

Camphor is a terpenoid compound with a strong aroma that in Leonardo's time was made by distilling the bark and wood of certain East Asian trees, especially *Cinnamomum camphora*. Imported from Asia, and traded by the Arabs, camphor became widespread in the medieval Mediterranean world (Amar and Lev, 2017). It was commonly used as a drug, a condiment and mentioned as an important ingredient of perfumes in sources, even considered by some Arab authors as one of the five most important aromatic substances. In addition to using camphor to improve the scent and taste of oil, Leonardo also mentions the role of camphor in making a type of firebomb, the so-called *flammea* (manuscript B, Institut de France, folio 30v). He writes that, to make this device, you mix a range of volatile substances, including camphor, saltpetre, brandy, and incense, another natural resin with a long history in perfume production. When mixing has occurred, a woollen thread is submerged in the volatile liquid. This thread is then wound onto a sharply pointed object. According to Leonardo, this firebomb will even burn under water. On the same folio, Leonardo records another recipe for making a firebomb. This one was also made with a variety of volatile materials, including liquid varnish (*vernice liquida*), petroleum oil (*olio petrolio*), and turpentine resin (*trementina*). Mixed by heating aromatic compounds on a fire, and deployed by setting fire to these volatile substances, we can only imagine the intense and intoxicating scent the making and using of these firebombs must have produced.

While Leonardo was likely not involved in the production and use of firebombs himself, he was certainly familiar with the volatile ingredients in their composition. The materials used to make the second firebomb, for instance, are all key ingredients in the production of painter's varnish (Bol, 2023). The first – *vernice liquida* – is the oldest type of varnish, typically made with

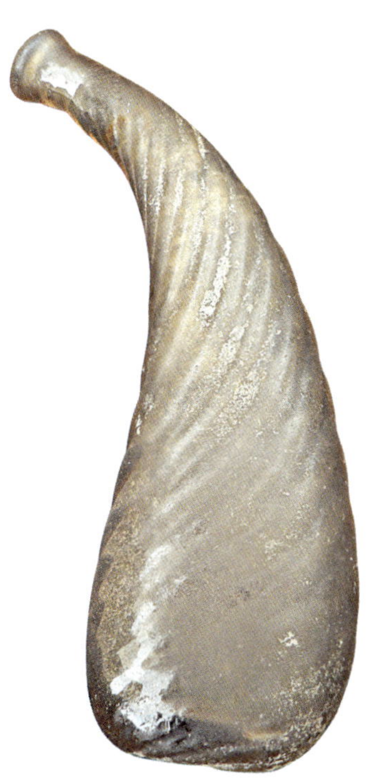

Ribbed perfume phial, 17th c., 10.6 × 6 cm, Aujac, Coll. Rigal, château du Cheylard d'Aujac

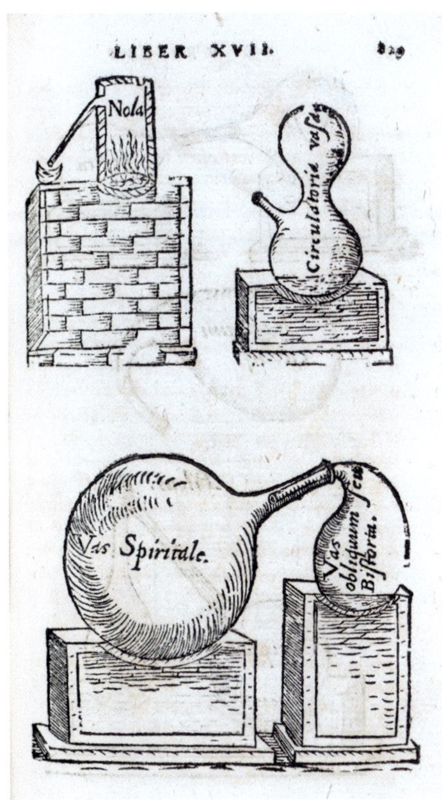

Girolamo Cardano, *De Subtilitate*, 16th c., printed text, 17.3 × 11.3 cm, Tours, Centre d'études supérieures de la Renaissance

a plant resin such as sandarac mixed with linseed oil over a heat source. *Vernice liquida* is described in the earliest collections of artisanal recipes that have come down to us and frequently appears in Leonardo's notebooks as well. Leonardo did not have to make *vernice liquida* himself as it could be bought ready-made from his local apothecary, but, in addition to this ready-made substance, the notebooks reveal that he was particularly interested in making his own varnish, even sourcing the raw materials himself. In the two recipes in question, contained in *Codex Forster I* (folio 44v) and *Codex Madrid I* (folio 191v), Leonardo discusses in rather remarkable detail how to source the resin used to make this varnish. We learn that an excellent varnish can be made by cutting the bark of a juniper tree (from the genus *Juniperus*) so that the resin flows from its cuts [fig. 1]. Seasonality determines when the juniper resin can be procured, and thus when this varnish can be made. Leonardo explains that the best time to cut the tree for juniper resin is at the end of March and in April. Upon extraction, while it is still liquid, the juniper resin is mixed with an aged walnut oil that needs to be "well purified and white". This last remark likely refers to Leonardo's concern with the proper extraction of walnut oil discussed earlier.

In another note, Leonardo explains how to make a carnival blouse (*vesto da carnovale*) by applying an "odoriferous varnish" (*vernice odorifera*) to a thin linen fabric. This varnish is made by dissolving a *vernice in grane* (a solid resin, possibly sandarac) in turpentine oil. Turpentine oil is made by distilling turpentine resin. And, as it is a volatile oil, Leonardo also lists it as an ingredient in his firebomb recipes. Turpentine oil had also been an important ingredient in painter's varnish

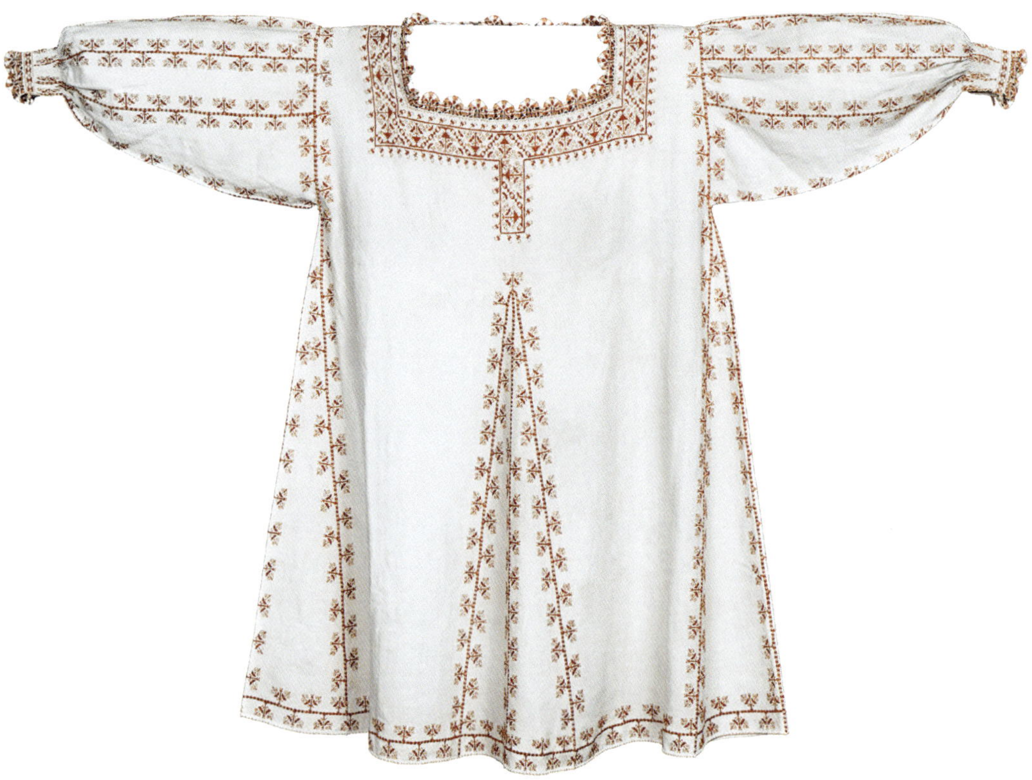

Women's shirt, 16th c., embroidered linen, needlepoint and bobbin lace, 110 × 159 cm, Prato, Museo del Tessuto, inv. n. 76.01.15

since the 16th century (Bol, 2023), but here it is used to imitate the black-and-white embroidery on a blouse [fig. 2].

To make the garment, thin linen is coated with the aromatic varnish described above. This varnish acts like a glue for the pattern which is applied in the second step of the recipe. To this end, a print with a geometric design is perforated so that the design can be transferred to the varnished cloth (probably using a method of dusting pigmented powder through the holes of the print, a technique known at the time as *spolvero*). The print is made wet so that it does not stick to the varnish.

The transferred design is then filled in with millet grains coloured black and white. This works because the varnish used to coat the linen is sticky, and, as such, the millet grains stick to it to form the black and white pattern in imitation of embroidery. The wearer of the garment would have certainly been enveloped in the aromatic scent of the resins used.

Leonardo's surviving paintings provide physical evidence that he regularly worked and experimented with oils and resins. But beyond his paintings, Leonardo's notebooks document how diverse his engagement with these aromatic materials really was. Leonardo used the strong and aromatic scent of volatile resins to perfume substances, as in the case of the varnished blouse

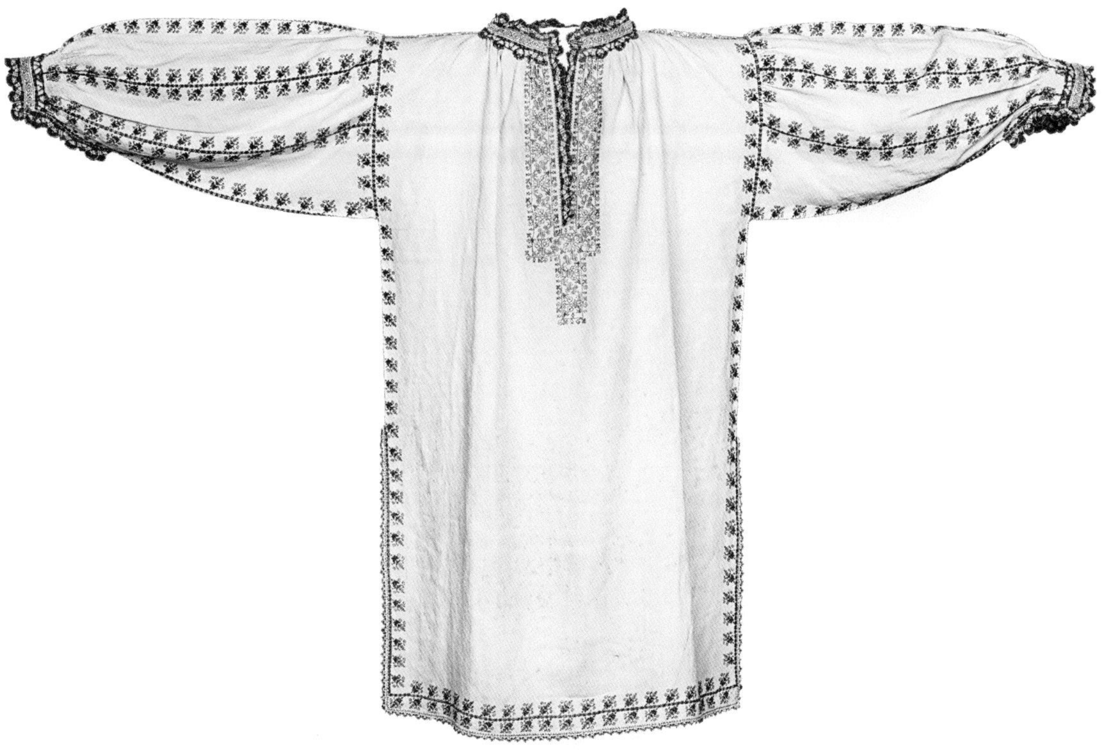

Fig. 2. Men's shirt, 16th c., embroidered linen, needlepoint and bobbin lace, 92.5 × 150 cm, Prato, Museo del Tessuto, inv. n. 76.01.19

with imitation embroidery discussed above, or, in the case of camphor, to improve the taste of walnut oil. In other examples, he used scent to establish the purity of a substance, such as to determine whether walnut oil is fresh or rancid. Leonardo's interest in oils and resins went beyond the pharmacy, where such aromatic compounds were typically bought. His notebooks show that he was interested in sourcing the raw materials for making varnish himself, conveying knowledge of how and when to tap trees for resin, and how to procure oil from walnuts through a process of decomposition. Indeed, the small kaleidoscope of the roles of aromatic oils and resins in Leonardo's practice presented here suggests that not only did their perfume pervade Leonardo's day-to-day practice, but also that he derived knowledge and expertise about materials and techniques from his olfactory experiences.

Bibliography

Amar Zohar and Lev Efraim, *Arabian Drugs in Medieval Mediterranean Medicine* (Edinburgh: Edinburgh University Press, 2018).
Bol Marjolijn, *The Varnish and the Glaze. Painting Splendor with Oil, 1100–1500* (Chicago: University of Chicago Press, 2023).
Donkin Robert Arthur, *Dragon's Brain Perfume. An Historical Geography of Camphor* (Leiden: Brill, 1999).
Farago Claire, "Léonard's *Battle of Anghiari*: A Study in the Exchange between Theory and Practice", *Art Bulletin*, vol. 76, no. 2 (1994), pp. 301–30.
Keith Larry, Roy Ashok, Morrison Rachel and Schade Peter, "Léonard da Vinci's 'Virgin of the Rocks': Treatment, Technique and Display", *National Gallery Technical Bulletin*, vol. 32 (2011), pp. 32–56.
Travers Newton Henry, "Léonard da Vinci as Mural Painter: Some Observations on his Materials and Working Methods", *Arte Lombarda* (Milan: Vita e Pensiero, no. 66, 1983), pp. 71–88.

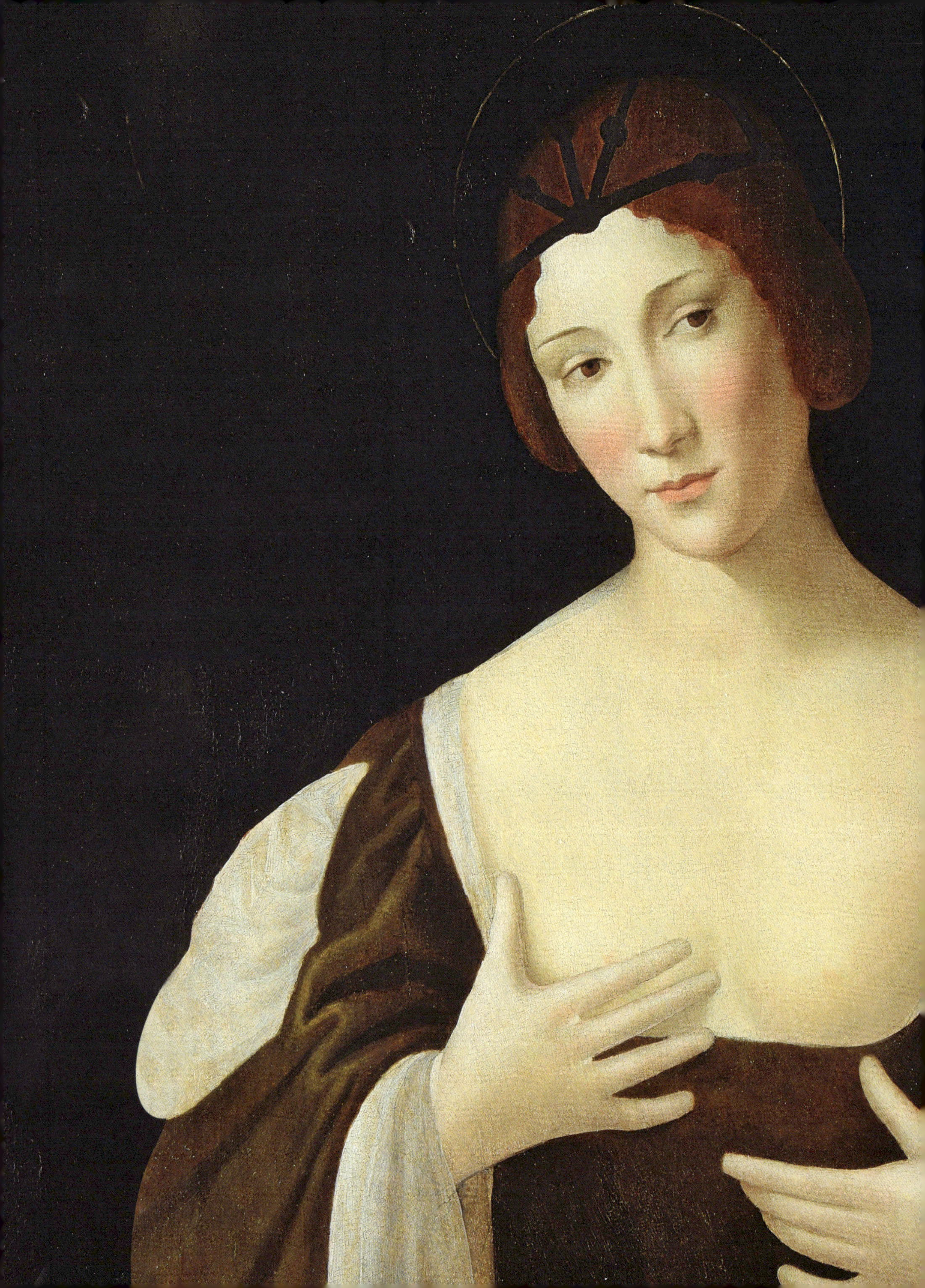

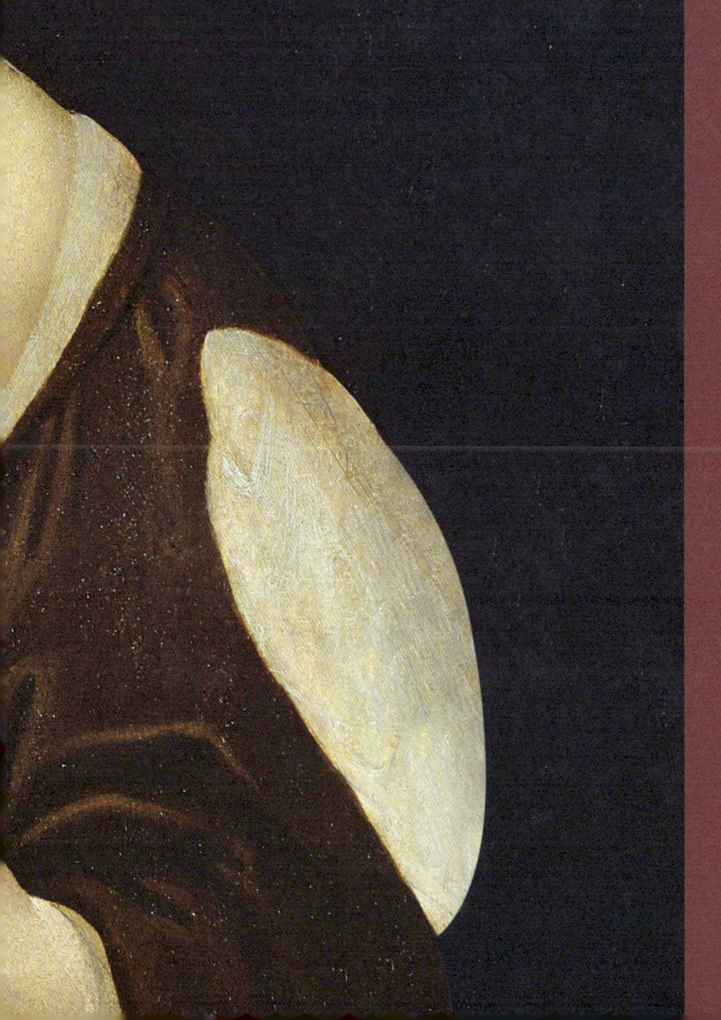

At the Sforza Court in Milan

Chapter IV

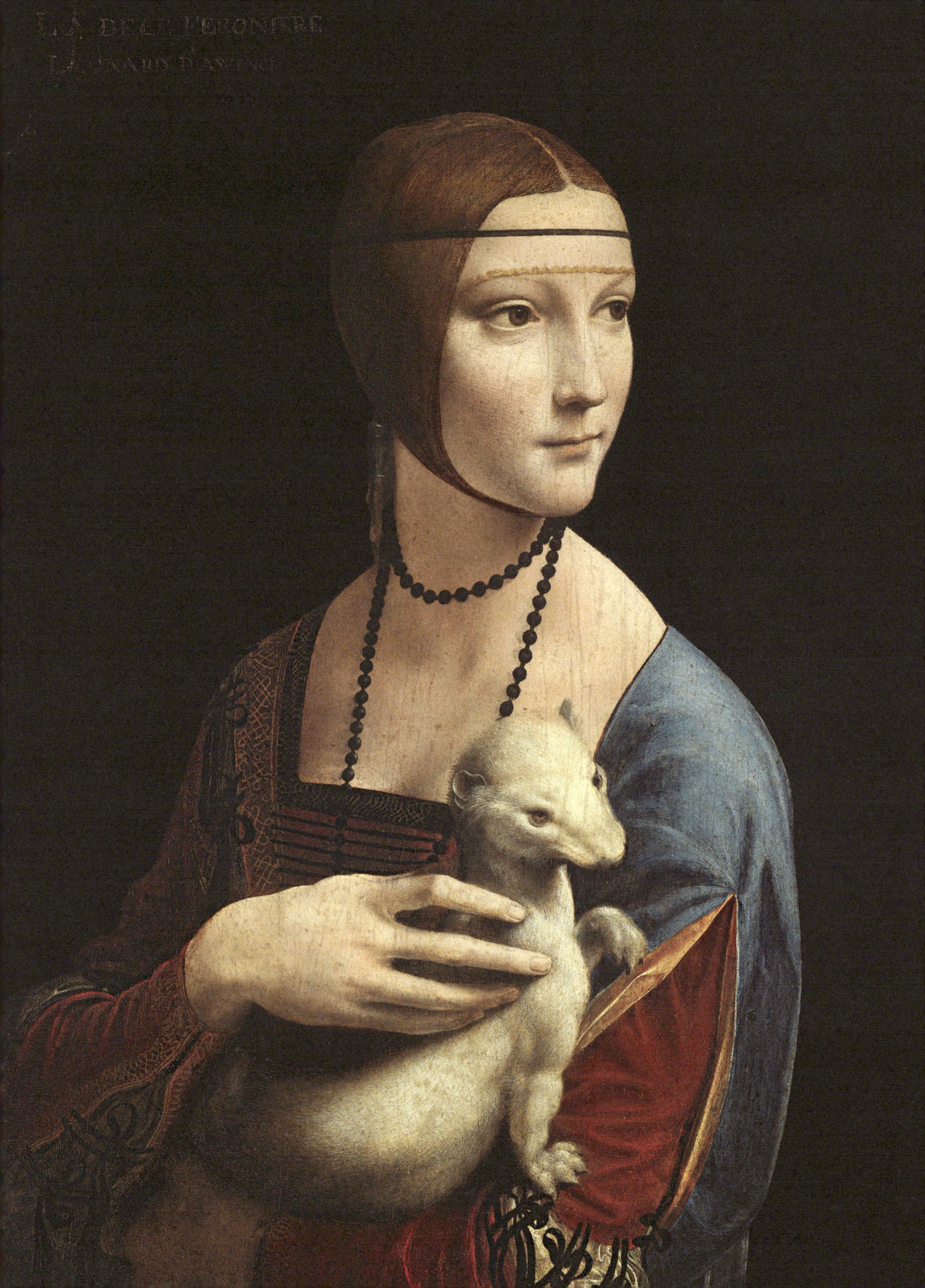

PERFUMED OBJECTS, JEWELLERY AND CLOTHES AT THE COURT OF THE SFORZA FAMILY AND OF ISABELLA D'ESTE

Paola Venturelli

On 6 March 1493, Bernardino Prosperi, a chancellor of the Este family, wrote to Isabella d'Este, Marchioness of Mantua, informing her of the visit to Vigevano castle that his mother, Eleonora of Aragon, Duchess of Ferrara, had paid to Isabella's sister Beatrice d'Este, the wife of Ludovico Sforza. He described three rooms that Beatrice had furnished for her personal use: one with numerous items of clothing, and two smaller ones, one dedicated to precious objects, the other to the "making or using of perfumes, products used in perfumery and fragrant waters". At the end of the visit, Eleonora received a gift of twenty "small phials of perfumed powder". Clearly much used by the young Beatrice, it is possible that some of these expensive materials were purchased from Ludovico Sforza's barber (whose trade combined the sale of cosmetics and perfumes), Giuliano de Imeratici from Alessandria, who in 1486 had been granted a space in the castle's clock tower in which to live and set up his workshop. We do not know whether Beatrice practised the art of perfumery, as other noblewomen did, but it is certain that the Sforza court was passionately interested in the art of perfume making. In the projected expenditure budget for the Duchy of Milan in 1476, no less than three hundred ducats was allocated to "perfumes, powders and scented waters", which were also prepared by the Neapolitan "master perfumer" Filippo dell'Oliva, employed by Duke Galeazzo Maria Sforza since 1474 (Venturelli, 2016).

Catarina Sforza, the famous author of *Experimenti*, spent her early years at this court. The daughter of Galeazzo Maria and his mistress Lucrezia Landriani, she was brought up by her grandmother Bianca Maria Visconti Sforza, who is remembered for the "very beautiful red blusher" that she took from a recipe in the Laurentian Codex Ashburnham 1388, a treatise on cosmetics by Chiara da Correggio compiled around the middle of the 16th century. After the death of Bianca Maria, Catarina found an affectionate teacher in Bona di Savoia, her father's wife; it was her apothecary, Cristoforo de Brugora, who created a botanical garden in Milan, one of the first of its kind (Ray, 2015, pp. 18–19, 178–79). Close to the Basilica di Sant'Ambrogio, it was bordered by the Nirone, the stream near which Leonardo had planned to build the villa of the governor of Milan, Charles II d'Amboise, adjoining a garden filled with "bitter oranges", lemons and citrons (*Codex Atlanticus*, folio 732v), citrus fruits used in perfume recipes, one of which was developed by Leonardo himself

PREVIOUS PAGE
Attributed to Giovanni Antonio Boltraffio
Female Figure, 16th c.
Oil on canvas, 63 × 51.5 cm
Pavia, Musei Civici del Castello Visconteo, inv. p. 111

LEFT
Leonardo da Vinci
Lady with an Ermine, 1488, oil on walnut board, 54 × 39 cm, Krakow, Czartoryski Museum

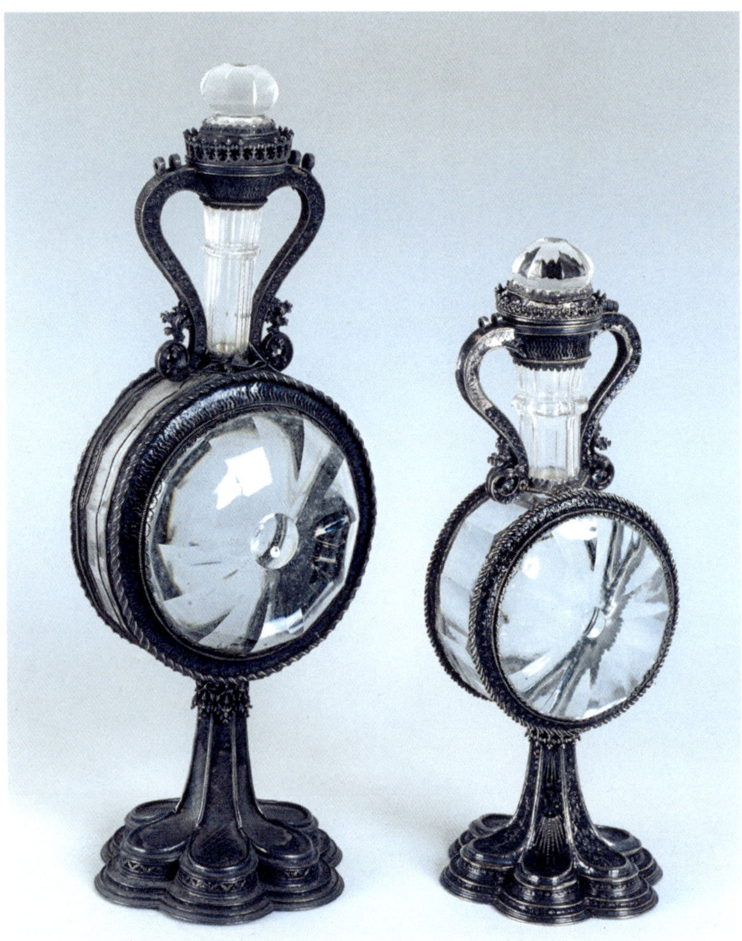

Fig. 1. Venetian workmanship, pair of small bottles, 3rd quarter of the 15th c., rock crystal, gilded silver and enamel, Modena, Galleria Estense, inv. 6918, 6919

(*Codex Atlanticus*, folio 195v). Chopped lemons, combined with other ingredients, appear in the recipe for a scented water "ideal for the face" that was used by Isabella of Aragon, wife of Duke Giangaleazzo Sforza from 1488. This recipe is described in a collection written at the beginning of the 16th century in northern Italy and intended for those wishing to "perfume their clothes or themselves" (Guerrini, 1883, p. 23).

Famous for her compositions of scented waters and pastes, Beatrice d'Este's sister Isabella had the necessary materials – musk, ambergris, civet – purchased in Venice, as well as Damask rose water and "eau de naffe" (distilled from orange blossoms), which arrived from the Orient by sea in large glass phials ("*zucche*") or smaller flasks ("*achaini*") made in the glassworks of Murano. From 1497 onwards, Isabella offered her blends to various illustrious figures. Among the lucky recipients were Chiara Gonzaga, sister of her husband Francesco, and Bianca Maria Sforza, wife of the Habsburg emperor, Maximilian I. In 1513, she gave "*bossoletti*" (small boxes) of fragrant pastes to Cardinal Pietro Bembo and on several occasions to Giuliano de' Medici. Members of the French court also received tributes from her. For example, on 18 May 1516 Isabella sent three "*busoletti*" containing perfumed substances: one in crystal, with a gold lid, to the Queen of France; the other two, in horn, to Louise of Savoy and the Duchess of Alençon (ASMn, AG* 2992, book 9, chap. 7r).

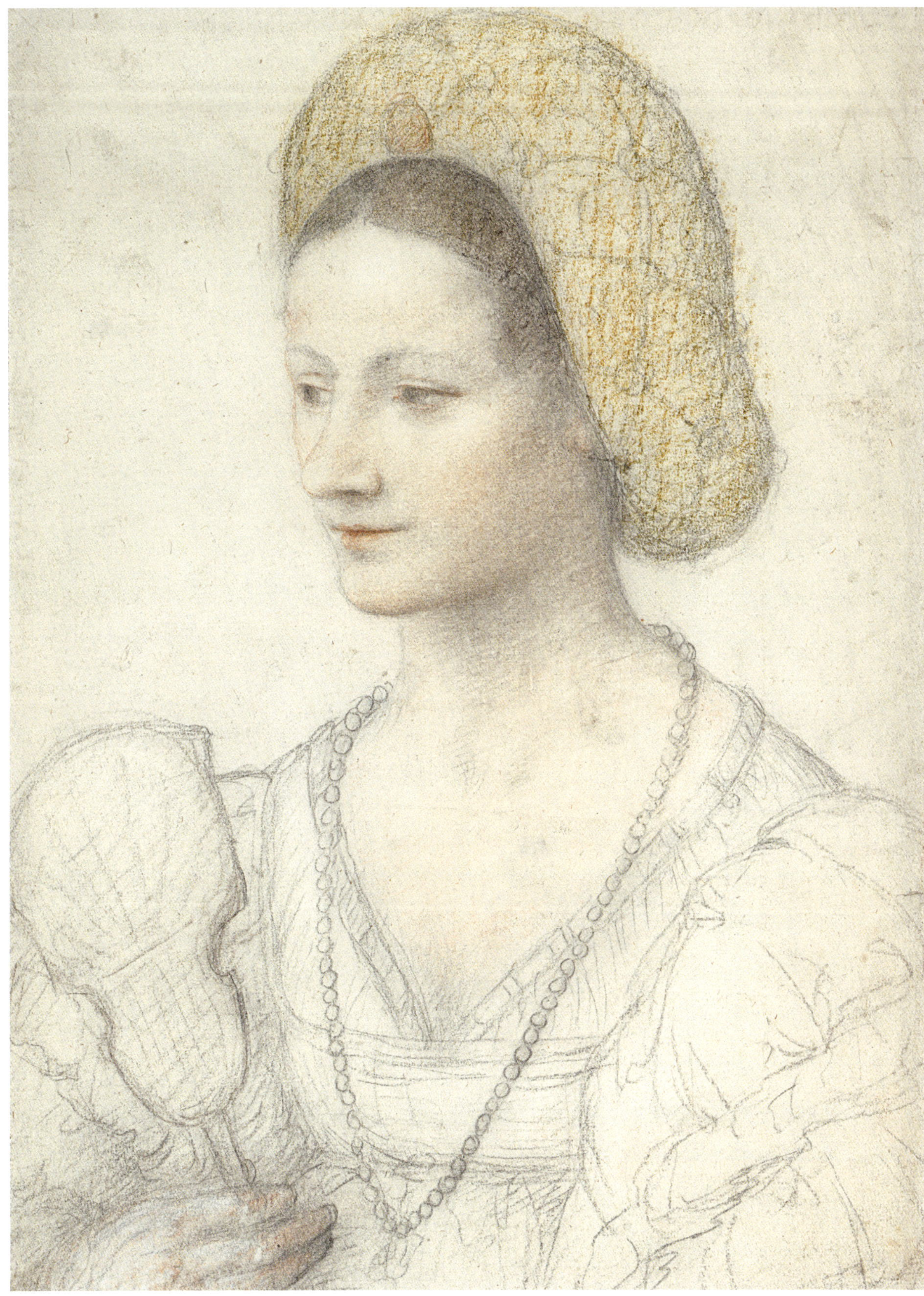

Fig. 2. Bernadino Luini, *Portrait of a Woman with a Fan*, 1520–25, Vienna, Albertina Museum

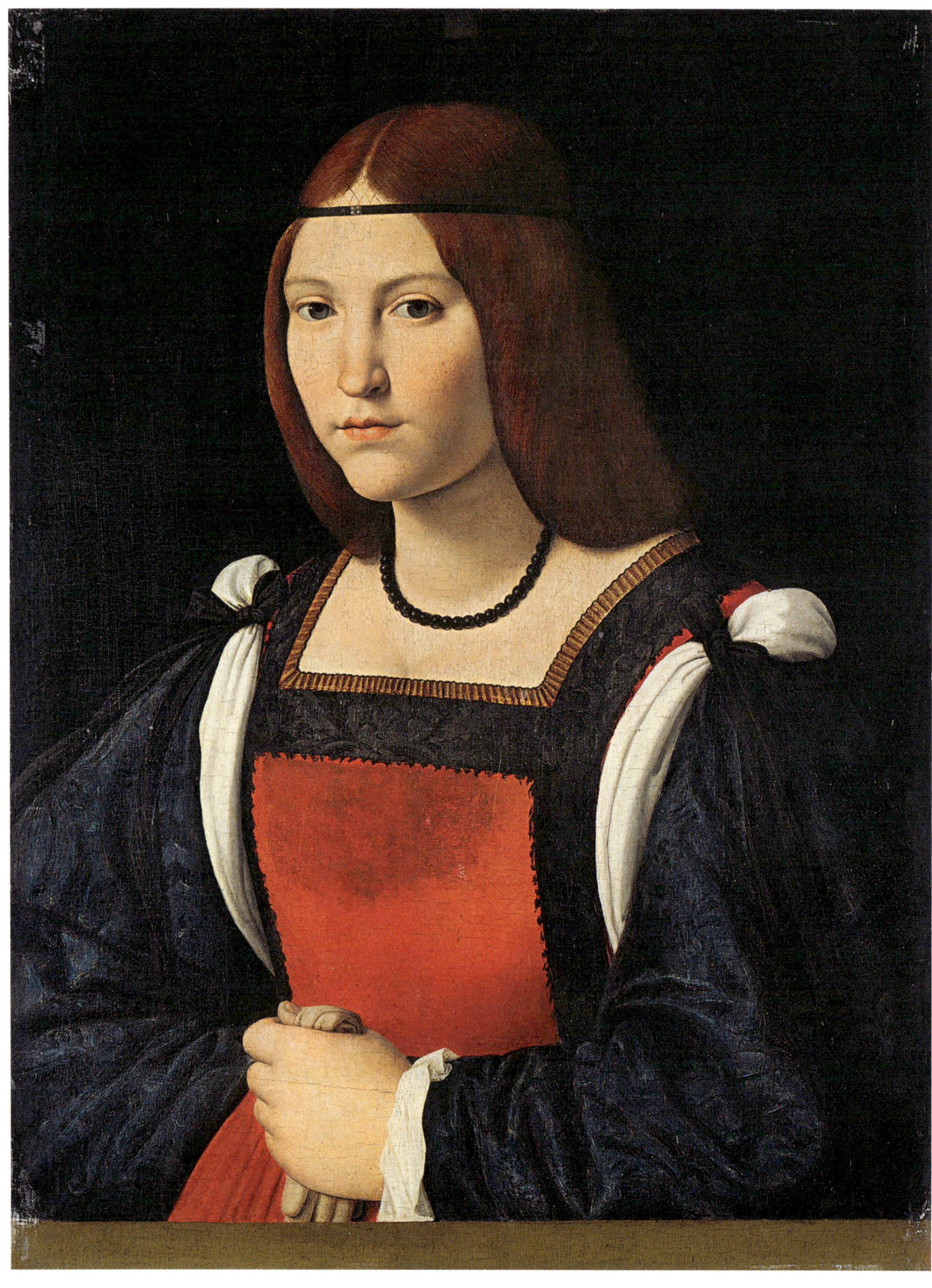

Fig. 3. Andrea Solario, *Portrait of a Woman with Gloves*, ca. 1505–07, Milan, Castello Sforzesco, Pinacoteca, inv. PIN 433

Isabella d'Este knew that her gifts would be greatly appreciated, as she believed that she had "never made a better mixture" and that she had no rival in the world "as far as the composition of these scents was concerned".

The containers for perfumes and the materials used to make them varied. Liquids were kept in glass or rock-crystal jars or flasks [fig. 1], while pastes or powders were placed in *bossoletti*, probably originally made of boxwood, and later in other containers of various shapes. The ebony container ordered by Isabella d'Este on 22 November 1498 was almost "square", a shape that the marchioness believed made it easier to extract the civet. Some of these small objects were made by the inventive Milanese turner and sculptor Cleofas de Donati, in the service of Isabella from 1508 to 1530. In the summer of 1511, he also produced a necklace made of fragrant aloeswood and a design for an ivory ball. Using wood and ivory, Cleofas also made handles for paper or ostrich feather fans, accessories that were worn attached to the belt with a small chain [fig. 2]. Lucrezia Borgia, sister-in-law of Isabella d'Este and wife of Alfonso I d'Este, had a "small" fan made of black ostrich feathers, created for her in 1516 by the Veronese maestro Alfonso; two filigree "small frames" containing "paste mixtures" were inserted into the gold structure. Fragrant substances such as aloeswood, amber, benzoin, musk or sandalwood were sometimes put into openwork spherical gold or silver cases of various sizes, used for necklaces, bracelets, or as pendants and buttons (Venturelli, 1999, pp. 7–8). Between 1515 and 1516, Isabella d'Este sent the Queen of France bracelets made of gold beads filled with these mixtures. She advised her to wear them all the time, especially at night. Larger beads could be hung from the belt, like the gold one ordered by Isabella d'Este on 20 May 1512 (ASMn, AG 2996, book 32, chap. 87r), designed to hold a "small ball of solid perfume". In the inventory of her famous "Grotto" in the Ducal Palace in Mantua, recorded between 1540 and 1542, we find a "pear-shaped button made of a perforated material to contain musk"; another, also in gold and filigree, is among the jewels received by her son Frederick II Gonzaga, as are a pair of gold bracelets with "small roses filled with paste" (ASMn, Estensioni notarili, vol. K 10, chap. 146v, 150r). In her jewellery, there were also scented beads ("paternoster beads") that did not require a valuable container; in Milan, the most fashionable were black. The necklace of Cecilia Gallerani in Leonardo da Vinci's portrait *Lady with an Ermine* is made of shiny spheres of this colour, and they also feature in the paintings of Giovanni Antonio Boltraffio and Andrea Solario [fig. 3], two "Milanese Leonardesque painters". It may be "black amber", as it was called, which was much sought after in jewellery in the late 15th and early 16th centuries, and may correspond to what Marbodo described as "*gagate*", i.e. modern jet, a black variety of lignite with a distinctive lustre (Venturelli, 1999; and 2021, pp. 255–57), or beads made from perfumed substances treated according to processes described by Giovanventura Rosetti in his *Notandissimi secreti de l'arte profumatoria*, published in Venice in 1555. The recipes in this work are the fruit of previous practical experiments, as illustrated by the preparation of a water for washing the face, which takes its inspiration from Catarina Sforza's *Experimenti*. According to Rossetti, to obtain beads of this colour, it was necessary to use "black earths", bile or charred bones, lampblack scraped from a boiler, charcoal, "soot" (from the calcination of conifers) or charred peach stones ground into powder. These were then mixed with fragrant oleaginous substances, moulded into balls and dried. The brilliance of these solid perfumes came from the application of a layer of egg white. Particularly hard, "stuccos" and pastes of this type were crafted on a potter's wheel (Rossetti, 1555, chap. 150–52, 213, 322–23).

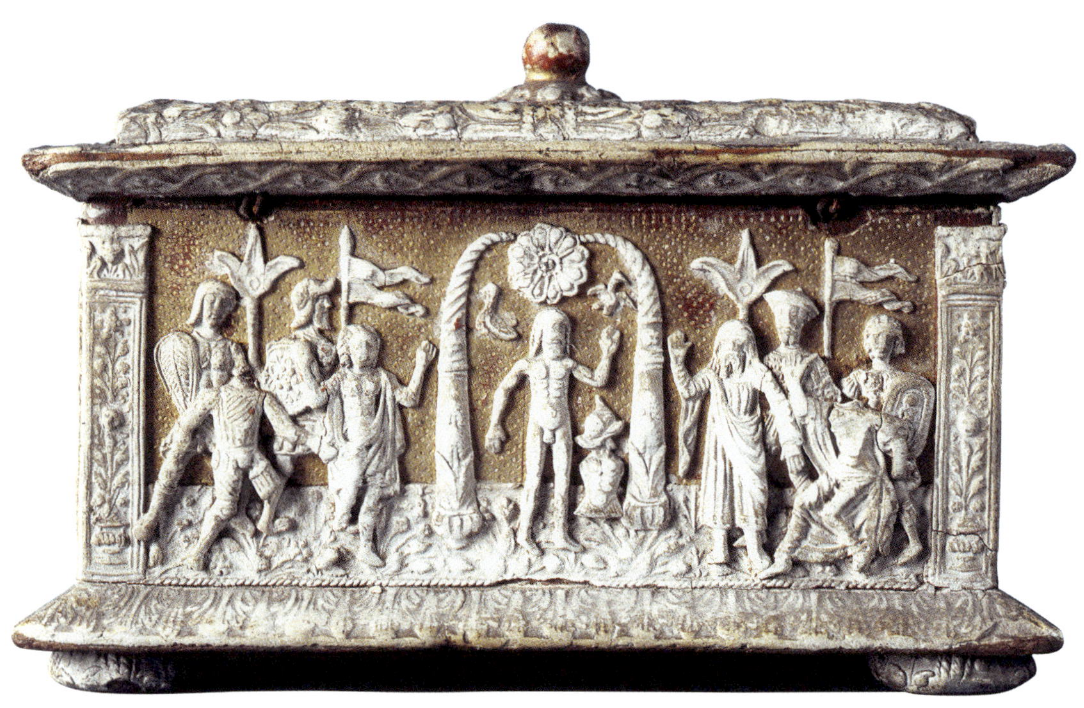

Fig. 4. Wooden casket decorated with gold leaf, ca. 1520–1530, 9.5 × 15.8 cm, Pavia, Musei Civici del Castello Visconteo, AM 33

Isabella d'Este often sent the Queen of France perfumed gloves, which were much appreciated by the monarch, especially if they were impregnated with "cedar flower" oil. A typical accessory of the upper classes, they were worn by both men and women in winter and summer, and were treated during the tanning process with perfumed formulations. The most richly coated gloves were intended to be worn at night to keep the hands soft. The best came from Spain, in particular Ocaña, not far from Toledo, or Valencia, but they were also produced in Rome, Genoa and Florence. Mixtures of different compositions were also used to create decorative objects: sacred altarpieces, statuettes, frames for mirrors and paintings, inkwells and caskets, the latter sometimes intended to contain perfumes. The inventory of Bianca Maria Sforza's dowry includes two small boxes with "soap compasses and carafes filled with powder", as well as a steel mirror decorated with "perfume paste". To decorate a wooden chest, the Breton Giovanni Carlo de Monlione, who had been working for the Este court since 1430, had made scented plaster figurines which were then gilded by the miniaturist Giorgio d'Allemagne with the help of the painter Cosmè Tura [fig. 4] (Venturelli, 1999, pp. 142–43). Small cloth sachets filled with perfumed powders were used to perfume linen, accessories and clothes stored in chests. Among the main ingredients were the precious "chypre powders", obtained from the lichens found on certain trees, such as oak, cedar and fir trees (Rossetti, 1555). They were also used to sprinkle on people and their horses, covering up bad smells caused by poor hygiene or dirty streets. Simpliciano, the protagonist of one of Matteo Bandello's novellas, is a good example of this: during a tryst, he wears an embroidered silk shirt, freshly "washed" [fig. 2, p. 125], which he covers with civet, ambergris, musk, "*oiselets de Chypre* (Chypre birdies) and other fine, sweet-smelling, prized powders".

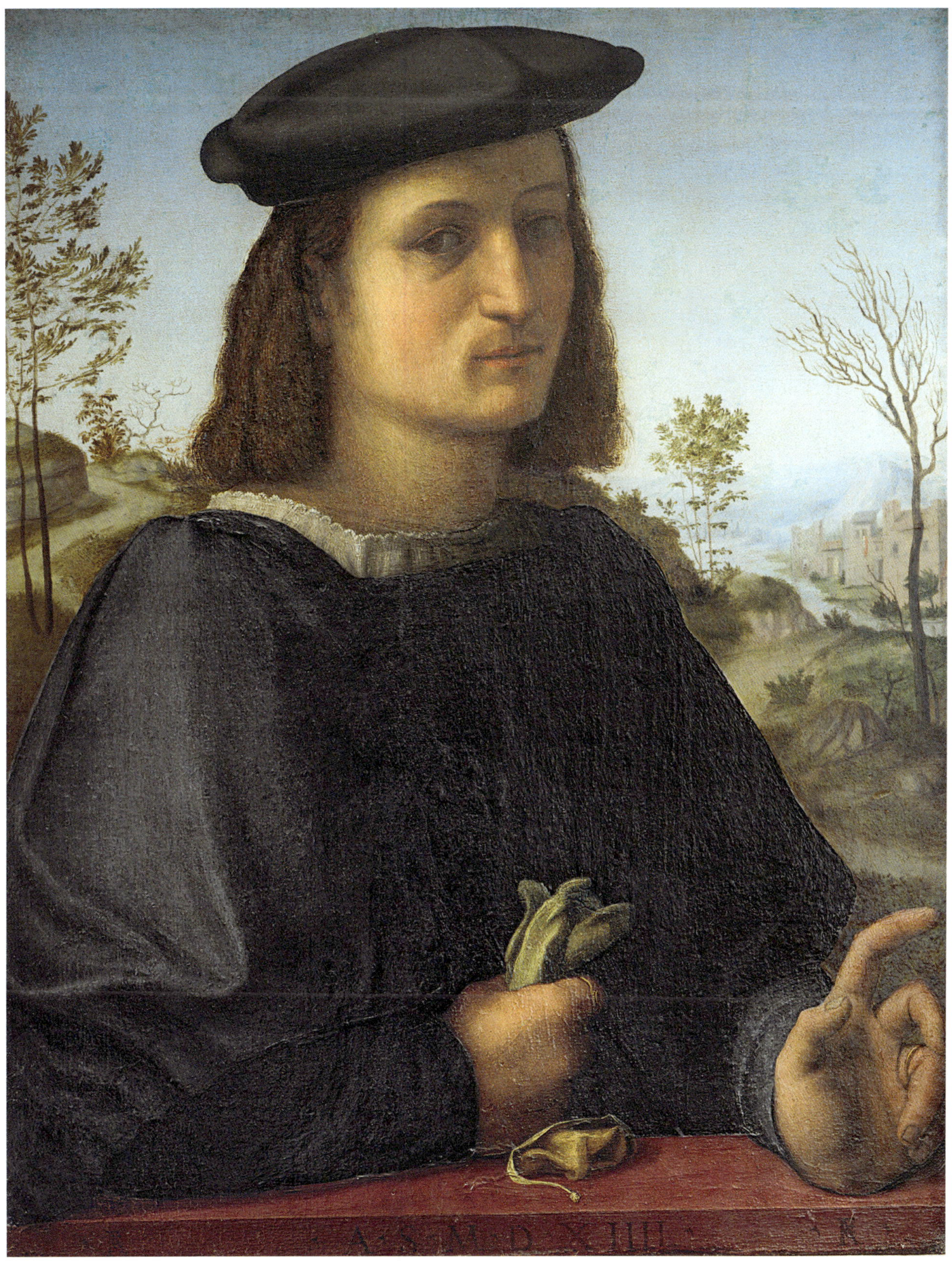

Francesco di Cristofano, known as Franciabigio, *Portrait of a Young Man*, 1514, oil on wood, 60 × 47 cm, Florence, Galleria degli Uffizi, inv. 1890 n. 8381

Bibliography

*ASMn, AG = Archivio di Stato di Mantova, Archivio Gonzaga

"I 'camerini' di Beatrice d'Este nel castello di Vigevano: un vecchio documento e nuove considerazioni", in *I Luoghi di Leonardo. Milano, Vigevano e la Francia*, proceedings of the Convegno Internazionale di Studi (Castello di Vigevano, 2 October 2014), Ferrari Simone (ed.), special issue of *Valori Tattili* (8 July–8 Dec. 2016), pp. 107–17.

Guerrini Olindo, *Ricettario galante del principio del secolo xvi* (Bologna: Gaetano Romagnoli, 1883).

Ray Meredith K., *Daughters of Alchemy. Women and Scientific Culture in Early Modern Italy* (Cambridge: Harvard University Press, 2015).

Rossetti Giovanventura, *Notandissimi secreti de l'arte profumatoria: a fare ogli, acque, paste, balle, moscardini, uccelletti, paternostri, e tutta l'arte intiera, come si ricerca, così ne la città di Napoli del Reame, come in Roma, e quivi in la città di Vinegia nuovamente impressi* (Venice: Francesco Rampazetto, 1555).

Venturelli Paola, *Glossario e documenti per la gioielleria milanese (1459-1631)* (Florence: La Nuova Italia, 1999) (updated online edition: Gioielli milanesi. Glossario 1459-1631, OADI Digitalia, 2019, http://www.oadi.it/wp-content/uploads/2019/06/venturelli.pdf).

Id., *La moda alla corte degli Sforza. Leonardo da Vinci tra creatività e tecnica* (Cinisello Balsamo: Silvana Editoriale, 2019).

Id., *Arte orafa milanese 1450-1527. Leonardo da Vinci tra creatività e tecnica* (Cinisello Balsamo: Silvana Editoriale, 2021).

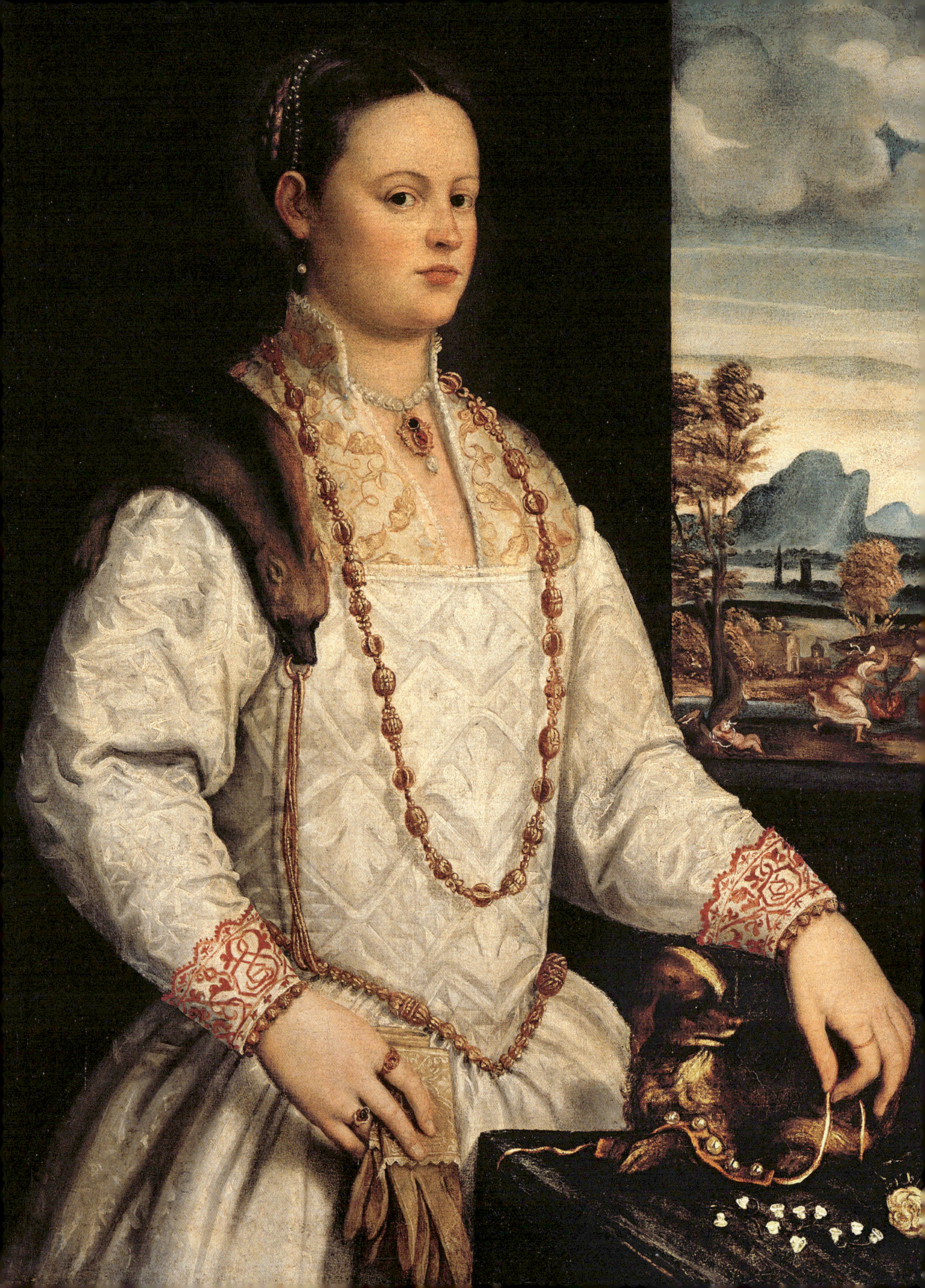

"*JUSTE AU CORPS* (CLOSE TO THE BODY) PERFUME", PERFUMED CLOTHES AND ACCESSORIES IN THE LATE MIDDLE AGES AND THE RENAISSANCE

Nicolas Baptiste-Anthore et Soline Anthore-Baptiste

While it is now common practice to apply perfumes, deodorants and other body odour masking products to the skin, societies in the late Middle Ages and the Renaissance did not have the same relationship with the smells of nature and the body, and therefore with the scents extracted from the former to complement the latter. The relationship with the body has evolved throughout history, and the world of fragrances is full of nuances.

Society in Leonardo da Vinci's time did not consider the body to be the primary medium for perfume. The reason for this is not clear, but it may lie in the importance attached to natural odours. Doctors in the modern era considered them to be symptomatic: sweat, for example, was a sign of good or bad health (Liébault, 1582). They therefore took a dim view of excessive cleanliness and the use of perfumes, insofar as they clouded their understanding of the physiology of the body. Knowing more about how ancient societies thought about the body and its emanations helps us to understand the fascinating figures of the past. This knowledge also helps us avoid the risk of devaluing certain essences and obscuring the "scents of history", just as we would deodorise the body with a fragrance that may well be heady, but is also composite.

Perfume Balls and Scents to Perfume Clothes in the Wardrobe

LEFT
Francesco Beccaruzzi, *Portrait of a Woman with a Dog*, 16th c.
Oil on canvas
97.8 × 76.2 cm, Bergamo, Accademia Carrara, inv. 81 LC 00193

During the Renaissance, unpleasant body odours were a fact of life. Society was beset by this nuisance: royal ordinances in 1366 regulated odours in the towns of Navarre and Laon; in 1564, the Medici ambassador Bartolomeo Concini called for scented tablets to counter the stench of dormitories; and Alessandro Orsini di Pitigliano ordered scented products to mask the odours of unclean guests...who didn't seem to know how to use soap!

So how does one adorn the body with a "pleasant" or at least "diverting" scent, without masking the body's natural odour? Water is not well thought of, so it is best to use herbs picked from around one's home, as well as aromatics, resins or preparations such as vinegar mixed with camphor. Some are reputed to have antibacterial properties, like incense, which is diffused in holy places. The fashion for "Chypre birdies" appeared as early as 1380: "Item, *Auzelles de Chipre* (Chypre birdies) for perfuming rooms" (Gay, 1883): these were sculptures made of perfumed paste and designed to be consumed like perfumes for burning, or scented sachets in the shape of small feather-covered birds that were placed in cages, like real exotic birds (Franklin, 1906).

Linen was also infused with scents in wardrobes, chests and bedrooms. In the 14th century, Queen Clementia of Hungary ordered rose and honeysuckle water, and even "vine shoots, roses and lavender...to put with the linen" (Vigarello, 2014). There are also references to myrrh, musk, storax and benzoin in various forms. From the 14th century onwards, one of the most common powders used was made from violets, such as the powder used by the Duke of Touraine in 1392: "white satin...to make cushions in which to put violet powder...to put between one's linen." These scented powders continued to be used, and were still to be found in the Household Ordinances of Henry VIII of England in 1526, when the laundress was required to "provide as much sweet powder...for the gentle care of the said stuffs". Thin, silk, violet-patterned taffeta was also purchased to make sachets for scented powders for Margaret of Navarre in 1549.

Powders for Pourpoints, Pomanders and Perfumed Gloves, Accessories for one's Dress

Sachets of scent were also carried on one's person: a portable version of those used in caskets, they became accessories for one's dress. The inventories of Louis, Duke of Orléans, mention pourpoint powders supplied by apothecaries from the end of the 14th century. These were probably the same perfumed powders found in sachets in wardrobes, with antiseptic and insecticide properties.

Appearing from the 14th and 15th centuries, pomanders became fashionable and quickly evolved from plant versions to jewelled versions in the form of small spheres enclosing fragrant products. They were a common sight at the French court. These jewels enjoyed lasting popularity at the European courts, and can be seen in many Renaissance portraits. They sometimes took on different forms, such as fruits, like the "Spanish-style, golden, pear-shaped pomander", mentioned in 1560 in the possessions of Francis II.

While their presence is certainly associated with pleasure of the senses, medical treatises also mention them as a means of warding off the pestilent odours of disease: the 1469 inventory of the Duchess of Milan's jewels lists "a ball for spreading perfumes against the plague", while Jean Goeurot (*L'Entretenement de vie...*, 1530) suggests "a singular regimen against the plague", comprising a quilted sachet with the power to resist venom. At the time, it was thought that "warm" perfumes such as musk could be used to combat the pathogenic odours generated by the sick body. In this context, perfumes play more of a repellent role than an attractive one, even if they provide olfactory pleasure in addition to their primary function of combating contagion (Muchembled, 2021).

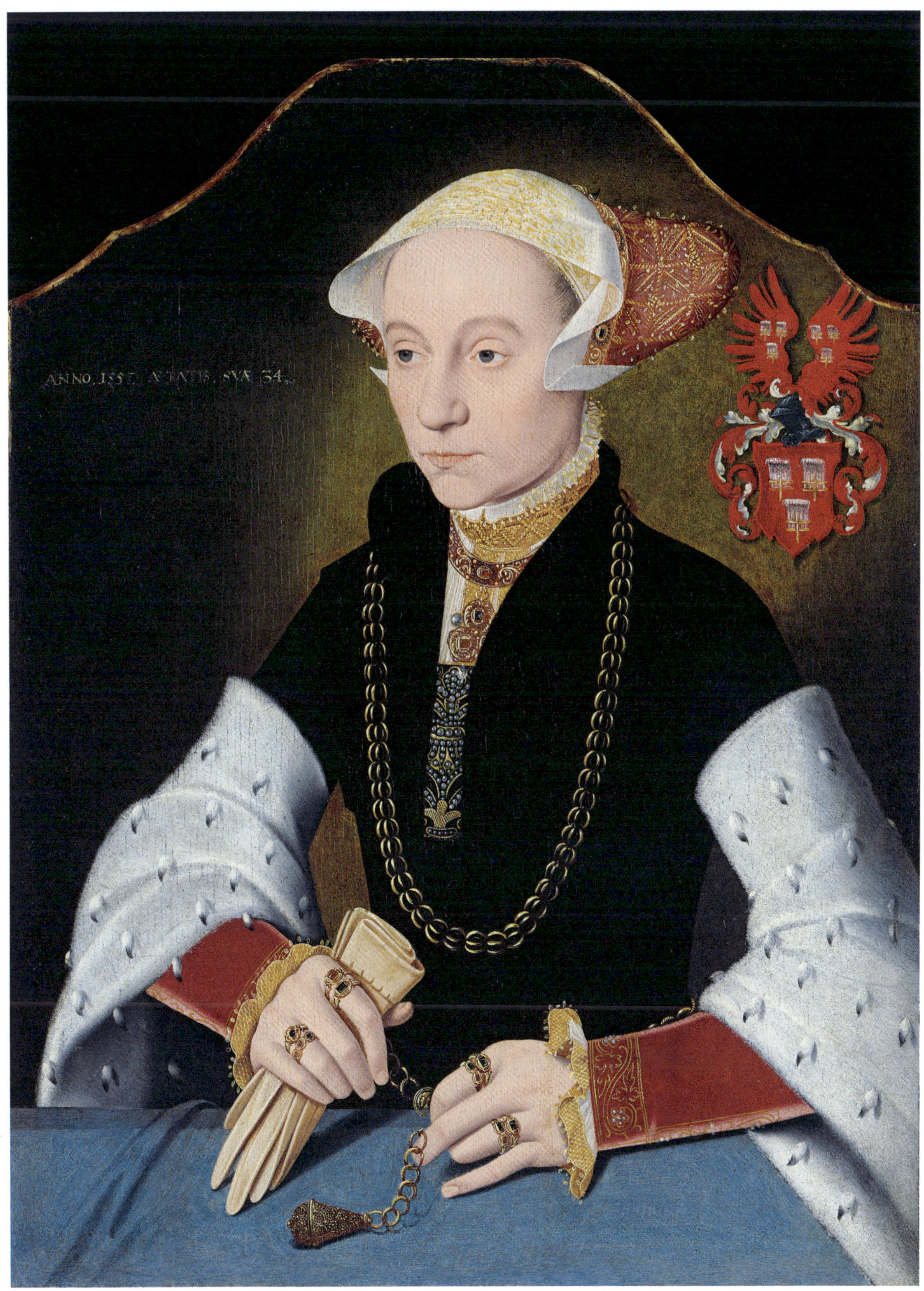

Barthel Bruyn the Younger, *Portrait of a Woman of the Slosgin Family of Cologne*, 1557, New York, Metropolitan Museum of Art, Friedsam Collection, bequest of Michael Friedsam, 1931

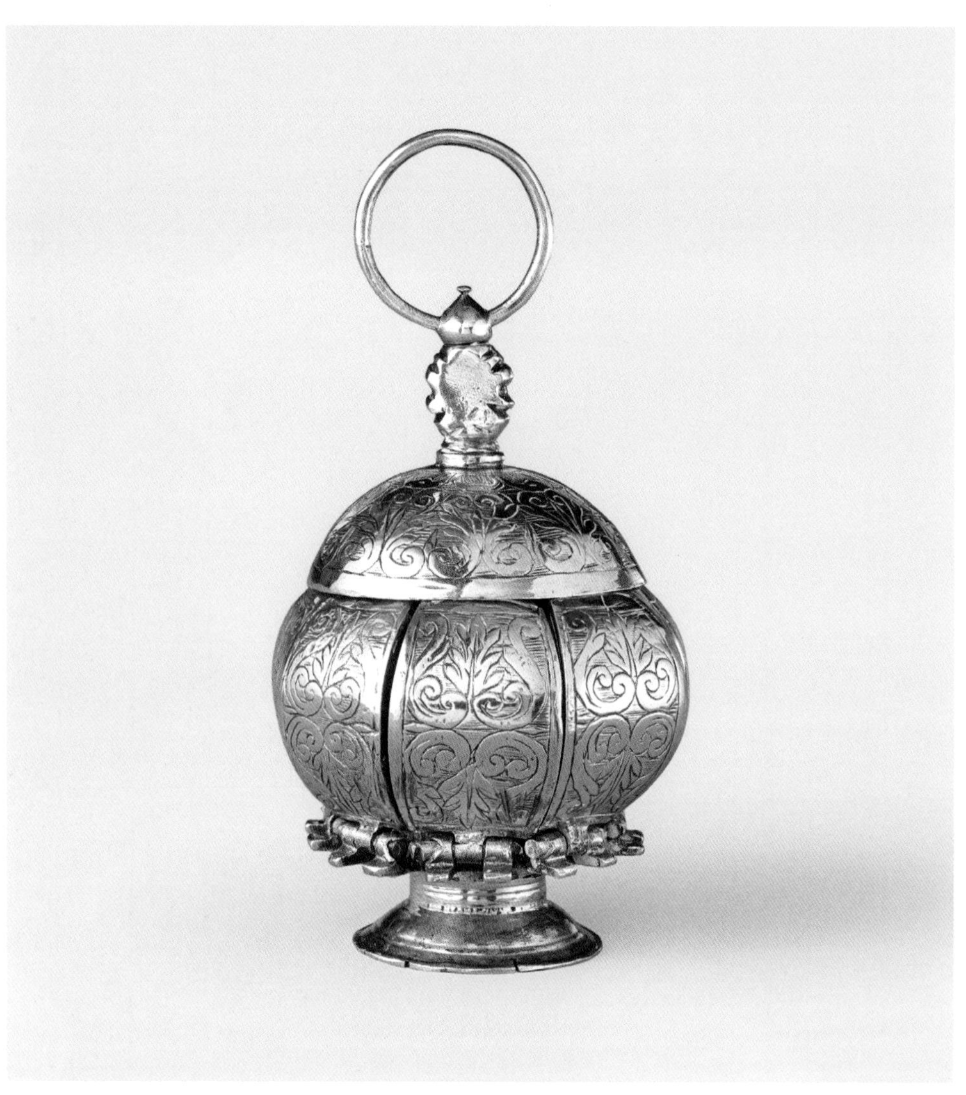

English silver pomander, initials S. B., ca. 1580, New York, Metropolitan Museum of Art, gift of Irwin Untermyer, 1968

In the second half of the 16th century, scented articles became widely available to all levels of society. Almost all leathers were treated, and perfumed gloves, which had been around since the Middle Ages, appeared in greater numbers during the Renaissance, sometimes carrying flirtatious overtones, but also as diplomatic gifts, as in the case of Eleanor of Toledo, who sent perfumed gloves to Pope Julius III in 1550 (Welch, 2011).

Montaigne's "scented collar", which "is at first scented for me: if I wear it for three days together, only other people notice the scent", will remain a mystery of fashion history: was it a garland of fragrant flowers, an item of jewellery, a garment, or even a scented leather pourpoint, like that worn by France's Charles IX in 1571 (Gay, 1883)?

There were fabrics, handkerchiefs and dresses, as well as a variety of jewellery: ambergris-embedded paternoster beads, earrings, bracelets, buttons, aiglets and belts filled with musk paste. Although such items were often preferred by the elite, they were not restricted to them. As lottery prizes, they were won by washerwomen, prostitutes, aristocratic men and women, as well as clerics and nuns (Welch, 2011).

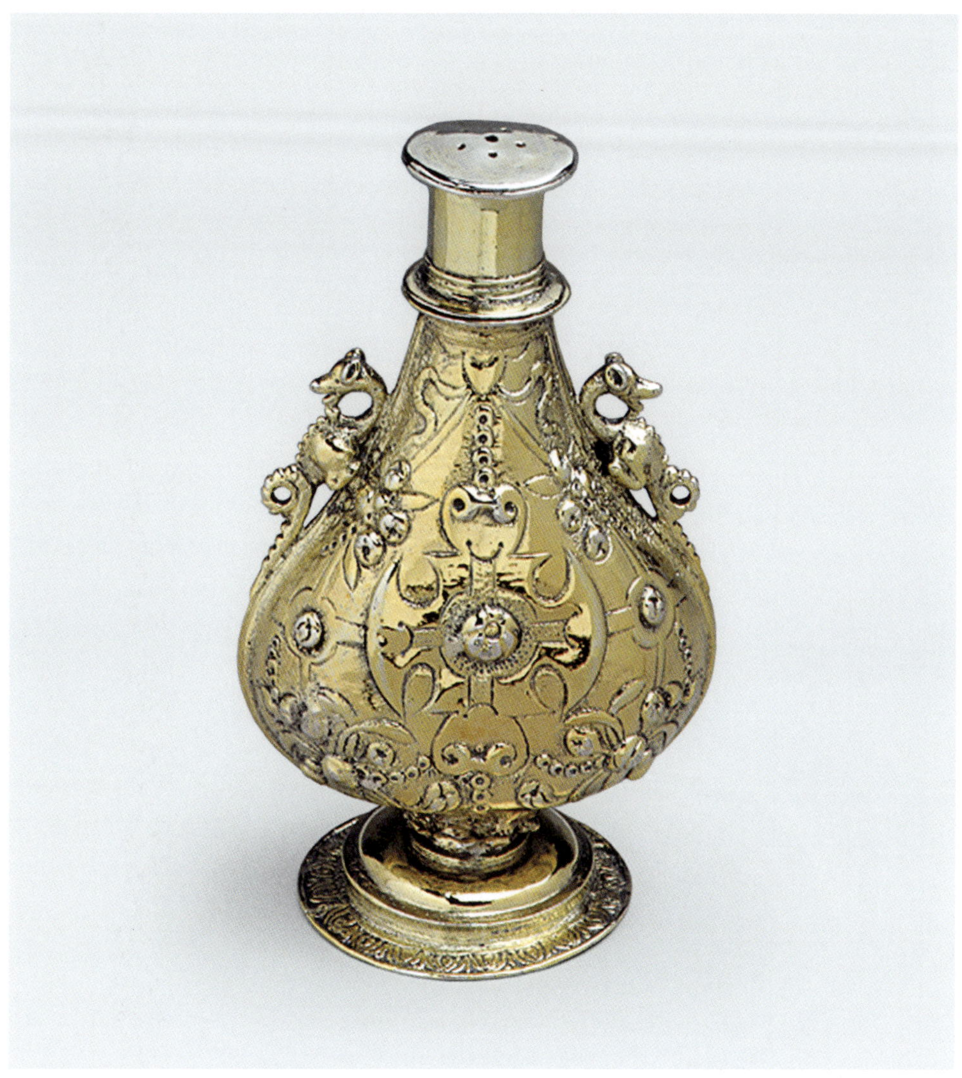

Silver gilt perfume bottle, English, possibly by Jasper Fysher Foot, 1577–78; body ca. 1585, New York, Metropolitan Museum of Art, gift of Irwin Untermyer, 1968

Beads were also made from ambergris or rose water incorporated into substances such as brick dust or resinous pastes. Works such as Rosetti's *Notandissimi Secreti de l'Arte Profumatoria* (Venice, 1555) give recipes for creating these pastes, beads, musks and rosaries in the home kitchen. Connoisseurs could find the ingredients they needed to make perfumes in apothecaries (Welch, 2011), and there were even reports of counterfeit products (Franklin, 1906).

Ointments, Waters and Balms, and a Revival of the Earliest Fragrances

Unctions, creams, balms and scented waters abounded. The inventory of Francesco, a *muschiero* (perfumer) in Venice, shows that in 1547 his shop was filled with bottles of perfumed waters and oils (Welch, 2011). Musk, amber and civet are often mentioned. Their natural properties did not serve to mask body odour but, on the contrary, to emphasise the fragrance of the body, and ancient societies were certainly discriminating on this subject. Moralists condemned these substances as inciting sensuality. In Renaissance literature, sumptuary laws regulated or even prohibited their use, and feminine odours, whether natural or artificial, were even demonised.

Flower waters made from rose, violet, bergamot, iris or clove were in plentiful supply, like the one made by the physician Antonio Mizauld in 1562, which was sold as a pleasant way of warding off infections. Like all doctors, he advised adding to the powerful – even heady – scents that protect, something to delight the wearer's senses (Muchembled, 2021). Tommaso Garzoni (*Piazza Universale*, 1585) tells us that we can sprinkle a little rose water on a shirt, handkerchief or pillow (Welch, 2011). These *eaux d'ange* were highly reputed in France from the end of the 14th century, and in 1380, the inventory of Charles V records "2 large jugs for *eau d'ange*". In 1418, the inventory of the Louvre mentions "a phial for storing Damask rose water". Special glass or silver "sprinkler" bottles were used to sprinkle these waters. It was also a common ingredient in many home remedies (Zoppino, *Operetta Nova de Cose Stupende in Agricultura Vere*, ca. 1520).

From 1500 onwards, barbers "had a small phial of fragrant water to throw over their customers' faces" (Leonardo Fioravanti, *Miroir universel des arts et des sciences*, 1598). Tournament combatants used a scented Holland cloth to refresh their faces between fights, for example in Ivrea in 1522 (Dondi, 1988).

Conclusion

Renaissance perfume came close to the body as if to charm it without actually touching it. It enveloped it powerfully, in a subtle interplay, as Montaigne testifies: "Whatever the smell is, it is wonderful how it clings to me and how my skin is simply made to drink it in... If I bring my glove or my handkerchief anywhere near it, the smell will linger there all day." But then, if we note that the use of perfume in past societies evolved to become closer and closer to the body itself, until its appearance in our contemporary world through the use of eau de Cologne and other alcohol-based perfumes, there is still some doubt as to the appeal of these fragrances and their exact role in social practices. How can we interpret with any certainty the real nature of odours in history and in the sensory register? It is not possible to come up with a clear answer, and one of the possible explanations, if the prejudices of a particular era are anything to go by, lies in human beings and their varied tastes, which are not specific to any particular era or obscurantism. Whether the attraction is for bodily odours or for perfumes, it is above all a question of the transformation of the body, and this interaction between odours is as evident in the lovers of the Renaissance as it is in the tales of tormented lovers of antiquity.

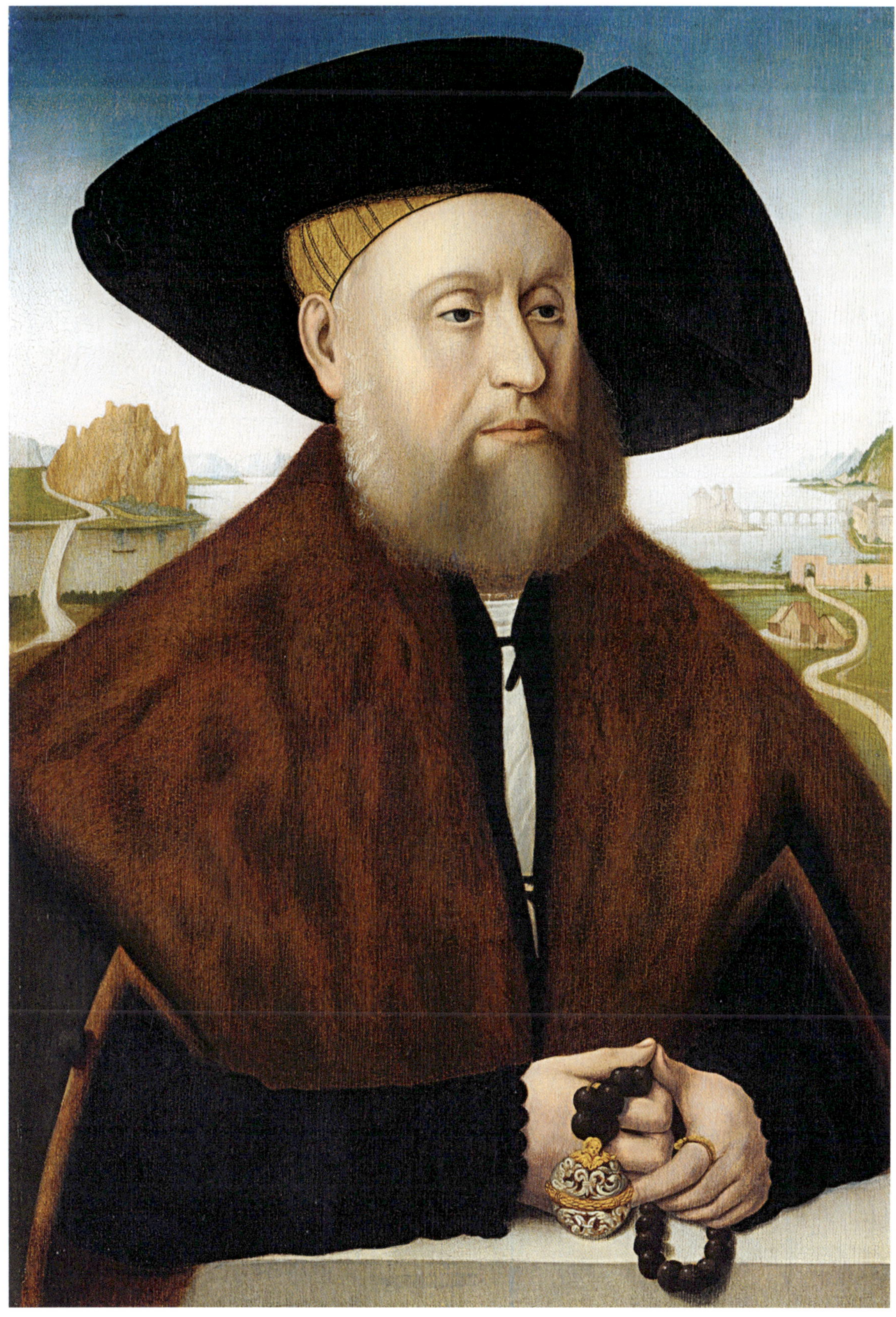

Heinrich(?) vom Rhein zum Mohren, copy after Conrad Faber von Creuznach, late 1520s, New York, Metropolitan Museum of Art, Jack and Belle Linsky Collection, 1982

Bibliography

Balard Michel, Hervé Jean-Claude & Lemaitre Nicole (eds.), *Paris et ses campagnes sous l'Ancien Régime* (Paris: Éditions de la Sorbonne, 1994).

Bonnaffe Edmond, *Inventaire de la duchesse de Valentinois, Charlotte d'Albret* (Paris: A. Quantin, 1878).

Dondi Giorgio, "Il Bagordo d'Ivrea" in *Armi Antiche* (Turin: Academia di S. Marciano, 1988-1989), pp. 3–32.

Franklin Alfred, *Dictionnaire historique des arts, métiers et professions exercées dans Paris depuis le treizième siècle* (Paris: H. Welter, 1906).

Gay Victor, *Glossaire archéologique du Moyen Âge et de la Renaissance* (Paris: Librairie de la Société bibliographique, 1882).

Havard Henry, *Dictionnaire de l'ameublement et de la décoration*, vol. 4, P-Z (Paris: Maison Quantin, 1878).

Jordan Édouard, "Adrien Harmand. 'Jeanne d'Arc, ses costumes, son armure'" (attempted reconstitution) in *Revue d'histoire de l'Église de France*, no. 72, pp. 398–401 (Paris: Ernest Leroux, 1930).

Lecoy de la marche Albert, *Le roi René, sa vie, son administration, ses travaux artistiques et littéraires* (Paris: Firmin-Didot frères, fils et Cie, 1875).

Liébault Jean, *Trois Livres de l'embellissement et ornement du corps humain* (Paris: Jacques du Puy, 1582).

de Montaigne Michel, *Les Essais*, Paris: Bibliothèque de la Pléiade, Gallimard, no. 14, 2007.

Muchembled Robert, *La Civilisation des odeurs* (xvie-début xixe siècle) (Paris: Les Belles Lettres, 2021).

Vigarello Georges, *Le Propre et le Sale – l'hygiène du corps depuis le Moyen Âge* (Paris: Points, 2014).

Welch Evelyn, "Scented Buttons and Perfumed Gloves: Smelling Things in Renaissance Italy", in *Ornamentalism: The Art of Renaissance Accessories*, Mirabella Bella (Ann Arbor: University of Michigan Press, 2011, pp. 13–39.

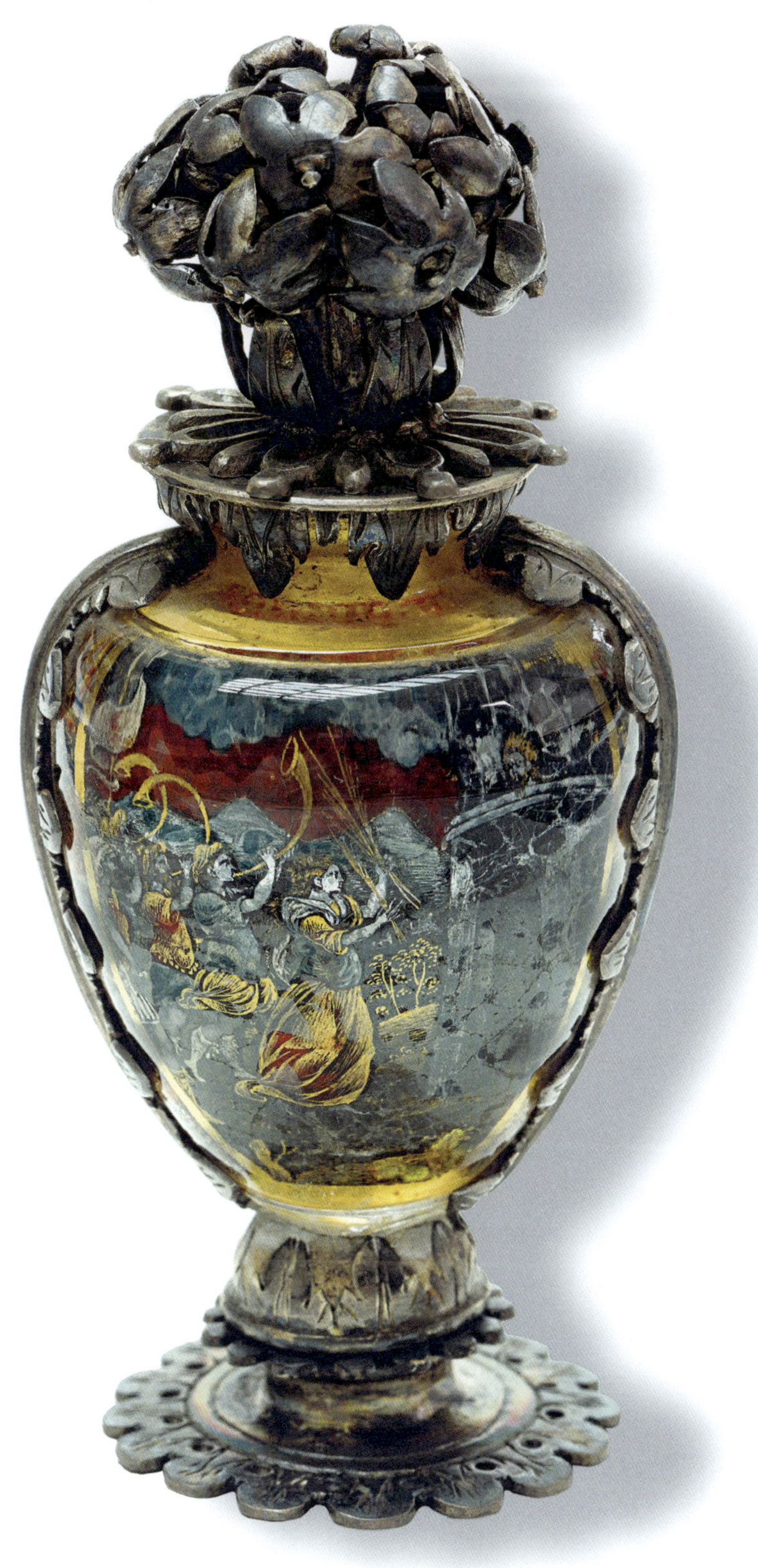

Reliquary bottle depicting a triumphal scene, 16th c., gold and silver painted rock crystal, 9 × 4 cm
Turin, Palazzo Madama – Museo Civico d'Arte Antica, inv. 107/VD

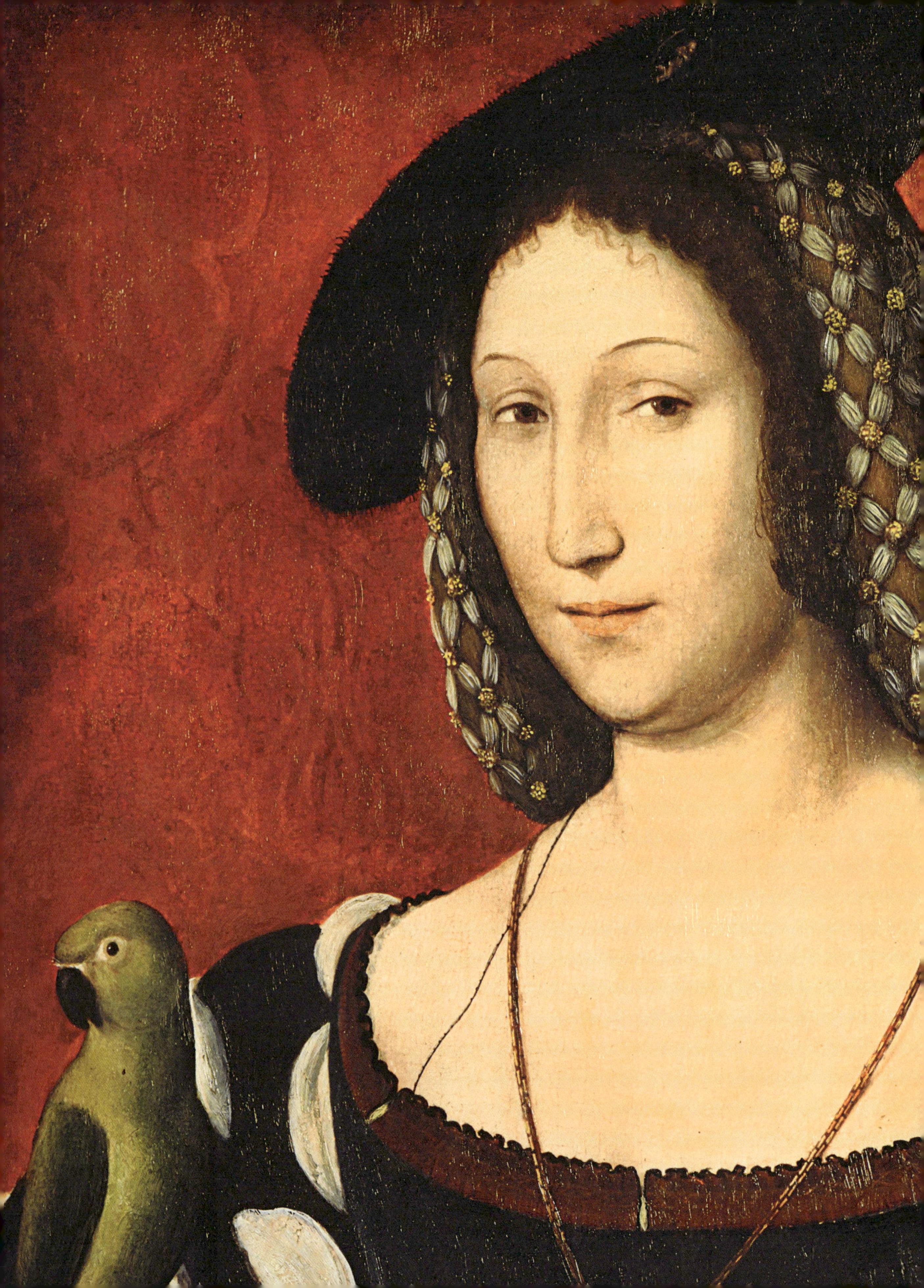

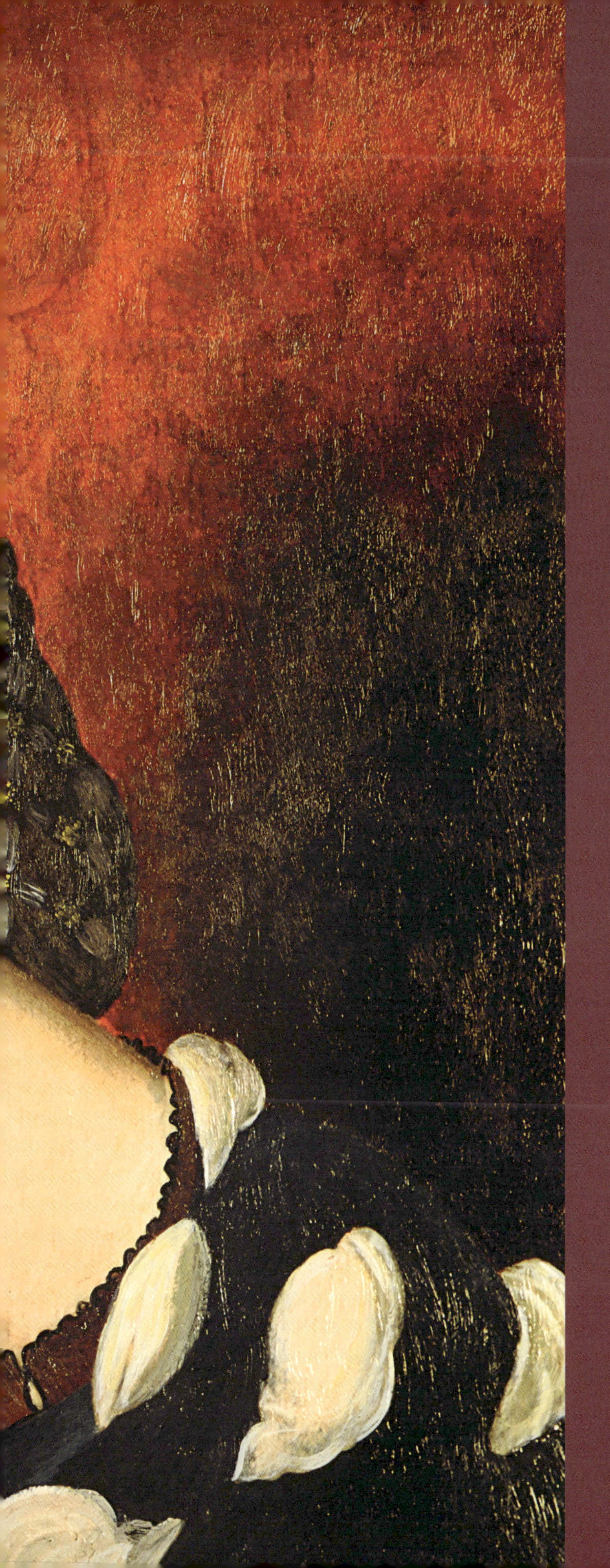

Perfumes at the Court of Francis I

Chapter V

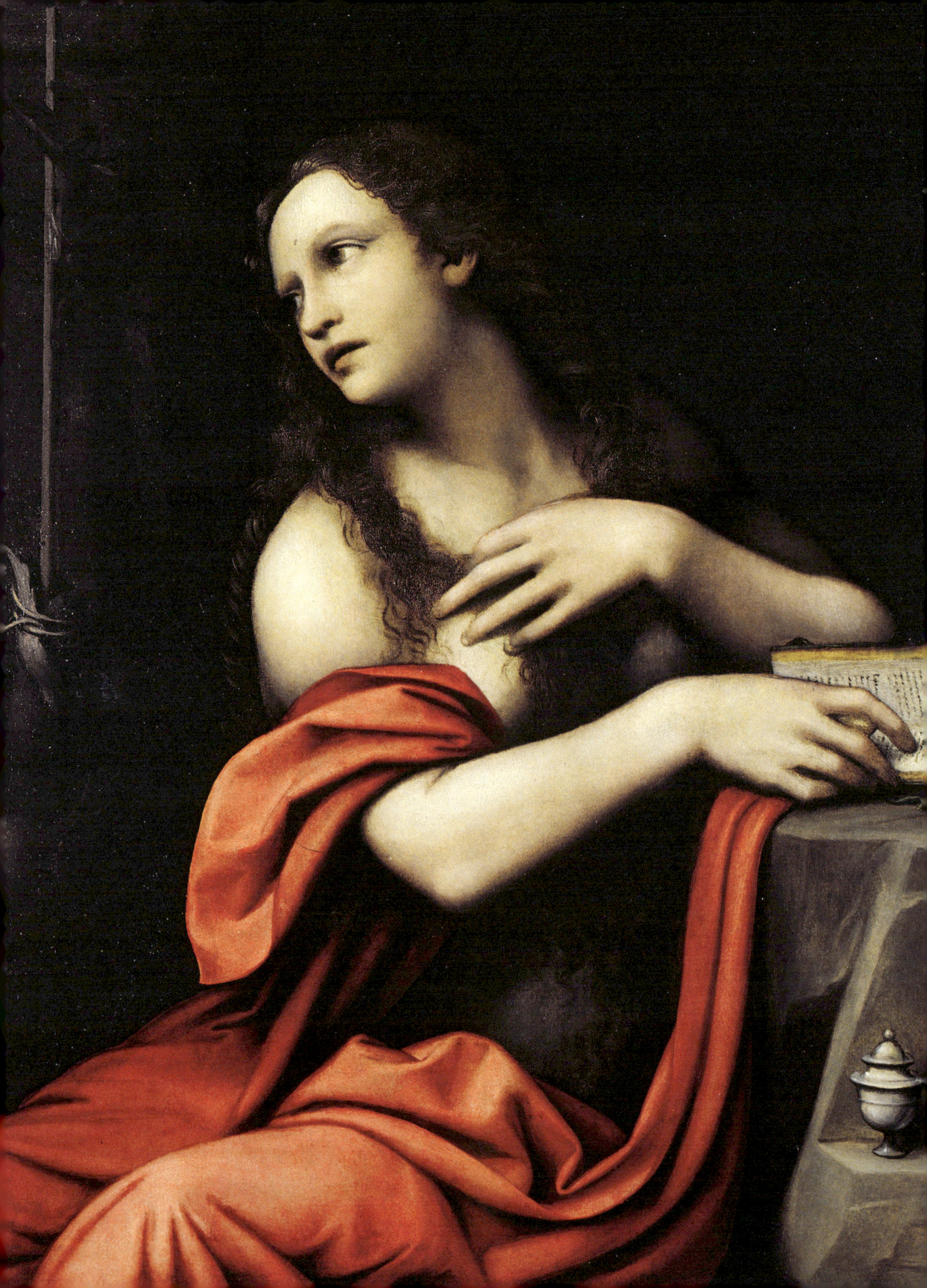

PERFUMES AT THE END OF THE 15TH CENTURY, FORMS AND ISSUES

ÉLODIE PIERRARD

As vehicles for social and cultural values, perfumes play a central role in the society and era that produces them. The end of the 15th century was a turning point, just before a 16th century that would be marked by an explosion of books of secrets and the empowerment of the profession of the perfumer. At the end of the Middle Ages, perfumes in the form of preparations that gave off a pleasant smell, with a variety of fragrances, featured in every aspect of daily life. They held aesthetic, medical, cultural and religious significance.

At the end of the 15th century, perfumes came in many forms. They could be applied directly on the skin or infused into objects worn on the body. The recipes of the period offer a glimpse into this rich olfactory universe. Perfumed oils and waters were used alongside fragrant cosmetic preparations, such as rosewater ointments to protect the face from the sun. Aromatic ingredients were also widely used in concoctions produced for personal hygiene. Mouthwashes with mint, deodorants with musk, soaps and other floral waters used for hand-washing all served to keep people clean and healthy, while also providing a pleasant scent. Fabrics also gave off pleasant smells, thanks to the use of scented powders or perfumed starches. Some buttons and pearls were covered in musk, forming a whole range of scented adornments, including pomanders or openwork balls filled with fragrant solid substances. The most prestigious of these contained amber, an odoriferous substance derived from the intestinal concretions of sperm whales. Another way of perfuming the body was through fumigation. *Oiselets de Chypre* (Chypre birdies) were particularly popular in the late Middle Ages. Made from a fragrant paste moulded into the shape of a bird, they were placed in a cage and then burnt to release their scent. The ashes left after they were burnt were sometimes used to make other aromatic preparations.

While the forms of perfume may have been varied, the range of scents was no less so. Animal substances played a key role, in particular amber, musk, secreted by male muskrats in Asia, and civet, extracted from the glands of a mammal native to Africa and India. Precious spices, rare and from far-off lands, were also used in perfumed products. In many recipes, cloves, nutmeg, cinnamon, cumin, ginger and other exotic aromas were accompanied by more common raw materials,

PREVIOUS PAGE
Jean Clouet
Portrait of Margaret of Navarre (reproduction of the original kept at the Walker Art Gallery, Liverpool), 16th c.
Oil on canvas, 79 × 69 cm
Amboise, château du Clos Lucé

LEFT
Giovan Pietro Rizzoli, also known as Giampietrino,
Mary Magdalene Seated in Prayer before the Crucifix,
1520–30, 73.3 × 57.5 cm
Milan, Pinacoteca del Castello Sforzesco,
inv. PIN 306

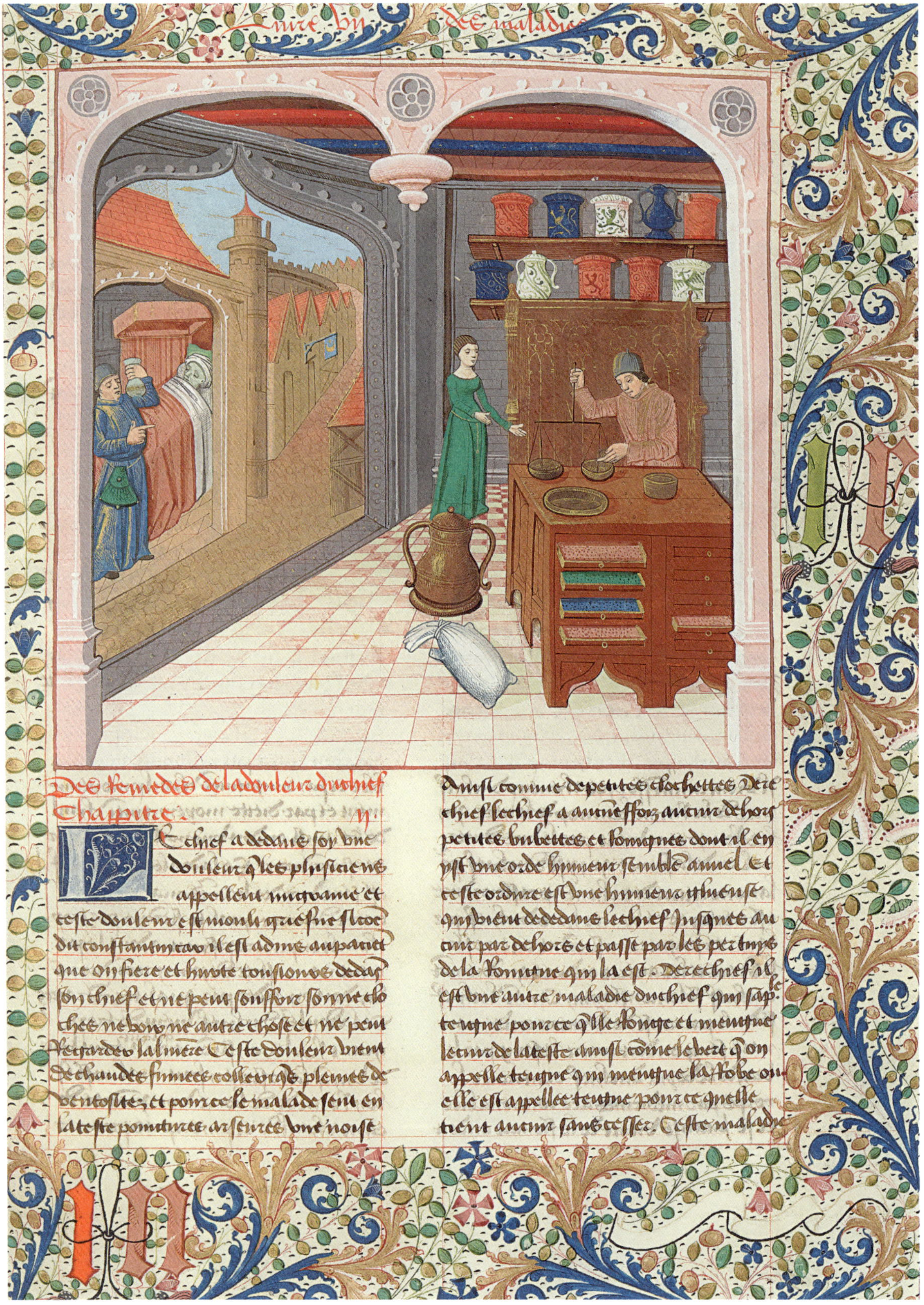

Fig. 1. Jean Corbechon, *Le Livre des propriétés des choses* (*On the Properties of Things*), Apothecary shop, late 15th c.
Paris, Bibliothèque nationale de France, Ms. fr. 218, f.111

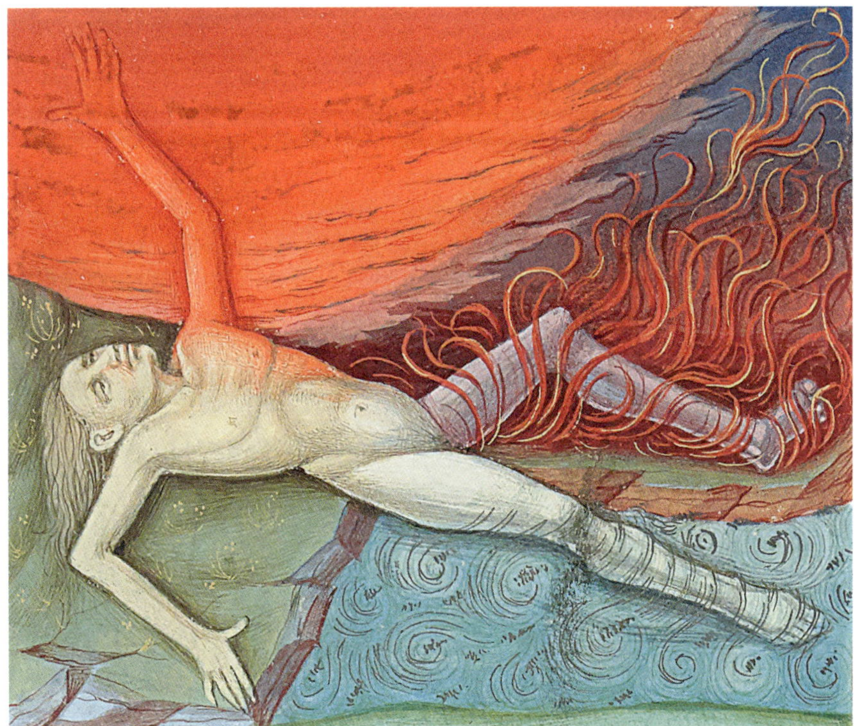

Fig. 2. *Constituent parts of bodies, in which man is represented at the centre of the four elements and the four humours*, 15th c., Paris, Bibliothèque nationale de France, Ms fr. 135, f. 91

in particular plants such as mint, basil, marjoram, sage, iris, violets, lavender and laurel. Rose was still the most common ingredient. Some recipes included more unexpected scents, with water lily and pomegranate flowers being two ingredients that might have featured in perfumes at the end of the 15th century.

Apothecaries were the main suppliers and makers of perfumes at the time [fig. 1]. The apothecary was the professional who prepared, dispensed and sometimes administered to the public the medicines prescribed by doctors. The profession first appeared in the West around the 13th century, and was gradually regulated. Aspiring apothecaries had to undergo several years of apprenticeship and pass an examination to reach the rank of apothecary. Their shops were inspected to check the conformity and quality of their medicines. The professions of apothecary and grocer could easily be confused, as they sold the same type of products. In 1484, Charles VIII issued a decree requiring any grocer wishing to become an apothecary to first complete an apprenticeship and pass the professional examination, thus distinguishing the two trades without separating them. Preparations made by apothecaries included products for both health and beauty.

Medieval perfumes were, in fact, not just aesthetic products. They were considered to have numerous prophylactic and therapeutic properties. Scents were used to ward off disease and heal sufferers. The Great Plague, which swept across Europe from 1348 and killed between a quarter and a half of the population, had a lasting impact on the use of perfumes in the late Middle Ages. Pomanders, used by doctors to protect against the Black Death, were still used to spread their protective scent in times of epidemic. As well as being a nuisance, bad smells were also a threat,

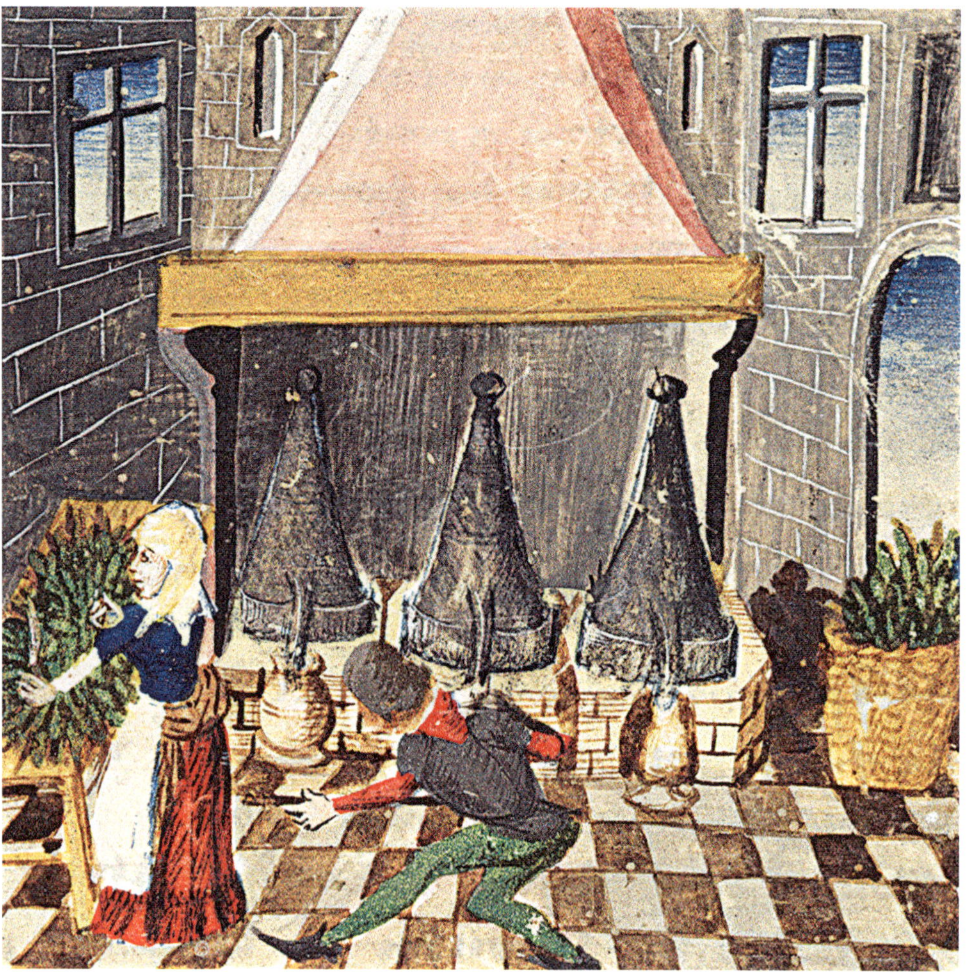

Fig. 3. Matthaeus Platearius, *The Book of Simple Medicines*, 2nd half of 15th c., Paris, Bibliothèque nationale de France, Ms fr. 623 f. 23

as medieval thought held that diseases were spread by fetid and foul-smelling air. Faced with the fear of epidemics, perfumes played a defensive role by blocking out this contaminated air.

Scented substances might well have been included when making remedies. Based on criteria drawn from humoral theory, medieval medicine believed they played an active role in keeping people healthy. Originating in antiquity, this doctrine played a dominant role in medicine until the 18th century. It was based on the idea that mental and physical health depended on the balance between the four fluids circulating in the body, known as "humours" (blood, phlegm, yellow bile, black bile), to which were associated four physical qualities (hot, cold, dry, moist) [fig. 2]. According to humoral theory, all illnesses stemmed from an imbalance in these elements. The physical qualities could have different intensities, classified in four degrees (degree zero qualifying a substance that was neither hot nor cold, neither dry nor moist). According to the same principle, an illness that was hot in the third degree and dry in the second had to be treated with a medicine that had the opposite properties, but in the same degree, i.e. cold in the third degree and moist in the second.

Fragrant raw materials and their scents were also classified according to these qualities and their intensity. These criteria were key to the descriptions and are the starting point for each entry

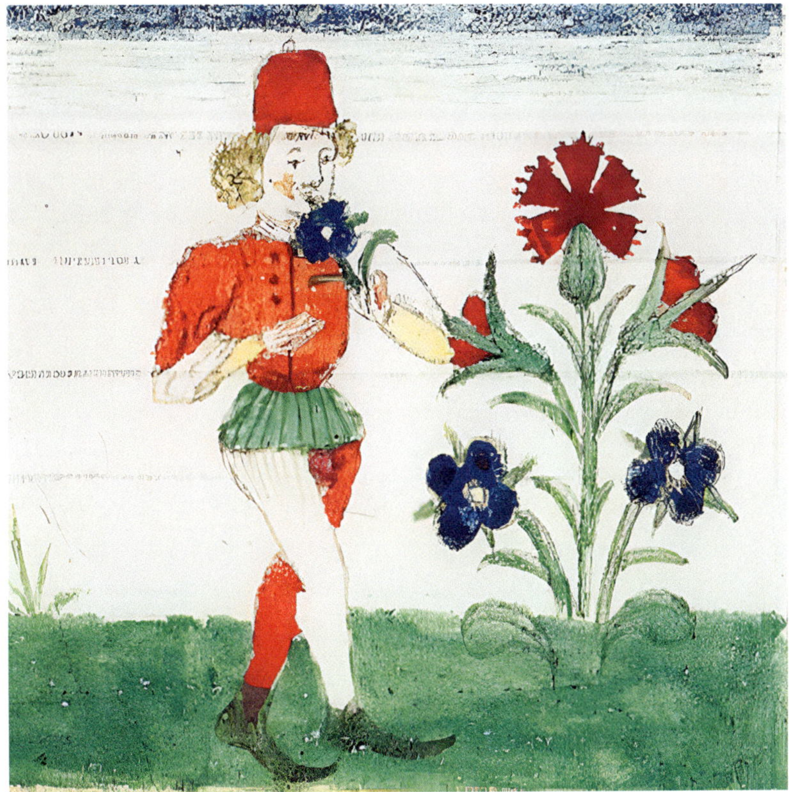

Fig. 4. Jean Corbechon, *Le Livre des propriétés des choses* (*On the Properties of Things*) ca. 1480–90, Tours, bibliothèque municipal, f. 417, Ms 703

in *The Book of Simple Medicines* [fig. 3]. This treatise details the characteristics of "simples", the term used to describe medicinal substances in their pure form, as they are found in nature. It is a translation of the *Tractatus de herbis*, a compilation of medical knowledge compiled in the 11th century by the Salerno School of Medicine. It was copied and expanded several times, culminating in *The Book of Simple Medicines* around 1480. The therapeutic properties attributed to a number of ingredients used in the perfumes of the time are meticulously described. We learn, for example, that rose is cold in the first degree and dry in the second, that rose water supports the body's natural warmth while expelling superfluous hot humours, and that inhaling the scent of musk combats weakness of the brain.

As well as having decorative and medicinal uses, perfumes also had an important cultural value. Smells and the sense of smell had a specific status, described in particular in the *Livre des propriétés des choses* (*On the Properties of Things*) [fig. 4], an encyclopaedic work that was copied several times over the course of the 15th century. At the end of the 14th century, Charles V commissioned the monk Jean Corbechon to write this French translation of the *Liber de proprietatibus rerum*, written in the 13th century by the Franciscan Bartholomaeus Anglicus. It divided smells into three main categories: first, those described as being "aromatic", strong and pleasant, such as amber and spices; then more discreet smells, considered "moderate", such as violet, which must come from pure substances to retain a good scent; finally odours described as "foul-smelling", resulting from putrefaction, which living beings instinctively avoid, and which

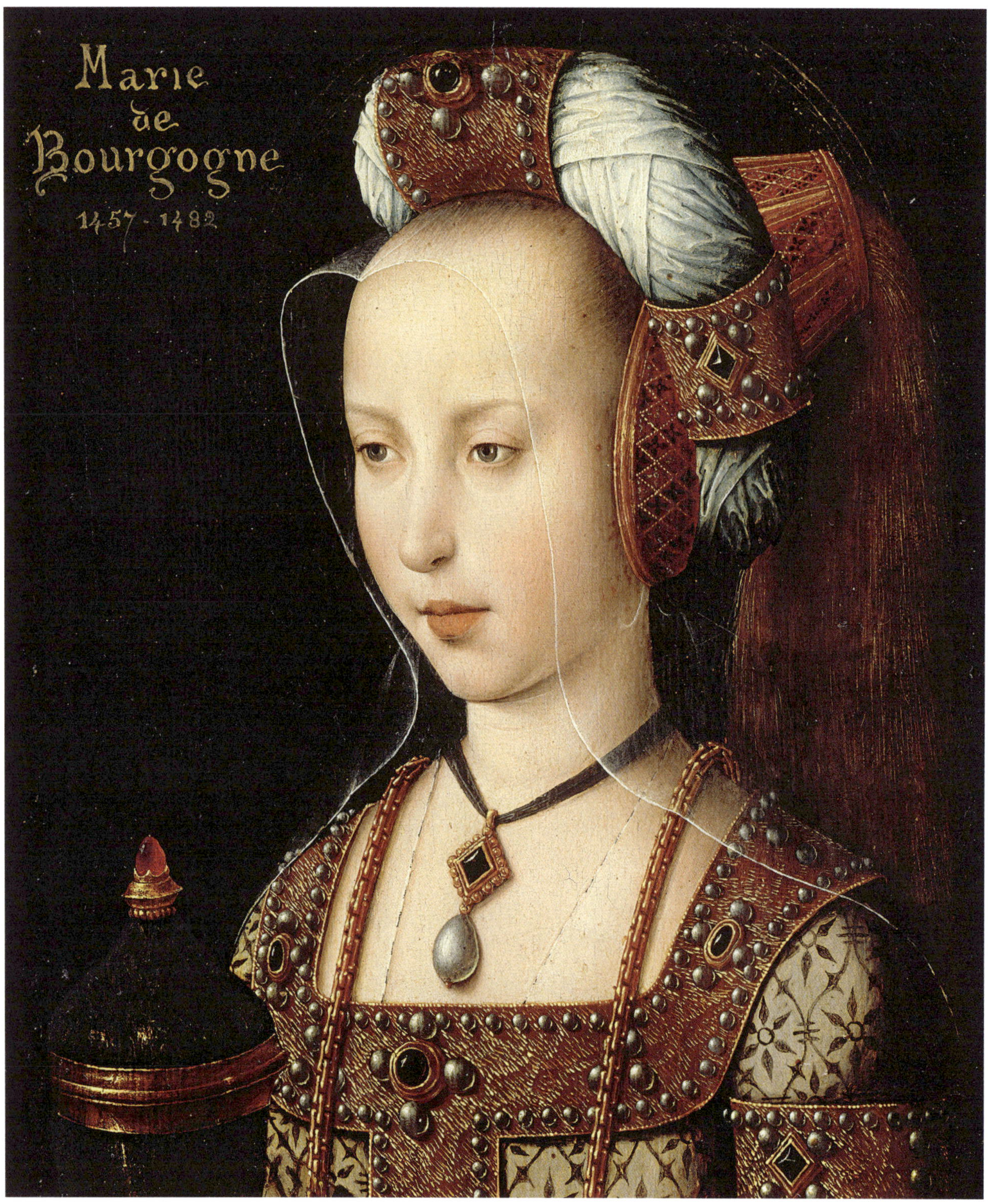

Fig. 5. The Master of the Legend of St Mary Magdalene (active 1480–1525), *Portrait of Mary of Burgundy as Mary Magdalene*, ca. 1510, oil on wood, 26.5 × 22.5 cm
Chantilly, musée Condé, PE588

were presented as dangerous to health. The *Livre des propriétés des choses* describes odour as "a smoky vapour arising from the substance of something odorable", echoing the Aristotelian notion that olfaction is a function of the soul. From this perspective, perfumes were perceived as revealing a person's inner self.

The cultural value of odoriferous preparations can also be seen in their religious function. Christ is depicted as a sweet-smelling being, one of the facets of his perfection. Invisible yet perceptible, perfume symbolises divinity. The use of incense during religious ceremonies gives concrete expression to his presence among the faithful. One of the first signs of sanctity is the wonderful scent that is presumed to emanate naturally from the body of a saint. This link between the soul and fragrance was believed to be expressed after death by the delightful scent of God's chosen ones, far removed from the stench of the corpses of the damned. Preserved from the decomposition that putrefies the bodies of mere mortals, saints die with an "odour of sanctity".

The figure of Mary Magdalene symbolises the prominent position held by perfumes in the spiritual life of the late Middle Ages. An important figure in Western Christianity in the second half of the Middle Ages, she occupied a special place in the society of the period, and her cult flourished throughout the 15th century. She embodied the figure of a sinner corrupted by a life of pleasure and vanity who, through love, renunciation and steadfast faith, achieved Christian salvation and holiness. Mary Magdalene established herself as a model of behaviour, offering a figure of redemption with whom the faithful could identify. During the 15th century, her cult spread throughout the Duchy of Burgundy, influencing the piety of the princesses and duchesses, who introduced the fashion of having themselves portrayed in the likeness of Mary Magdalene, a trend that marked portraiture among the female aristocracy until the early 16th century [fig. 5]. The symbolic attribute of this iconography was none other than the perfume jar with which the saint was traditionally portrayed. The image of Mary Magdalene is closely associated with perfume: according to Christian tradition, it was by anointing the feet and head of Jesus that she demonstrated her repentance and conversion to a holy life. In allegorical terms, the perfume sprinkled by Mary Magdalene was an offering, a sacrifice, a symbol of God's love and a path to salvation. In the 15th century, Mary Magdalene also became the patron saint of apothecaries, her vase of aromatics evoking those found in their shops.

Perfumes were very much a part of the sensory world in the late Middle Ages, enhancing every aspect of the body and helping to keep it healthy. Available in a wide range of fragrances, they were valued for their aesthetic, hygienic, medical, moral and cultural functions. They reveal a rich and complex history, with multiple facets, closely tied to our relationship with our bodies.

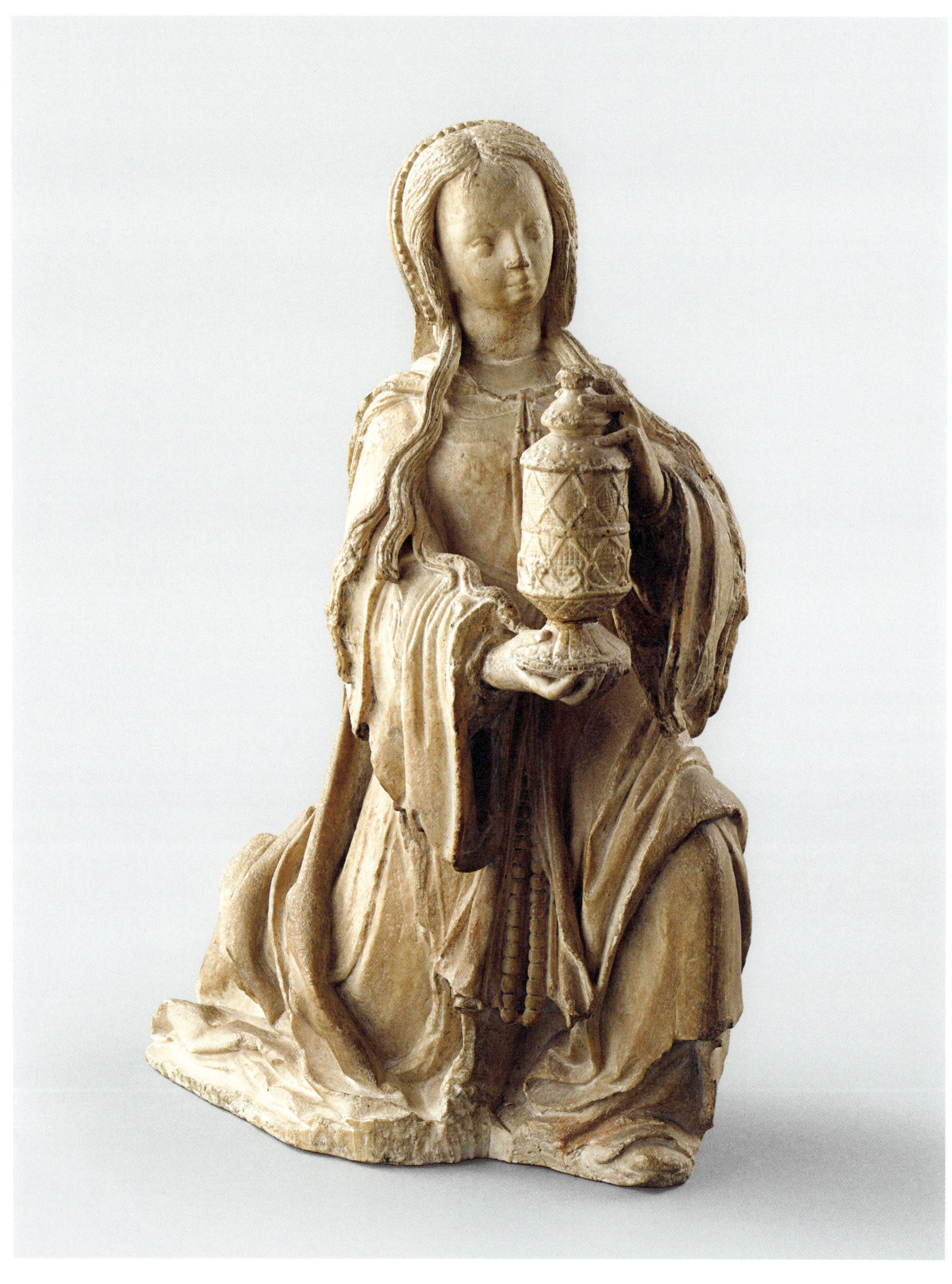

St Mary Magdalene Kneeling, 16th c., polychrome marble, 44.5 × 33 cm, Paris, musée de Cluny – musée national du Moyen Âge, inv. Cl. 19382

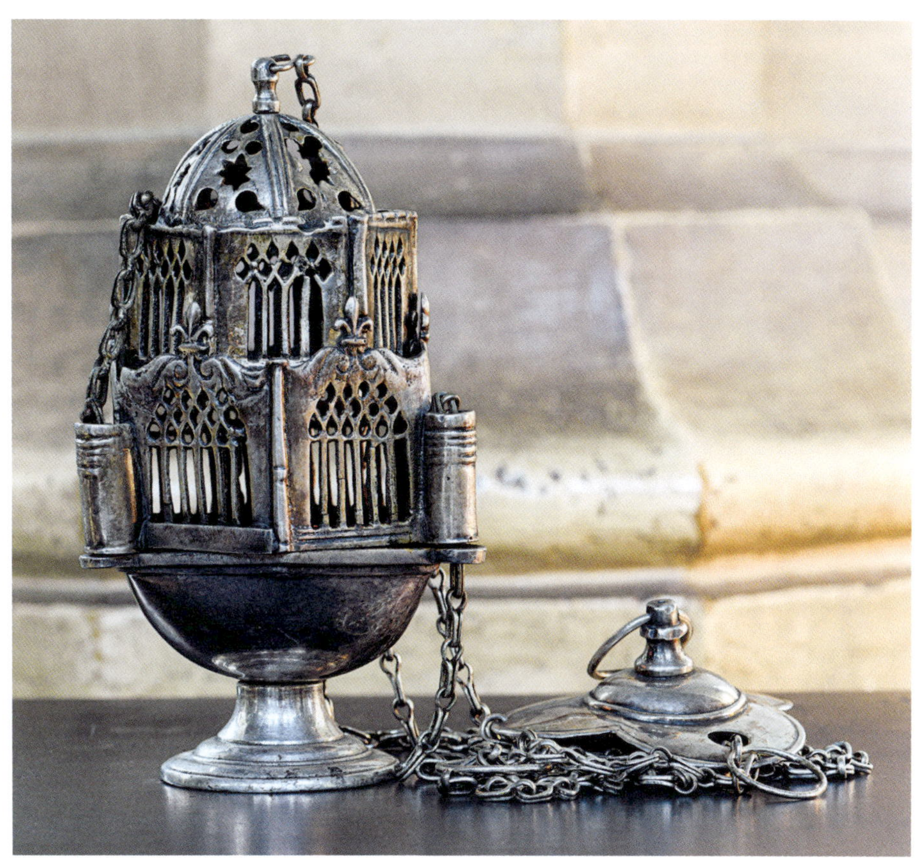

Censer, 16th c., cast brass, 21 × 11 cm, Blois, paroisse de la cathédrale Saint-Louis

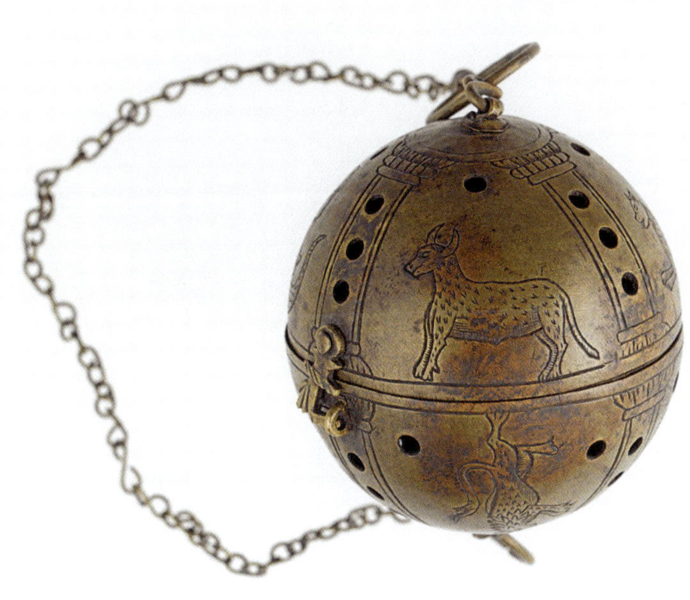

Hand warmer, 16th c., copper, 8 cm, Écouen, musée national de la Renaissance – château d'Écouen, inv. E.CL. 2825

ALBERT Jean-Pierre, *Odeurs de sainteté – La mythologie chrétienne des aromates* (Paris: École des hautes études en sciences sociales, 1990).

BALARD Michel, *Histoire des épices au Moyen Âge* (Paris: Perrin, 2023).

BOUCHET Florence & KLINGER-DOLLÉ Anne-Hélène (eds.), *Penser les cinq sens au Moyen Âge. Poétique, esthétique, éthique* (Paris: Classiques Garnier, 2015).

LAFONT Olivier, *Apothicaires et Pharmaciens – L'histoire d'une conquête scientifique* (Arcueil: John Libbey Eurotext, 2021).

LANOË Catherine, LAURIOUX Bruno & DA VINHA Mathieu (eds.), *Cultures de cour, Cultures du corps, XIVe-XVIIIe siècle* (Paris: PUPS, 2011).

LE GOFF Jacques, TRUONG Nicolas, *Une histoire du corps au Moyen Âge* (Paris: Liana Levi, 2003).

LORCIN Marie-Thérèse, "Humeurs, bains et tisanes : l'eau dans la médecine médiévale" in *L'Eau au Moyen Âge* (Aix-en-Provence: Presses universitaires de Provence, 1985), pp. 259—73 (*Senefiance*, no. 15).

MENJOT Denis, *Les Soins de beauté – Moyen Âge, début des temps modernes*, actes du IIIe colloque international de Grasse (26-28 April 1985) (Nice: Centre d'études médiévales de l'université de Nice, 1987).

PARAVICINI BAGLIANI Agostino (ed.), *Parfums et Odeurs au Moyen Âge – science, usage, symboles*, (Florence: SISMEL-Edizioni del Galluzzo, "Micrologus' Library" no. 67, 2015).

TACCONE Raphaëlle, *Marie-Madeleine en Occident : les dynamiques de la sainteté dans la Bourgogne des IXe-XVe siècles*, doctoral thesis under the supervision of LOBRICHON Guy and RUSSO Daniel (Avignon: Université d'Avignon et des Pays du Vaucluse, 2012).

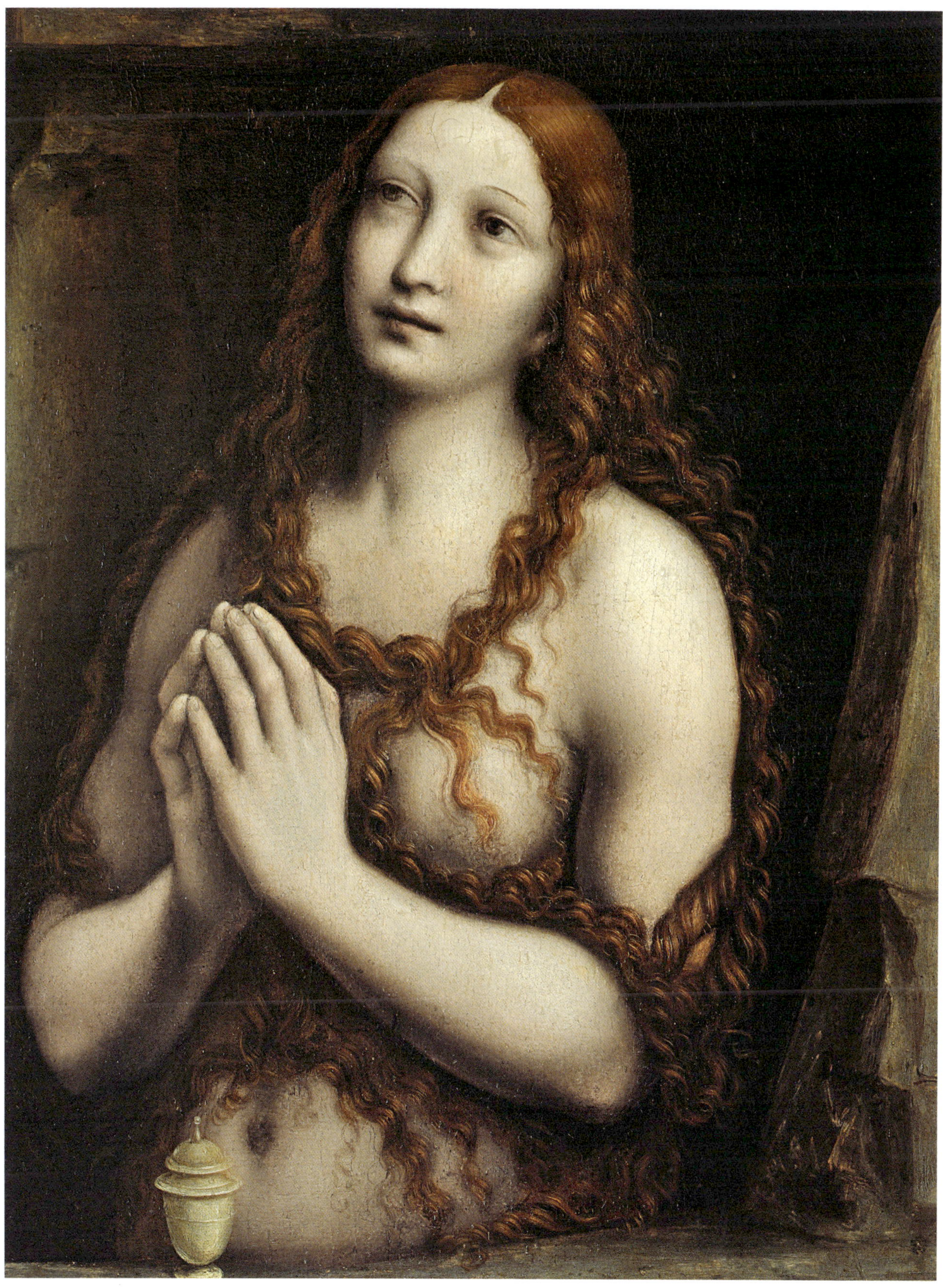

Attributed to Giovanni Pedrini, also known as Giampietrino, *St Mary Magdalene*, 16th c., oil on wood, 55 × 43 cm, Pavia, Musei Civici del Castello Visconteo, inv. p.121

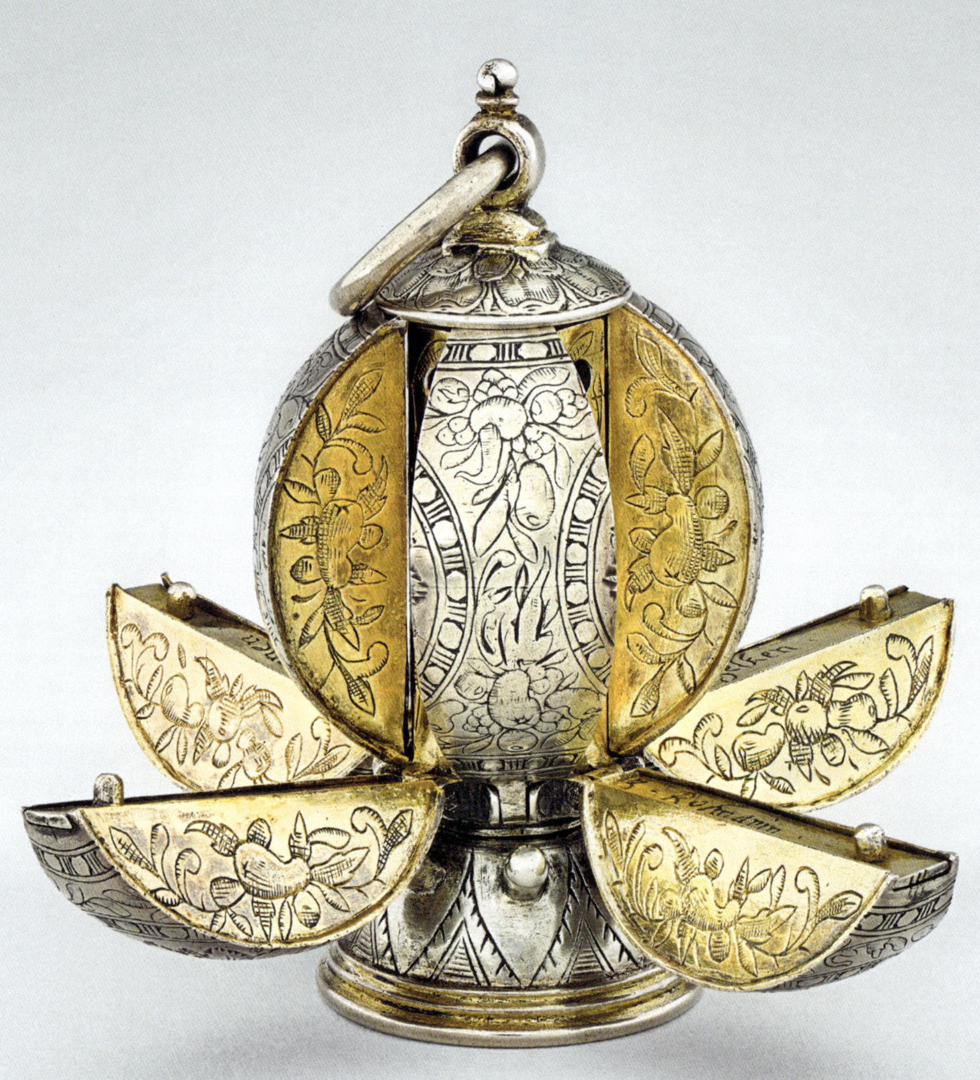

PERFUMES AT THE COURT OF FRANCIS I

Océane Fontaine Cioffi

During the Renaissance, perfumes circulated throughout Europe, either as gifts or as merchandise. From Italy to Amboise, they preceded and followed Leonardo da Vinci to the court of Francis I, where they were traded with Italy, England and Spain. Rather than considering perfume as an aromatic remedy, or a barrier against foul odours – often described as such in historiography – the aim of this article is to examine perfume as a precious commodity: a luxury product, a product of the imagination and of *savoir-faire*.

Valuable diplomatic gifts

In the royal invitation letter of 14 March 1516 to the French ambassador in Rome, Antonio Maria Pallavicini, containing instructions for Leonardo's journey to France, Admiral Guillaume Gouffier de Bonnivet first asks about the shipment of a painting and perfumes that Pallavicini had promised him:

> The King has asked me to write to you...I pray Sir, to give instruction that my Florentine painting be sent to me, and do not forget to send me at the same time the little vases and perfumes that you promised me. And also I beg you to urge Master [or Messer] Leonardo that he should come to the King's presence, as he is expected by this Lord's great devotion... (Jan Sammer, *Leonardo da Vinci: The Untold Story of His Final Years*, 2019)

LEFT
Fig. 1. Pomander, 17th c., partially gilded silver, 6 × 3.3 cm, Écouen, musée national de la Renaissance – château d'Écouen, inv. E.Cl.12521

A *pomme de senteur*, also known as a pomander, contains scented balls of animal, vegetable or floral matter in small compartments that open with a hinge and spring.

A few months later, at the end of October, Leonardo da Vinci and a ship carrying fragrances reached Amboise. The Venetian ambassador, Zoan Badoer, informed Louise of Savoy of the arrival of these perfumes sent from Venice, contained in two cases, each locked by key. The recipients of the scents were given precise instructions, with some items reserved for Louise of Savoy. On the morning of 31 October, she asked Badoer to bring the much-vaunted fragrances. In the presence of the King's mother and her daughter Margaret, the diplomat opened a box. The two women looked at each bottle and tested its scent, an examination that kept them busy until the evening. Badoer presented Margaret with a perfume diffuser in private. It may have been a perfume burner like the one shown in an engraving by Marcantonio Raimondi [fig. 2], a design by Raphael for

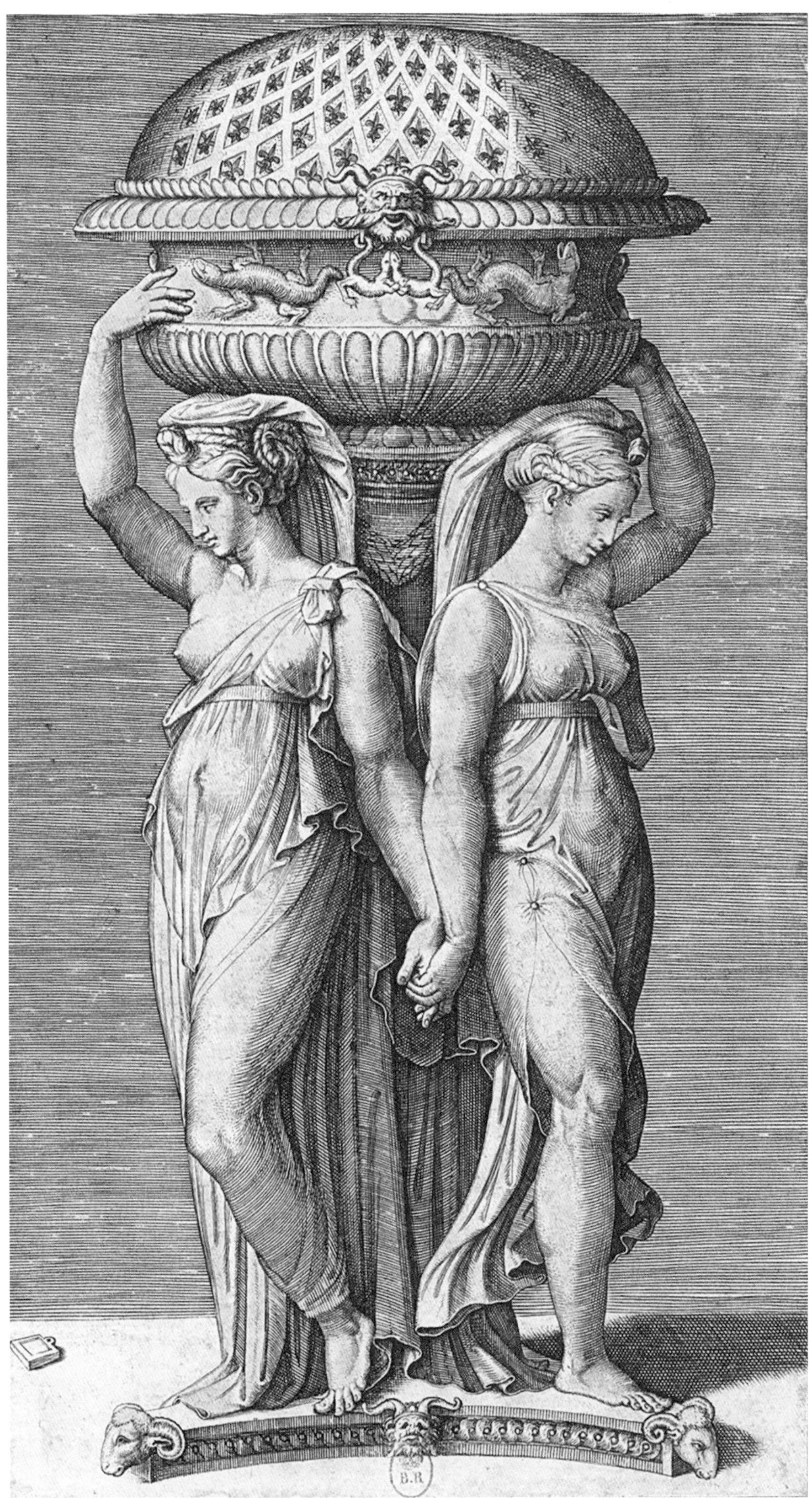

Fig. 2. Marcantonio Raimondi, after Raffaello Sanzio, *Perfume burner*, 16th c., engraving, 30.1 × 16.8 cm, Pavia, Musei Civici del Castello Visconteo, inv. St. Mal. 1764

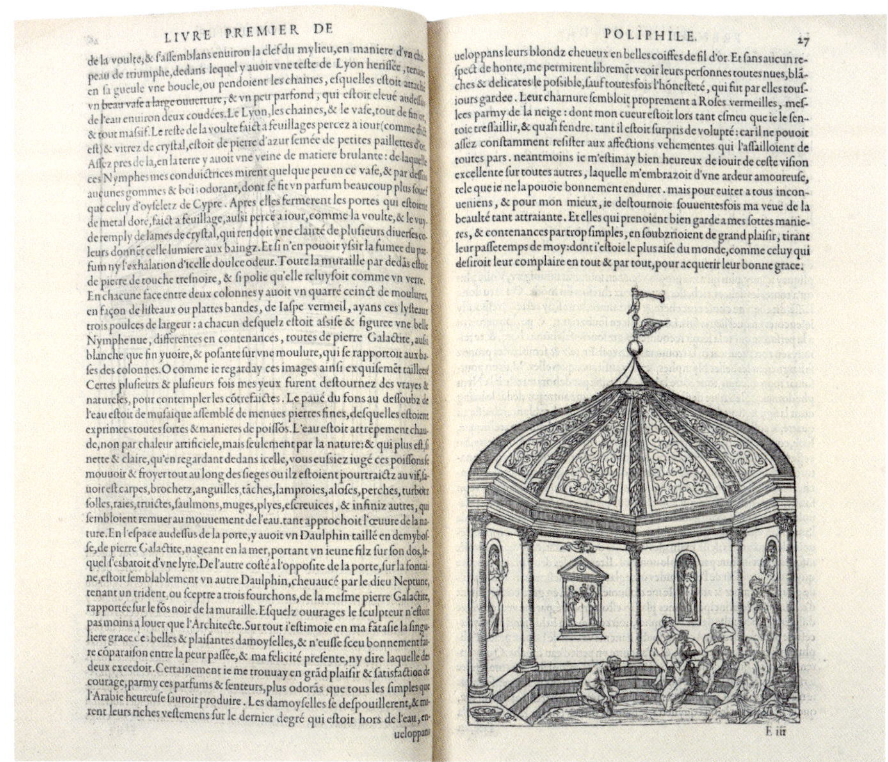

LIVRE PREMIER DE

de la voulte,& s'assemblans enuiron la clef du mylieu,en maniere d'vn chapeau de triumphe,dedans lequel y auoit vne teste de Lyon herissée, tenant en sa gueule vne boucle,ou pendoient les chaines, esquelles estoit attaché vn beau vase a large ouuerture, & vn peu parfond, qui estoit eleué audessus de l'eau enuiron deux coudées.Le Lyon,les chaines,& le vase,tout de fin or, & tout masif.Le reste de la voulte faict a feuillages percez a iour(comme dict est)& vitrez de crystal,estoit de pierre d'azur semée de petites paillettes d'or. Assez pres de la,en la terre y auoit vne veine de matiere brulante: de laquelle ces Nymphes mes conduictrices mirent quelque peu en ce vase,& par dessus aucunes gommes & bois odorant,dont se fit vn parfum beaucoup plus souef que celuy d'oyseletz de Cypre. Apres elles fermerent les portes qui estoient de metal doré,faict a feuillage,aussi percé a iour,comme la voulte,& le vuyde remply de lames de crystal,qui rendoit vne clairté de plusieurs diuerses couleurs donnẽt celle lumiere aux baingz.Et si n'en pouoit ysir la fumee du parfum ny l'exhalation d'icelle doulce odeur. Toute la muraille par dedãs estoit de pierre de touche tresnoire, & si polie qu'elle reluysoit comme vn verre. En chacune face entre deux colonnes y auoit vn quarré ceinct de moulures, en façon de listeaux ou plattes bandes, de Iaspe vermeil, ayans ces lysteaux trois poulces de largeur : a chacun desquelz estoit asise & figuree vne belle Nymphe nue, differentes en contenances, toutes de pierre Galactite, aussi blanche que fin yuoire,& posante sur vne moulure,qui se rapportoit aux bases des colonnes.O comme ie regarday ces images ainsi exquisemẽt taillees! Certes plusieurs & plusieurs fois mes yeux furent destournez des vrayes & natureles, pour contempler les cõtrefaictes. Le paué du fons au dessoubz de l'eau estoit de musaique assemblé de menues pierres fines,desquelles estoient exprimees toutes sortes & manieres de poissõs. L'eau estoit attrẽpement chaude,non par chaleur artificiele,mais seulement par la nature:& qui plus est,si nette & claire,qu'en regardant dedans icelle,vous eusiez iugé ces poissons se mouuoir & froyer tout au long des sieges ou ilz estoient pourtraictz au vif,sauoir est carpes,brochetz,anguilles,tâches,lamproies,aloses,perches,turbotz, solles,raies,truictes,saulmons,muges,plyes,escreuices, & infiniz autres, qui sembloient remuer au mouuement de l'eau.tant approchoit l'œuure de la nature.En l'espace audessus de la porte,y auoit vn Daulphin taillé en demybosse,de pierre Galactite,nageant en la mer,portant vn ieune filz sur son dos,lequel s'esbatoit d'vne lyre.De l'autre costé a l'opposite de la porte,sur la fontaine,estoit semblablement vn autre Daulphin,cheuaucé par le dieu Neptune, tenant un trident,ou sceptre a trois fourchons,de la mesme pierre Galactite, rapportée sur le fõs noir de la muraille.Esquelz ouurages le sculpteur n'estoit pas moins a louer que l'Architecte.Sur tout i'estimoie en ma fãtasie la singuliere grace de ces belles & plaisantes damoyselles,& n'eusse sceu bonnement faire cõparaison entre la peur passée,& ma felicité presente,ny dire laquelle des deux excedoit.Certainement ie me trouuay en grãd plaisir & satisfaction de courage,parmy ces parfums & senteurs,plus odorãs que tous les simples que l'Arabie heureuse sauroit produire. Les damoyselles se despouillerent,& mirent leurs riches vestemens sur le dernier degré qui estoit hors de l'eau,enueloppans

POLIPHILE. 27

ueloppans leurs blondz cheueux en belles coiffes de fil d'or. Et sans aucun respect de honte,me permirent libremẽt veoir leurs personnes toutes nues,blãches & delicates le posible,sauf toutesfois l'hõnesteté, qui fut par elles tousiours gardee. Leur charnure sembloit proprement a Roses vermeilles, meslees parmy de la neige : dont mon cueur estoit lors tant esmeu que ie le sentoie tressaillir,& quasi fendre. tant il estoit surpris de volupté : car il ne pouoit assez constamment resister aux affections vehementes qui l'assailloient de toutes pars. neantmoins ie m'estimay bien heureux de iouir de ceste vision excellente sur toutes autres, laquelle m'embrazoit d'vne ardeur amoureuse, tele que ie ne la pouoie bonnement endurer. mais pour euiter a tous inconueniens, & pour mon mieux, ie destournoie souuentesfois ma veue de la beaulté tant attraiante. Et elles qui prenoient bien garde a mes sottes manieres, & contenances par trop simples, en soubzrioient de grand plaisir, tirant leur passetemps de moy:dont i'estoie le plus aise du monde,comme celuy qui desiroit leur complaire en tout & par tout,pour acquerir leur bonne grace.

E iii

Fig. 3. Francesco Colonna, *Hypnerotomachia Poliphili or The Dream of Poliphilus*, late 15th c., bound paper work, 33 × 22 cm, Tours, bibliothèque municipale, Rés. 7873, f. 26v-27r

Francis I: the censer, with salamanders – the emblem of the King of France – on its rim, rests on three graces (only two of whom are visible in the image) with fleur-de-lys-shaped perforations on the lid through which the fragrant smoke could pass.

In the accounts of the Menus plaisirs (entertainment expenses) of Francis I, we find several items of expenditure on such perfume diffusers, or perfume-burners made of precious metals, as well as pomanders [fig. 1]. These adornments could take a variety of forms and contain different substances. The accounts often omit to reveal their use, particularly when used as a prophylactic against bad air. Their shapes do, however, suggest some remarkable uses. While the three round pomanders "for fragrant preparations" delivered by the Parisian goldsmith Guillaume Castillon in December 1528 obviously appeal to the sense of smell, they also appeal to the sense of sight, and not just because of their aesthetic appeal: in each "there is a mirror and a dial", the latter term referring to a measuring instrument. In this way, the multi-sensory accessory becomes a scholarly item. More devoutly, in November 1529, the sovereign bought from the same goldsmith "two flat golden apples used to hold fragrant preparations, inside of which there are two small booklets in which are written the seven '*seaulmes*' [psalms], and two mirrors on either side" (Archives nationales, KK//100). Rather than a passive ornament, this combines olfaction, devotion and contemplation.

Valuable perfumes, as gifts, played a role in political and social relations, but also revealed the taste for luxury of the court and its sovereign, a luxury recalling that of an idealised antiquity.

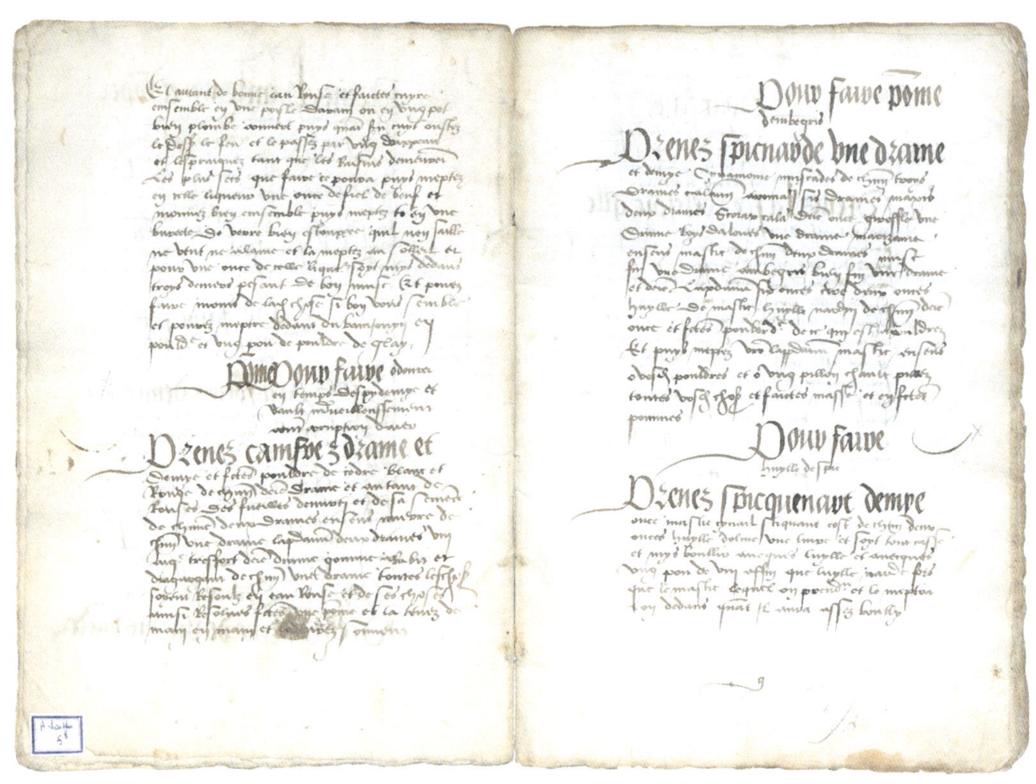

"Pommes pour faire odourer en temps d'espydeme et vault merveilleusement contre corruption d'aier",
Register of empirical, therapeutic and household formulae, 15th–16th c., manuscript, 19.5 × 27.5 cm,
Le Mans, Archives départementales de la Sarthe, booklet no. 8, f. 9v and booklet no. 9, f. 1r

Olfactory fancy, between indulgence and sensual pleasure

Francis I was one of the first known French readers of Francesco Colonna's *Hypnerotomachia Poliphili* (1499), adapted into French by Jean Martin under the title *Discours du songe de Poliphile* (*The Dream of Poliphilus*) (1546) [fig. 3]. The first book recounts the quest of Poliphilus to find his beloved, Polia, during which he traverses landscapes filled with ruins and ancient temples. In the allegorical kingdom of Free Will, Poliphilus meets five young girls – personifications of the five senses – carrying "vases full of muscat soap, & other scents", who take him to the baths:

> Not farre of, there was a cleft in the earth, the which continually did cast foorth burning matter, and taking of this, and filling the bottome of the vessel, they did put certaine ginnes and sweet woods which made an inestimable suffumigation, as of the sweetest past. (Francesco Colonna, *The Dream of Poliphilus*, translation by Jean Martin, 1546)

The scent of these substances burnt in a golden vase is compared to that of an *oiselet de Chypre* (Chypre birdy). This was the name given to sculptures made of scented paste that were intended to be burnt. The fragrant resins in the formulation held them together and allowed them to be moulded into shapes. These luxury products already existed in the Middle Ages, reflecting the taste of the elite for oriental luxury. Placed in beautifully crafted cages or on lavish displays, these birds perfumed interiors.

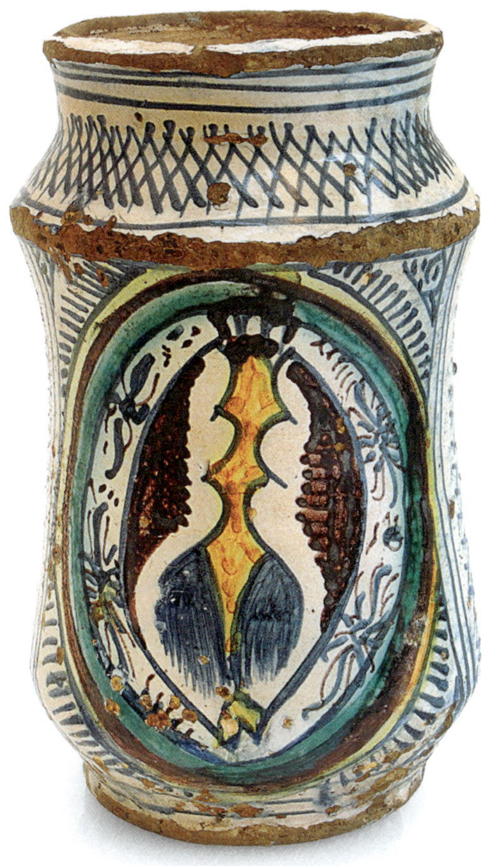

Albarello, Monteluppo Fiorentino, 15th c., polychrome earthenware,
19 × 9.5 cm, Grasse, musée international de la Parfumerie, inv. 0192

The Dream of Poliphilus had a great influence on the court of Francis I and on François Rabelais. Colonna's kingdom of Free Will was mirrored by *Gargantua*'s Abbey of Theleme, where:

> At the going out of the halls which belong to the ladies' lodgings were the perfumers and trimmers through whose hands the gallants passed when they were to visit the ladies. Those sweet artificers did every morning furnish the ladies' chambers with the spirit of roses, orange flower water, and angelica; and to each of them gave a little precious casket vapouring forth the most odoriferous exhalations of the choicest aromatical scents. (François Rabelais, *Gargantua*, 1534)

Like the members of the Abbey of Theleme, a Renaissance prince would at times call on the services of a skilled craftsman to create the most subtle fragrances: the perfumer.

The perfumer and the apothecary: Perfume makers in the service of the king

Although the profession of perfumer had no official status at the beginning of the 16th century, its practitioners were nonetheless specialised craftsmen. François d'Escobart, a Spaniard originally from Valencia, who lived in Paris from 1519 until his death in 1539, was honoured with the

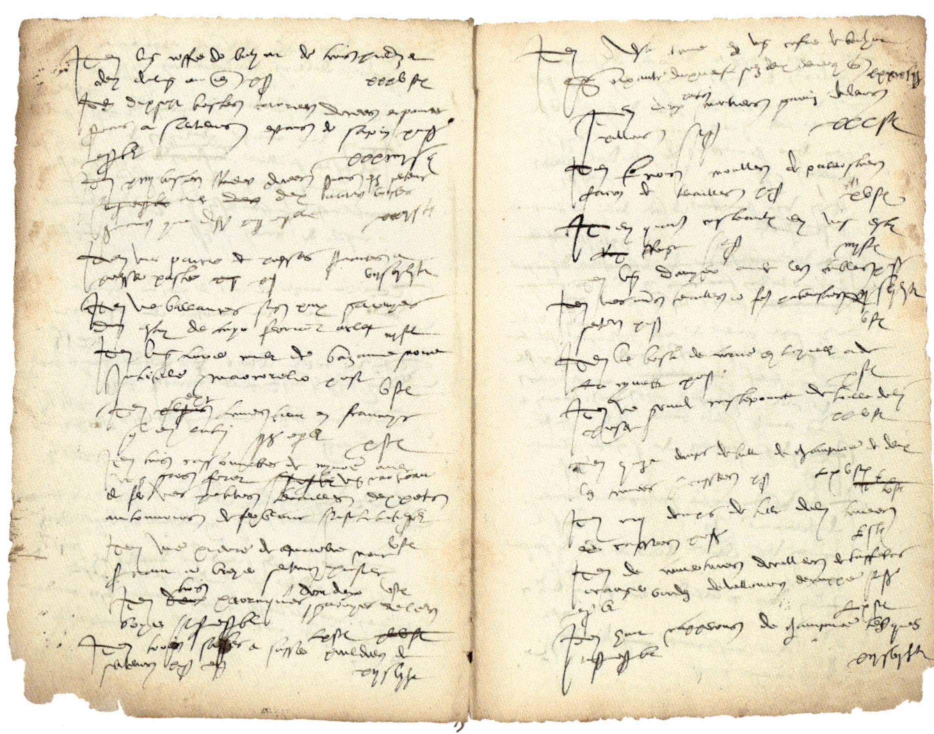

Fig. 4. Pierre Poutrain, *Post mortem inventory of François d'Escobart, Valet de Chambre and Perfumer to the King, dated 1st October 1539*, 16th c., manuscript, 29 × 20 cm, Paris, Archives nationales, MC/ET/LXXXVI/89, f. 5v-6r

title of Valet de Chambre and Perfumer to King Francis I. The equipment recorded in the inventory of his home in the Rue Saint-Honoré shows the specialised nature of his tools and receptacles [fig. 4]. In addition to scales, pestles and mortars, the inventory mentions a black marble stone used "to grind fragrances"; three "sieves for sifting fragrant powders"; several moulds for making "scented paternoster beads"; and four "wooden rods for shaping gloves" (AN, MC/ET/LXXXVI/89), gloves which François d'Escobart would perfume. In February 1529, he had already delivered to Francis I compositions "prepared and to be used for both gloves and in pomanders" for his pleasure and to offer as gifts to the king of England. A month later, the perfumer had supplied "perfumes, musk scented *eau de naffe* (orange blossom water), *cassolettes* and perfumed gloves" for the English sovereign (AN, KK//100). Among the scent containers in François d'Escobart's workshop was a horn box for civet, and another containing violet powder. During the Renaissance, the latter composition, placed among the linen, impregnated it with its delicate scent, with no undermining of virility implied by the use of this adjective:

> And when he had put on the handsomest and best-scented shirt he had, and a nightcap so well adorned that nothing was lacking in it, it seemed, to him, as he looked at himself in his mirror, that no lady in the world could deny herself to a man of his comeliness and grace. (Margaret of Angoulême, *The Heptameron*, 1559)

The clothes of Francis I – like the character in *The Heptameron* written by Margaret of Angoulême, the king's sister – were perfumed. According to the *Comptes de l'Argenterie* accounts, Benoist Gautheret, the king's apothecary, made purple taffeta and satin sachets on several occasions in 1536. He filled them with rose of Provins and violet powder and musk respectively; these scented sachets were then placed in the king's wardrobe (AN, KK//91). Scented sachets were also used to perfume the king's bed (AN, KK//92), and most likely the table linen (AN, KK//93).

In most cases, violet powder did not contain the flower of the same name. Its scent would have come mainly from the rhizomes of certain irises, with that of the Florentine iris being preferred at the time. The two plants are linked by their olfactory properties and sometimes by the colour of their flowers. For these two reasons, they may have been represented in the work by Francesco Melzi, a pupil of Leonardo. In this depiction of *Vertumnus and Pomona* (1518–22) [fig. 5], inspired by the Ovidian myth, violets bloom at the feet of the two figures, while iris flowers frame Pomona's beautiful face.

During the Renaissance, fragrances with refined compositions and sumptuous containers were offered and consumed in courtly circles. Fragrances were sent from Italy to the court of Francis I. He himself sent the king of England scented products made by a Spanish perfumer, who was undoubtedly responsible for exporting techniques from the Iberian Peninsula, which was renowned at the time for its perfumed gloves. The study of perfumes as precious items thus helps to decompartmentalise the world of the court, and to consider literary and pictorial representations, testimonies to a certain imagination. Finally, for Francis I, a protector of humanism and the arts, scents were perhaps less a protection against foul odours and more a pursuit of aestheticism and hedonism.

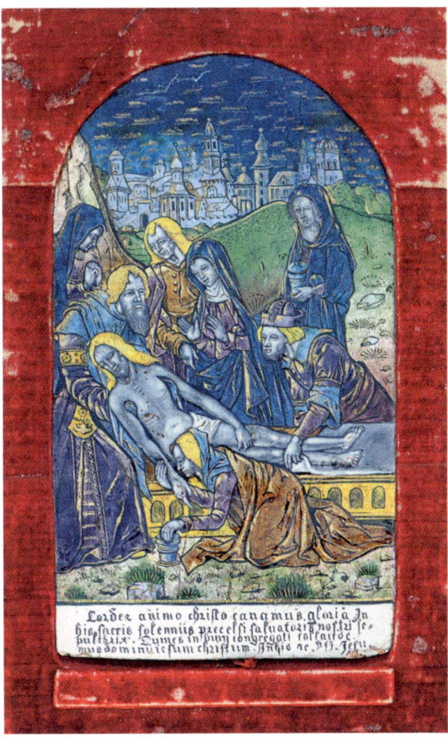

Attributed to Jean I Pénicaud, large curved polychrome plaque in painted enamel, with a depiction of the Entombment, ca. 1530, 25 × 14.6 cm, Amboise, château du Clos Lucé

Primary sources

Compte des Menus plaisirs, Archives nationales, Paris, KK//100.
Inventaire après décès de François d'Escobart, 1st october 1539, Archives nationales, Paris, MC/ET/LXXXVI/89.
Comptes de l'argenterie (1536), Archives nationales, Paris, KK//91.
Comptes de l'argenterie (1541), Archives nationales, Paris, KK//92.
Comptes du paiement des meubles, linges et autres fournitures nécessaires à l'hôtel du roi et à ses officiers (1533-1540), Archives nationales, Paris, KK//93.
d'Angoulême Marguerite, *L'heptameron des nouvelles de tresillustre et tresexcellente princesse Marguerite de Valois, royne de Navarre, remis en son ordre, confus au paravant en sa premiere impression : & dedié à tresillustre & tresvertueuse princesse Jeanne de Foix royne de Navarre, par Claude Gruget parisien*, Paris, 1559.
Rabelais François, *Gargantua* (Lyon: François Juste, 1534).

Bibliography

Bénézet Jean-Pierre, *Pharmacie et Médicament en Méditerranée occidentale* (xiiie-xvie *siècles*), (Paris: H. Champion [coll. 'Sciences, techniques et civilisations du Moyen Âge à l'aube des Lumières'], 1999).
Colonna Francesco, *Le Songe de Poliphile*, translation of the *Hypnerotomachia Poliphili* by Jean Martin (Paris: Kerver, 1546), presented, transliterated and annotated by Gilles Polizzi (Paris: Imprimerie nationale [coll. 'La salamandre'], 1994).
Magnier Océane, "Violet Powder: The Perfume of the Flower and the Scent of the Iris", in *The Power of Flowers* (1500-1750), Ghent University, 14-15 June 2023.
Sammer Jan, *Leonardo da Vinci: the Untold Story of his Final Years*, 2nd ed. (1st ed.: May 2019) (Prague: Amazon KDP, 2020).
Stabel Peter, "'Le goût pour l'Orient'. Demande cosmopolite et objets de luxe à Bruges à la fin du Moyen Âge", in *Histoire urbaine*, (2011), vol. 30, n° 1, pp. 21–39.
Welch Evelyn, "Scented Buttons and Perfumed Gloves: Smelling Things in Renaissance Italy" in *Ornamentalism: The Art of Renaissance Accessories*, Bella Mirabella (ed.) (Ann Arbor: University of Michigan Press, 2011), pp. 13–39.

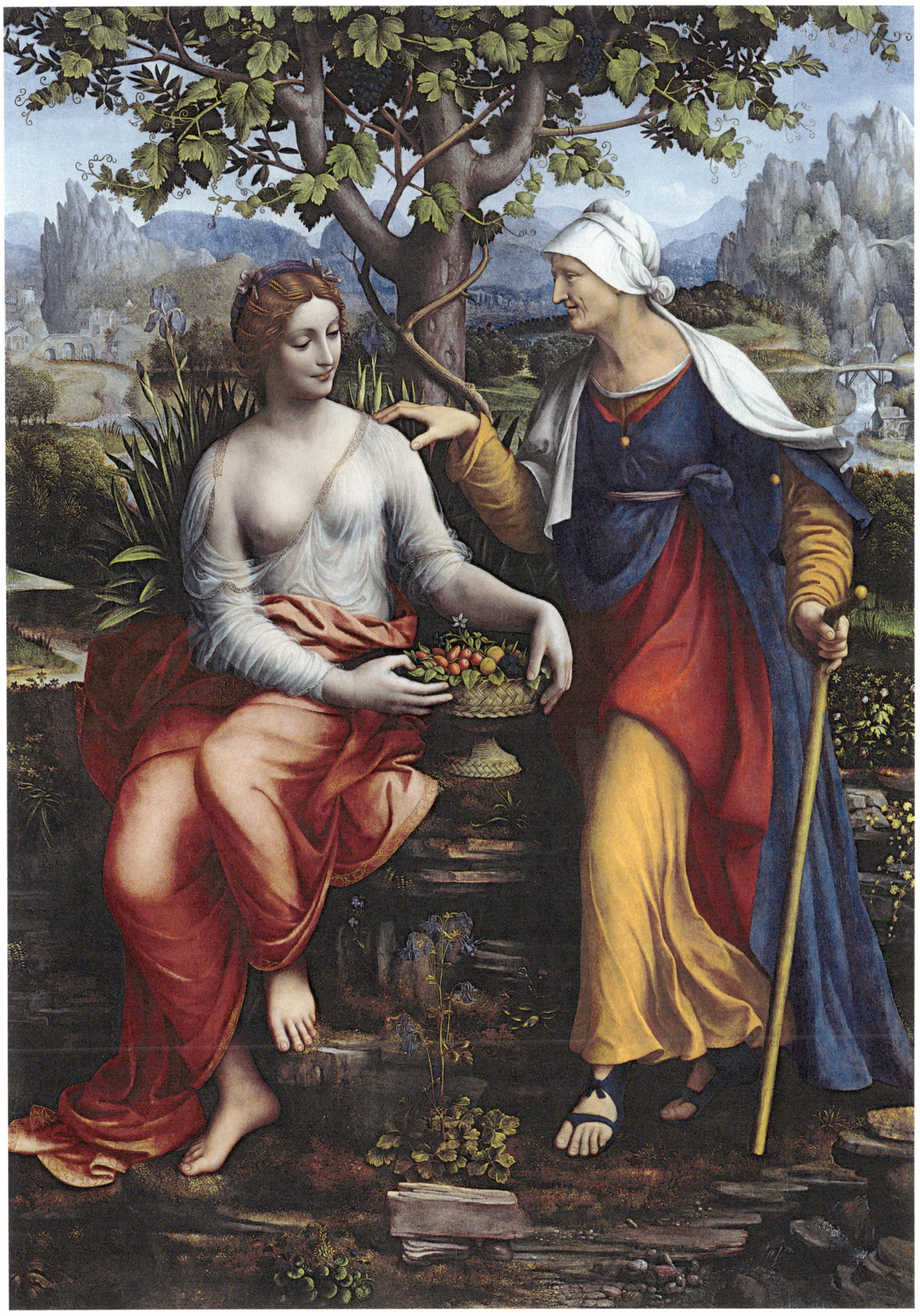

Fig. 5. Francesco Melzi, *Vertumnus and Pomona* (reproduction), 16th c., oil on canvas, 186 × 135.5 cm, Berlin, Gemäldegalerie

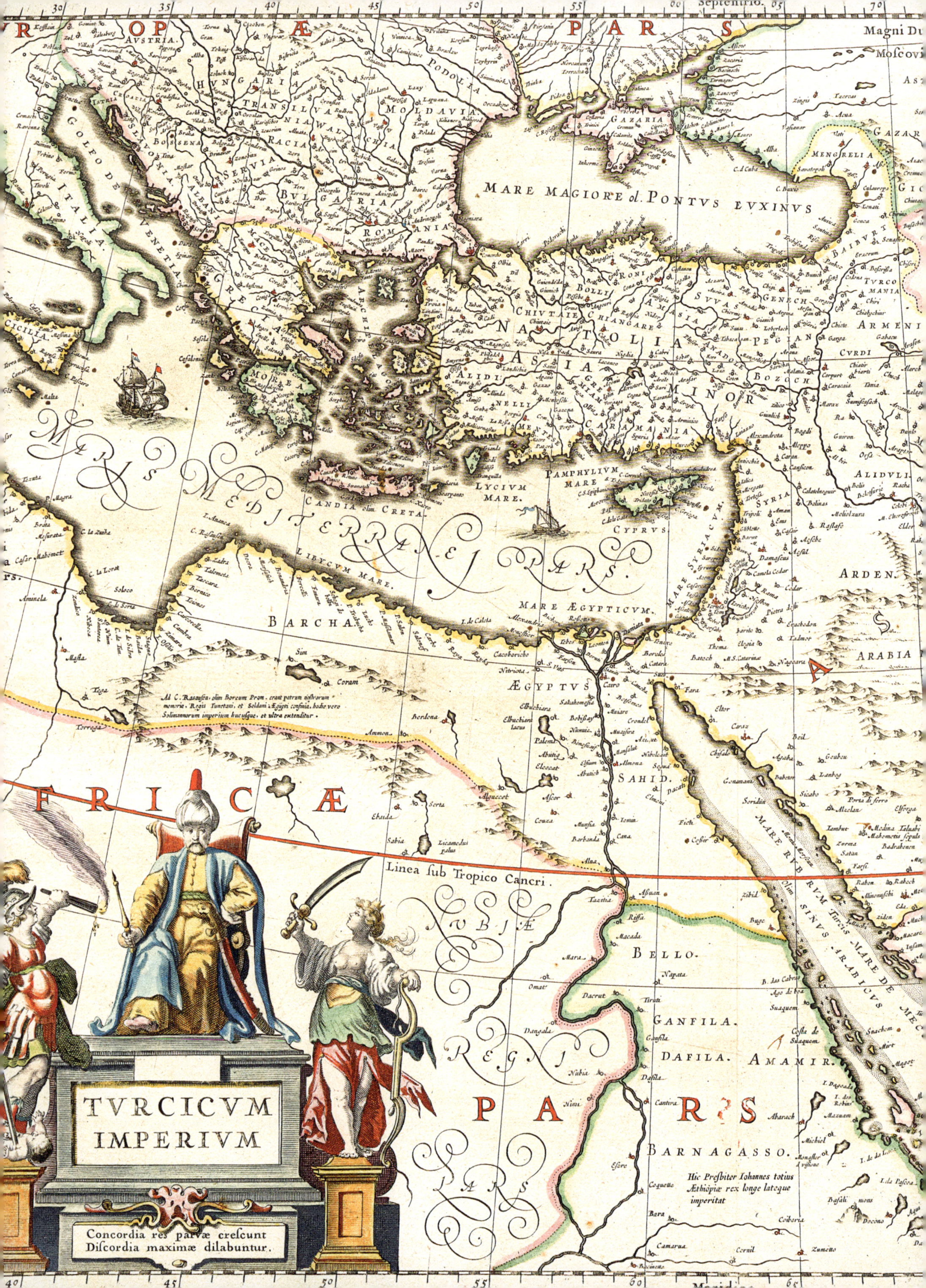
TVRCICVM IMPERIVM
Concordia res parvæ crescunt
Discordia maximæ dilabuntur.
EVROPÆ PARS
AFRICÆ
ASIA
MARE MAGIORE ol. PONTVS EVXINVS
MARIS MEDITERRANEI PARS.
LIBYCVM MARE.
MARE ÆGYPTICVM.
CANDIA olim CRETA.
LYCIVM MARE.
PAMPHYLIVM MARE
CYPRVS
NATOLIA
ASIA MINOR
ÆGYPTVS
BARCHA
ARABIA
ARDEN.
SYRIA
MOLDAVIA
PODOLIA
HVNGARIA
TRANSILVANIA
VALACHIA
BVLGARIA
ROMANIA
SERVIA
RACIA
BOSSENA
GRECIA
MOREA
ITALIA
GOLFO DE VENETIA
SICILIA.
AVSTRIA.
MENGRELIA
GAZARIA
ARMENIA
CVRDI
BOZOCH
CARAMANIA
SAHID.
Linea sub Tropico Cancri.
NVBIÆ REGNI PARS
BELLO.
GANFILA.
DAFILA.
AMAMIR.
BARNAGASSO.
Hic Prester Iohannes totius Æthiopiæ rex longe lateque imperitat
MARE RVBRVM SINVS ARABICVS
Ad C. Razaufa, olim Boreum Prom. erant patrum nostrorum memoria Regis Tunetani, et Soldani Ægypti confinia, hodie vero Solimannorum imperium huiusque, et ultra extenditur.
Septentrio.
Magni Du
Moscovi

TARTARIÆ
MARE DE BACHU ol. CASPIUM MARE ET HYRCANUM.
PERSIÆ PARS.
GILAN.
MEDIA
SERVAN.
ASYRIA
DIARBECH
PERSIÆ
FARCI
CVSISTAN
CALDEA.
ORMVS
MARE ELCATIF, ol. SINVS PERSICVS.
YAMAN.
ELCATIF.
ARABIA
MASCALAT.
FELIX.
AMANSIRIFDIN.
ALIBINALI.
GVBELLAMAN.
IRMIN.
ZIBIT
HERIT.
ADEN.
Magnifico Pruden
DAVIDI DE
Tabulam hanc
Milliaria

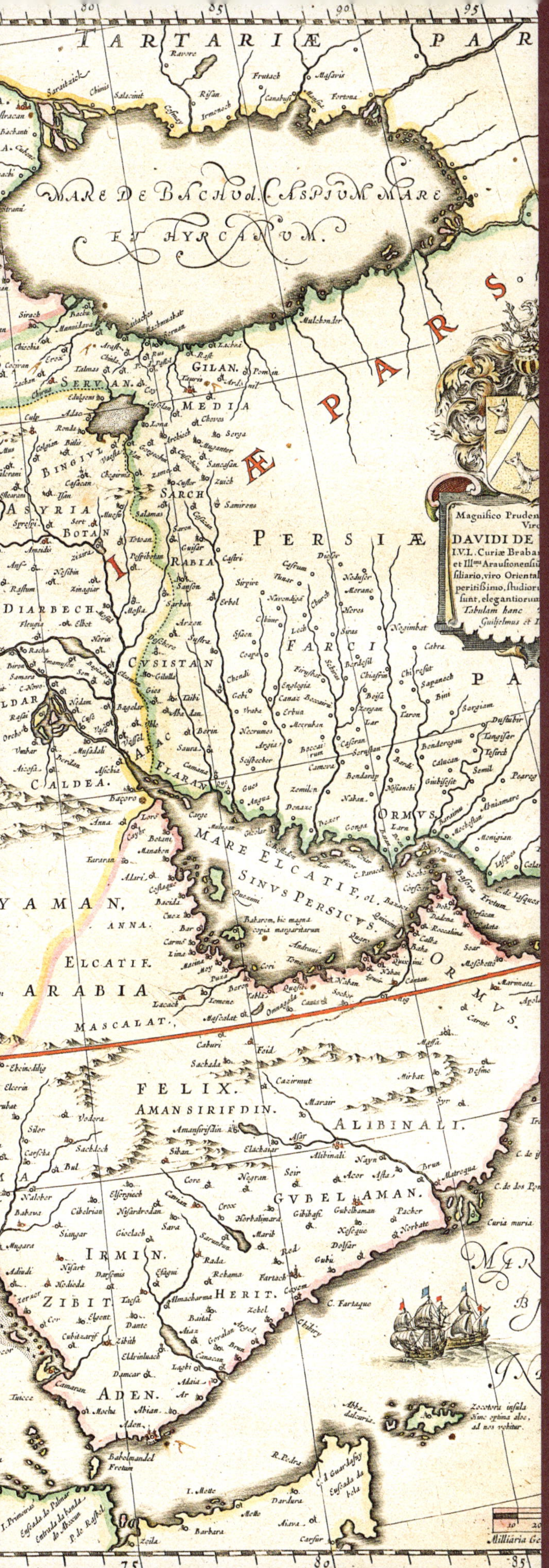

Annexes

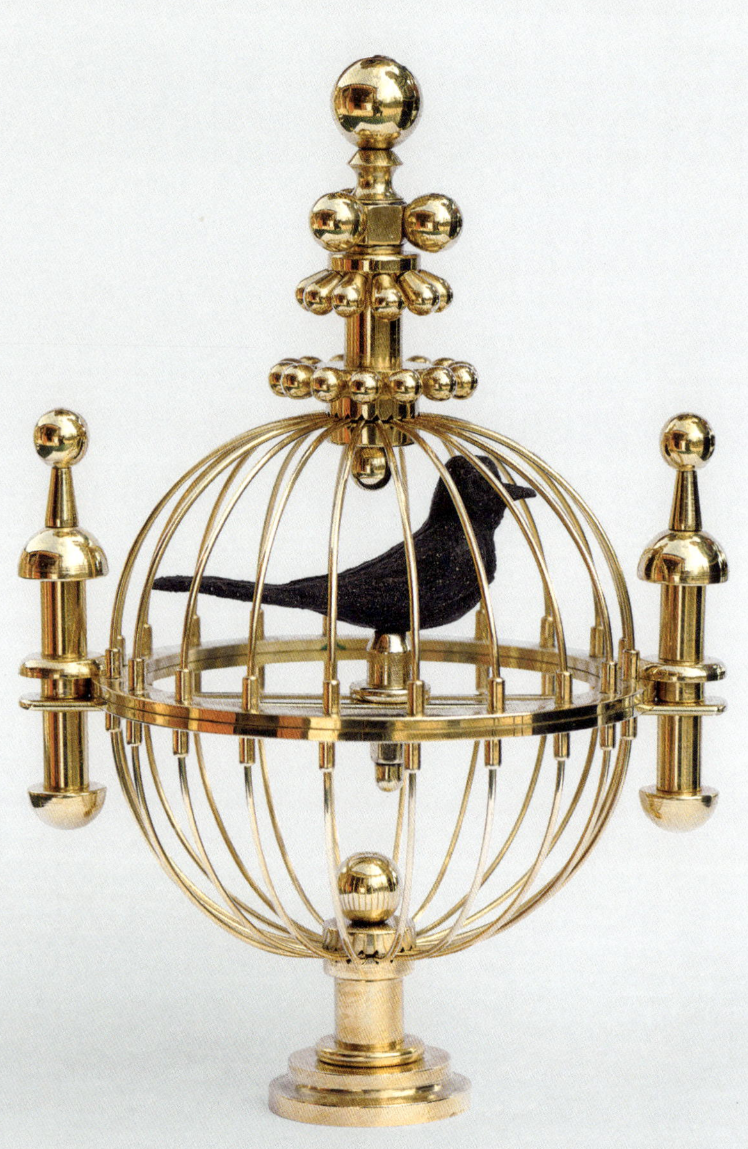

SOME RECIPES FOR RENAISSANCE PERFUMES

PASCAL BRIOIST

Chypre birdies

I secreti de la signora Isabella Cortese, ne quali si contengono cose minerali, medicinali, arteficiose & alchemiche, e molte de l'arte profumatoria, appartenenti a ogni gran Signora (Venice: Giovanni Bariletto, 1561).

Oiselets de Chypre (chypre birdies) perfume for burning. Chapter 137

Take 2 pounds of labdanum, powdered wood and styrax; 1 pound of storax calamita; 4 pounds of willow charcoal; the desired quantity of tragacanth gum soaked in *eau de vie* (fruit brandy) or rose water. After heating the pestle and mortar, place the labdanum in the mortar with the styrax, and carefully pound the mixture, adding the desired quantity of tragacanth until the mixture becomes liquid. Then add the willow charcoal, crushing it little by little; do the same with the wood powder. Stir this mixture until you obtain a good paste and spread it on a stone or a walnut table, as is done to make candles. Should you require more gum, add some; and as you pour in the boiling water, make a good paste. Finally, shape the *oiselets* or little birds according to your fancy.

PREVIOUS PAGE
Willem Janszoon Blaeu
Turcicum Imperium – Ottoman Empire
ca. 1640
Hand-coloured copper engraving
Amboise, château du Clos Lucé

LEFT
Michel Campana, reconstruction of a *oiselet de Chypre* (Chypre birdy) in its cage after a drawing by Leonardo da Vinci, *Codex Atlanticus*, f. 190v, Milan, Veneranda Biblioteca Ambrosiana – Pinacoteca

Oiselets more suited to another use. Chapter 138

Take very pure labdanum and good quality storax calamita, 6 ounces of each; benzoin, 3 ounces; rough aloeswood, 2 ounces; vegetable charcoal, 1 pound 5 ounces; tragacanth gum ground and moistened in the desired quantity of *eau de vie* or rose water, and reduce the whole to a fine powder; then proceed as above.

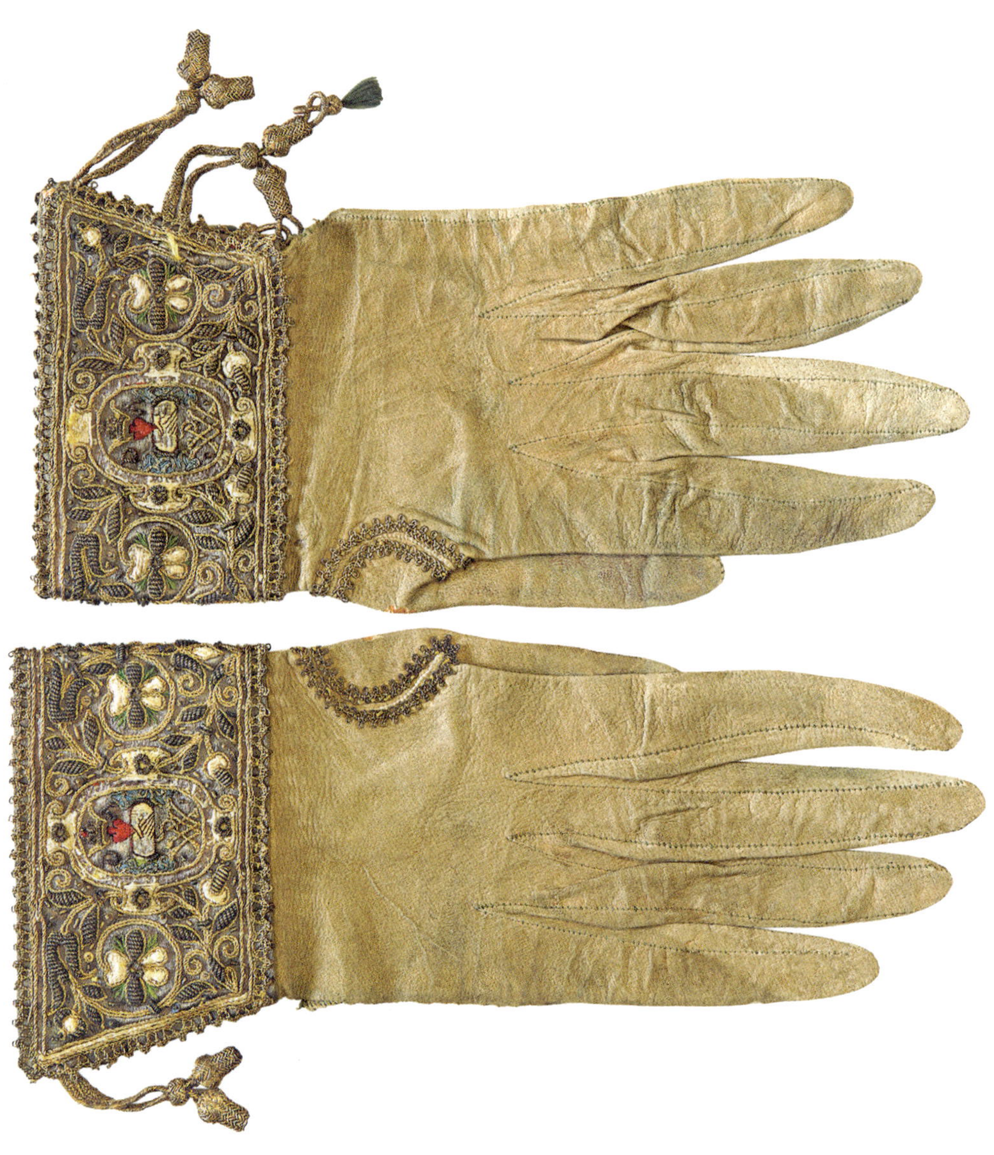

Gloves, 17th c., leather with satin insets and silk trim, embroidery and gold drawstrings, 24 × 10 cm, Florence, Musei del Bargello, inv. 2221 Carrand

Perfect tanning of gloves without using musk. Chapter 146

Take gum benzoin and styrax in equal quantities of 5 ounces; storax calamita, cinnamon, in the same quantities; 1 ounce of dried orange peel; 5 ounces of cloves; half a choice nutmeg; grind together, sift and sprinkle with rose water. Then place the mixture in a sealed glass vase. Take the quantity of jasmine or wild rose oil you need, or citron oil, or another oil suitable for tanning a pair of gloves, then add the required amount of civet musk and wipe your gloves several times so that they can be washed with either eau d'ange or rose water. Dry them after each wash until they lose the smell of leather. Then apply a little tanning grease. To give them a yellow colour, use a little ground turmeric mixed with the aforementioned jasmine oil. As a possible alternative to grease, use ointment by carefully rubbing the gloves in your hands with this composition, then mount them as desired on wooden shaping rods. Make sure the ointment and oil remain liquid so that you can grease the entire surface of the gloves by hand. Rub them with your hands, tanning them to shape them to your liking using the wooden rods, and leave them to dry in the shade – they will be perfect.

Anonymous, *Le Bâtiment des recettes* (Paris: Jean du Pré, 1540)

This book of secrets is the French translation of the Venetian collection *Dificio di ricette* (1525).

To perfume gloves
take sweet almond oil
and pour it into a phial.
grind the following to a fine powder: a quantity
of musk, storax calamita, iris root: once
all are thoroughly ground, add them to the phial
which should then be left to macerate in the
sun for eight days, taking care every day to stir the said
powders together with the oil using a stick,
then take musked rose water & your gloves
& moisten them very well with the same water
on a board & leave them to dry: do this three or four times,
& the last time the gloves are dried,
anoint them with said oil
and you shall behold the
smell they take on...

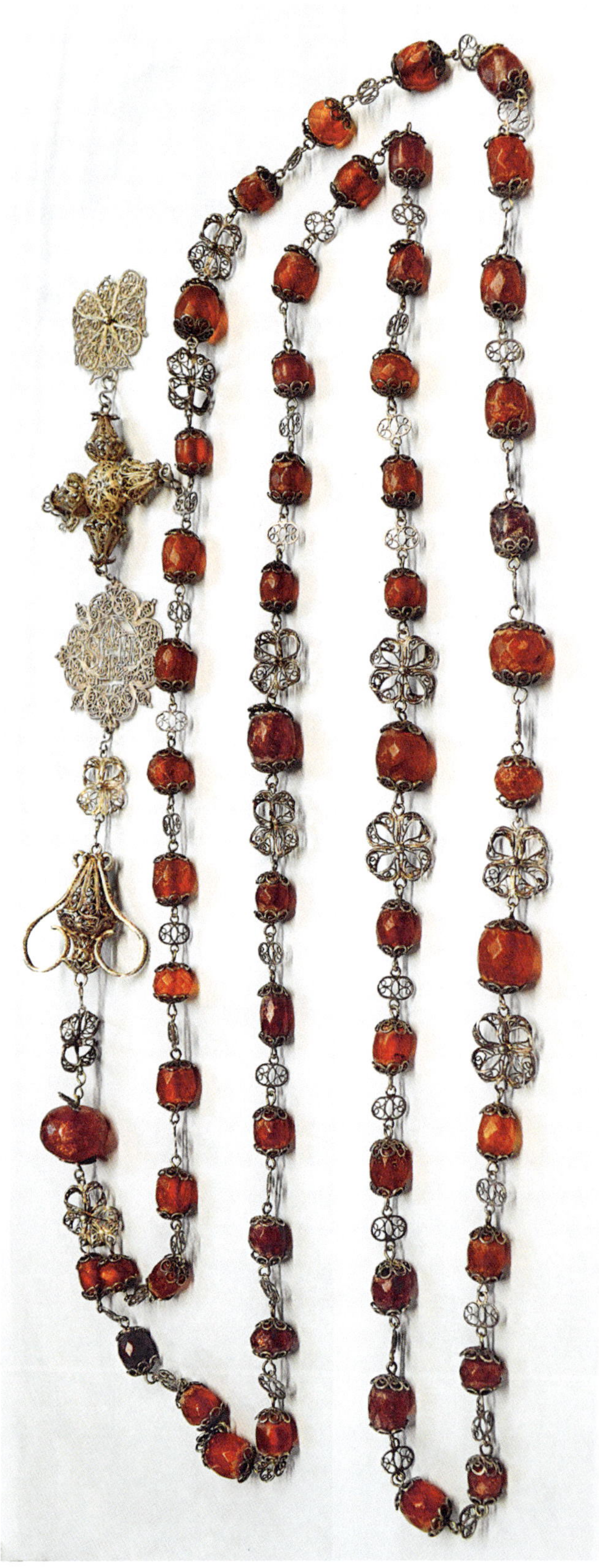

Rosary said to have belonged to Mary Stuart, 16th c., amber and silver, Roscoff, Notre-Dame-de-Croaz-Batz church and enclosure

Paternoster beads

Manuscript 1213 (Bibliothèque de Bordeaux), folio 128 r°

To make paternoster beads which shall have such a smell
as you should desire & also such a colour.
Take freshly milled bread crumb and add to it such colour
as you should desire & wine and egg yolk to your liking
then adjust the smell such as you should wish using heavily scented powder
also to your liking & beat the mixture together
to form a paste as easy to handle as wax & for moulding
according to your talents you may also fashion other items
that you might desire and set them to dry
in a dry place & it will be most pleasant & hard; it can also be used
to fashion knife handles and they too shall smell extremely good.

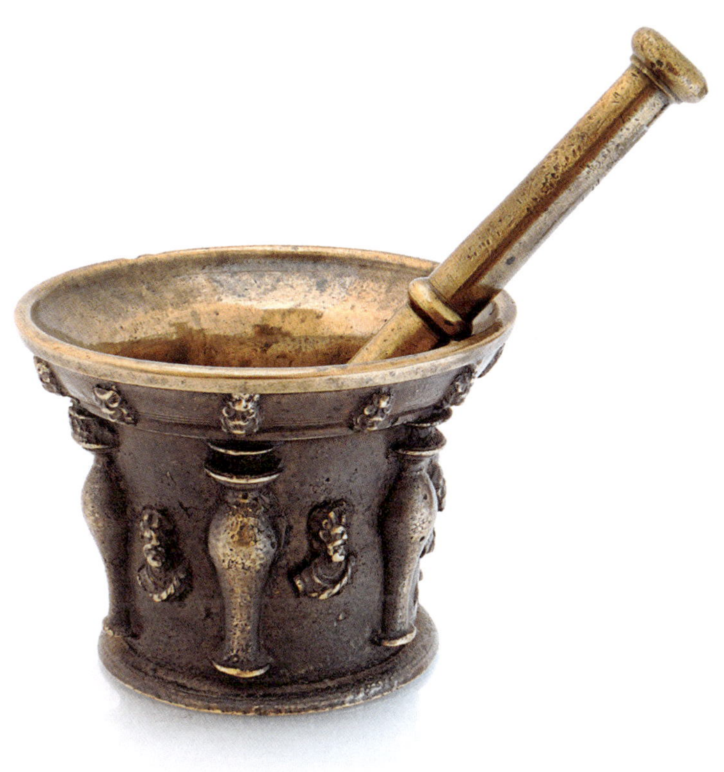

Pestle and mortar, late 15th–early 16th c., cast and hammered bronze, 20.7 × 3.2 cm, 13.5 × 10 cm, Grasse, musée international de la Parfumerie, inv. M0877.01 95 and M0877.01 96

LIST OF LOANED WORKS

SECTION 1 – THE ORIENT AND THE SEA

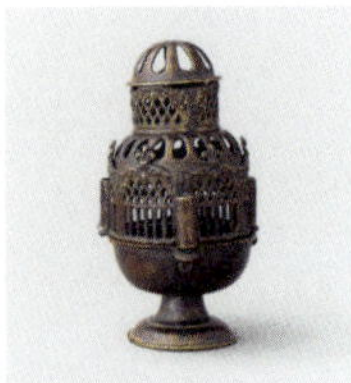

Censer
First quarter of the 17th c.
Copper
19.3 × 11 cm
Écouen, musée national de la Renaissance, château d'Écouen, inv. E.CL. 1007

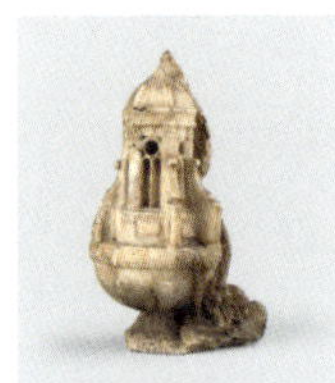

Censer
16th c.
Alabaster, 19 × 12.4 cm
Écouen, musée national de la Renaissance – château d'Écouen, inv. E.CL. 19310

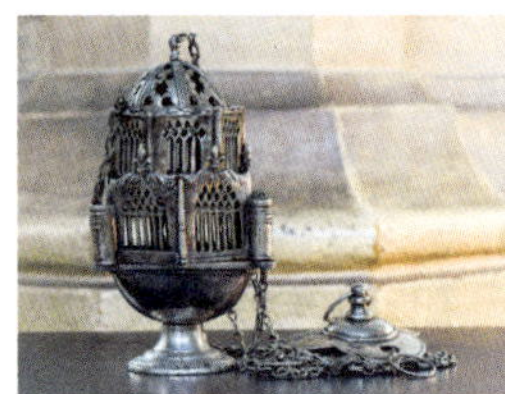

Censer
16th c.
Cast brass
21 × 11 cm
Blois, paroisse de la cathédrale Saint-Louis

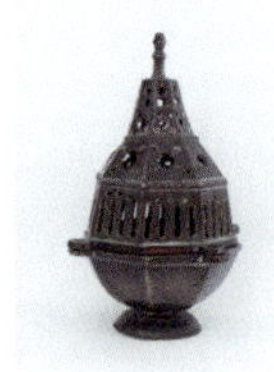

Gothic censer
16th c.
Bronze
19 × 12 cm
Amboise, château du Clos Lucé

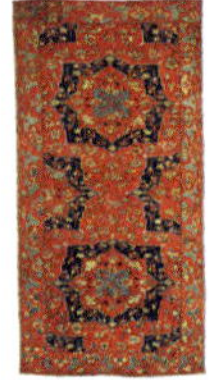

Star Ushak carpet from West Anatolia
15th c.
Wool, 297 × 148 cm
Milan, Galleria Moshe Tabibnia, inv. 124326

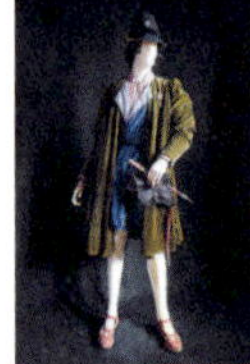

Costume of a Genoese merchant in Constantinople
Coll. MERCURIUS More Curious

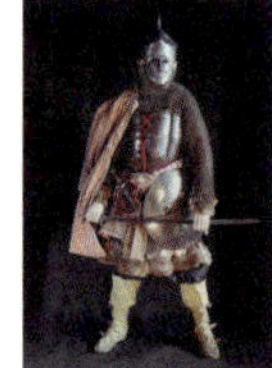

Circassian men's costume
Coll. MERCURIUS More Curious

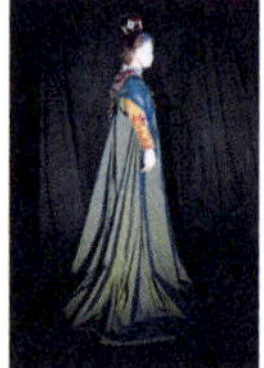

Circassian women's costume
Coll. MERCURIUS More Curious

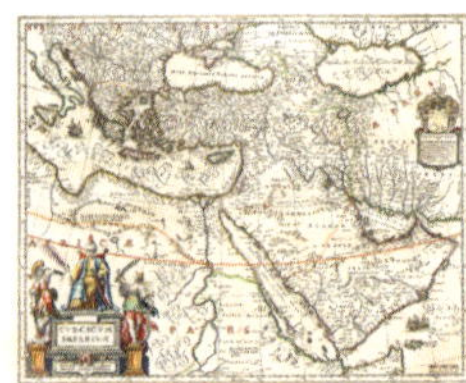

Willem Janszoon Blaeu
Turcicum Imperium – Ottoman Empire
ca. 1640
Hand-coloured copper engraving
Amboise, château du Clos Lucé

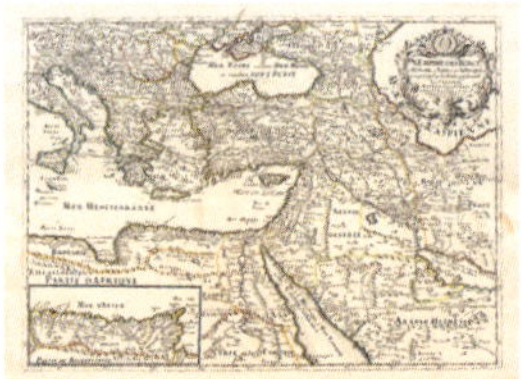

Pierre Duval, King's geographer
The Empire of the Turks in Europe, Asia and Africa, with the main routes used by caravans
1686
Amboise, château du Clos Lucé

SECTION 2 – **VENICE, GATEWAY TO THE ORIENT**

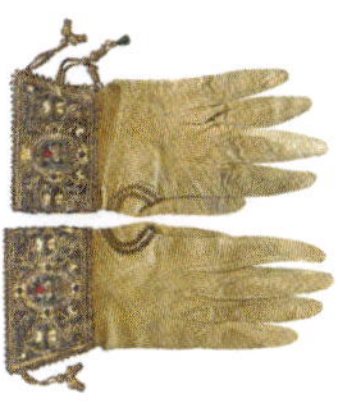

Gloves
17th c.
Leather with satin insets and silk trim, embroidery and gold drawstrings
24 × 10 cm
Florence, Musei del Bargello, inv. 2221 Carrand

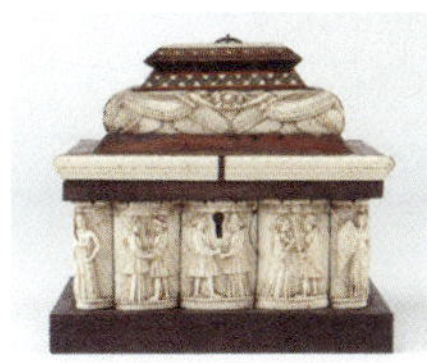

Balthazar Embriachi's workshop
Ivory casket
Early 15th c.
17 × 20 cm
Pavia, Musei Civici del Castello Visconteo, AM 28

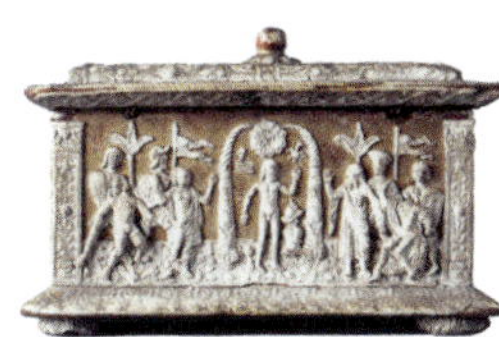

Wooden casket decorated with gold leaf
ca. 1520–1530
9.5 × 15.8 cm
Pavia, Musei Civici del Castello Visconteo, AM 33

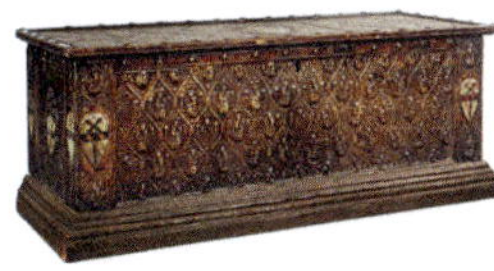

Cassone with noble coat of arms of the Segardi-Cristofori family
ca. 1460
Polychrome pastiglia decoration
186 × 71 cm
Amboise, château du Clos Lucé

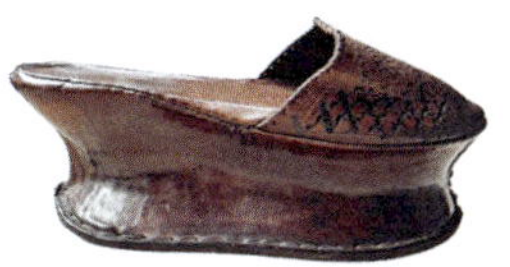

Pianelle belonging to Béatrice d'Este (reproduction)
Leather
23 × 10 cm
Vigevano, Museo Internazionale della Calzatura, inv. 3167

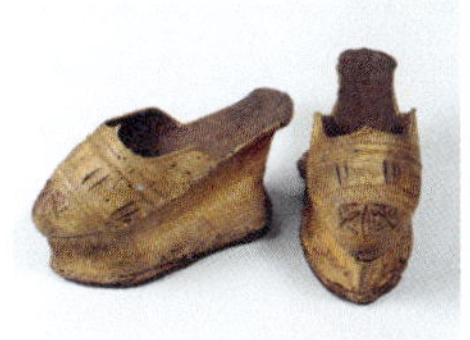

Pianelle
Venetian workmanship
16th c.
Wood and leather
10 × 21 cm
Florence, Museo Stefano Bardini, inv. MCF-MB 1922-812

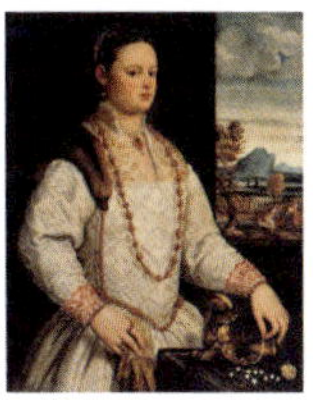

Francesco Beccaruzzi
Portrait of a Woman with a Dog
16th c.
Oil on canvas
97.8 × 76.2 cm
Bergamo, Accademia Carrara, inv. 81 LC 00193

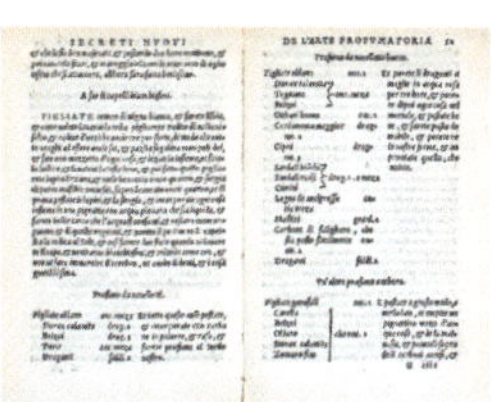

Giovanventura Rosetti
Notandissimi secreti de l'arte profumatoria
1555
Printed text
16 × 11 cm
Paris, bibliothèque Sainte-Geneviève, inv. 8 T 1692 INV 4483 FA, f. 51v-52r

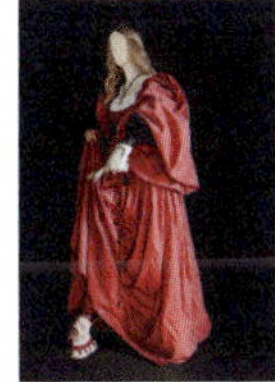

Venetian woman's costume after a work by Titian
Coll. MERCURIUS More Curious

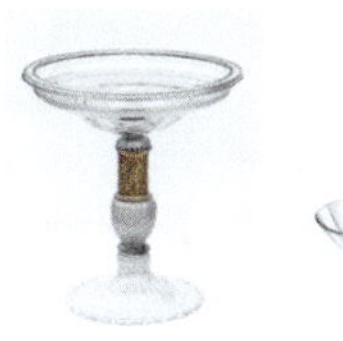

Set of Venetian glassware
End of the 16th c.
Amboise, château du Clos Lucé

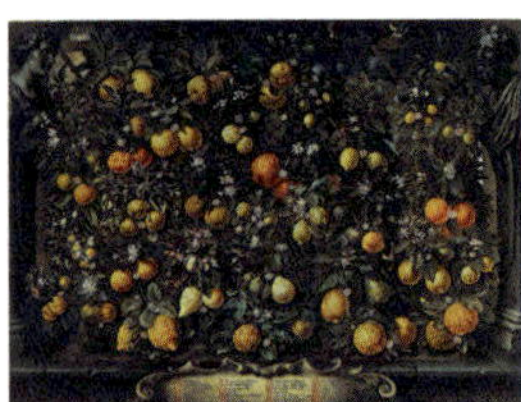

Bartolomeo Bimbi
Oranges, Limes, Lemons and Citrus lumia, 1715
Oil on canvas
198 × 257 cm
Direzione regionale musei della Toscana – Villa medicea di Poggio a Caiano e Museo della natura morta, inv. Castello n° 594

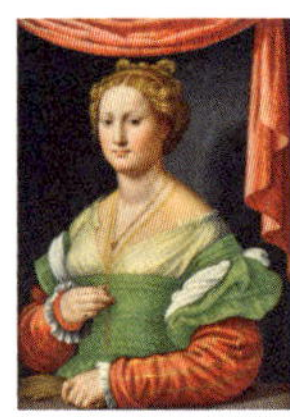

Francucci Innocenzo, also known as Innocenzo da Imola
Portrait of a Woman (thought to be Vannozza Cattanei)
16th c.
Oil on wood
97.5 × 77 cm
Rome, Galleria Borghese, inv. 416

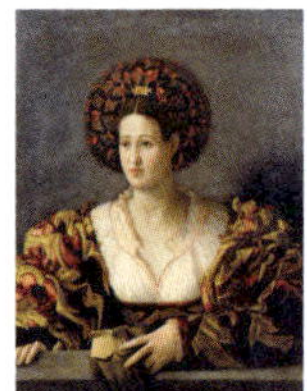

Paolo Morando, also known as Cavazzola
Portrait of a Woman
16th c.
Oil on canvas
74.2 × 96.4 cm
Oil on canvas
Bergamo, Accademia Carrara, inv. 58MR 00036

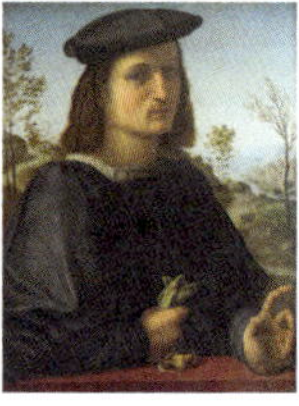

Francesco di Cristofano, known as Franciabigio
Portrait of a Young Man
1514
Oil on wood
60 × 47 cm
Florence, Galleria degli Uffizi, inv. 1890 n. 8381

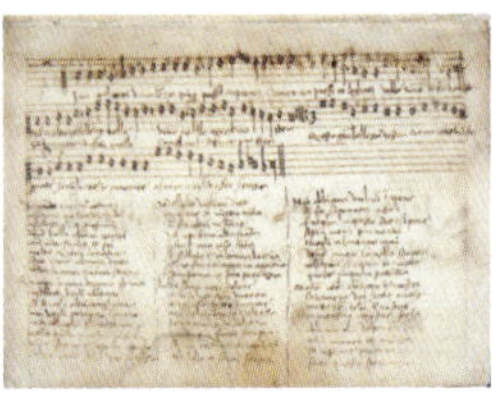

Collection of musical songs (Song of the Perfumers)
16th c.
Manuscript
33.5 × 26 cm
Florence, Biblioteca Nazionale Centrale, Banco Rari 230, inv. 230

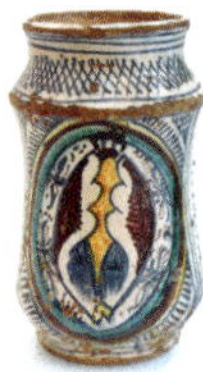

Albarello, Montelupo Fiorentino
15th c.
Polychrome earthenware
19 × 9.5 cm
Grasse, musée international de la Parfumerie, inv. 0192

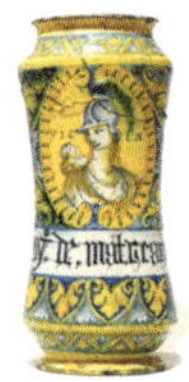

Albarello
16th c.
Polychrome earthenware
45 × 14 cm
Amboise, château du Clos Lucé

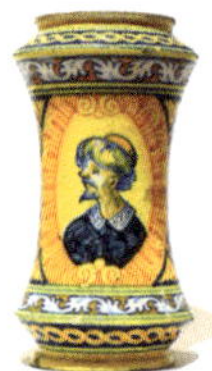

Albarello
16th c.
Polychrome earthenware
31 × 14 cm
Amboise, château du Clos Lucé

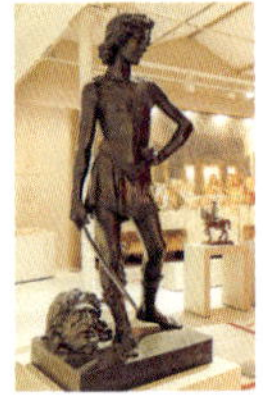

Andrea del Verrocchio
David (19th c. replica)
Bronze
132 × 59 cm
Amboise, château du Clos Lucé

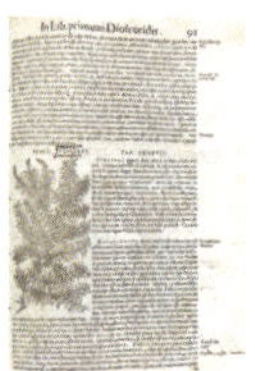

Pietro-Andrea Mattioli
Commentarii secundo aucti, in libros sex Pedecii Dioscoridis anazarbei de Medica Materia
1558
Printed text
33.3 × 22.5 cm
Romorantin-Lanthenay, centre de documentation du musée de Sologne, inv. FM 254, p. 91

Leonardo da Vinci
Notes on the usefulness of spectacles, and study of an asphodel (leaflet by Leonardo, drawing by Francesco Melzi?)
ca. 1508
34.7 × 24.2 cm
Milan, Veneranda Biblioteca Ambrosiana – Pinacoteca, Codex Atlanticus, f. 663r

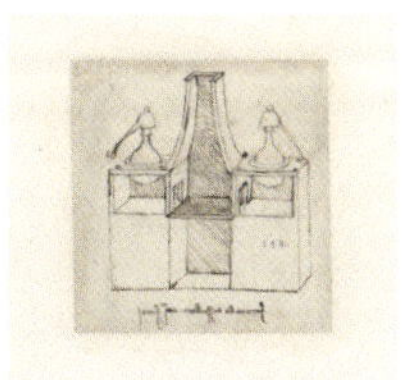

Leonardo da Vinci
Study of a tower furnace for the distillation of aqua fortis
ca. 1479–80
11.9 × 11.6 cm
Milan, Veneranda Biblioteca Ambrosiana – Pinacoteca, Codex Atlanticus, f. 912r

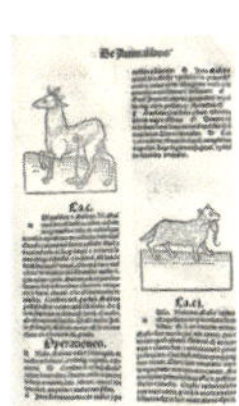

Johannes de Cuba (presumed author)
Ortus sanitatis
1491
Printed text
32 × 22.7 cm
Strasbourg, bibliothèque nationale et universitaire, réserve Joffre K.2.057, page E ii r

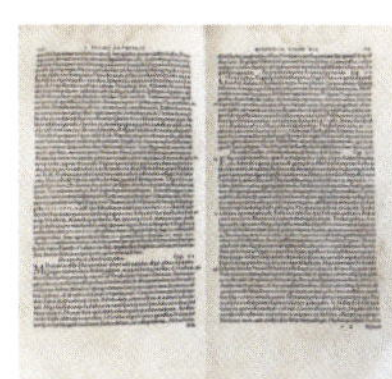

Pliny the Elder
Historiae naturalis
16th c.
Printed text
France, private collection

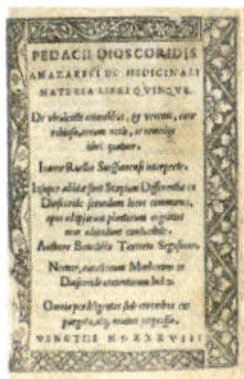

Dioscurides Pedanius
De medicinali materia libri quinque
16th c.
France, private collection

Section 4 – **At the Sforza court in Milan**

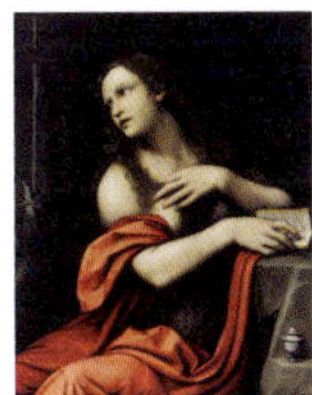

Giovan Pietro Rizzoli, also known as Giampietrino
Mary Magdalene Seated in Prayer before the Crucifix
1520–30
73.3 × 57.5 cm
Milan, Pinacoteca del Castello Sforzesco, inv. PIN 306

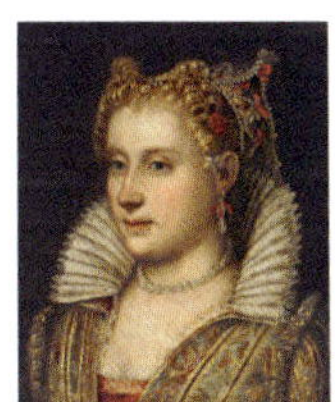

Veronese school
Portrait of a Lady
16th c.
Oil on canvas
95 × 80 cm
Pavia, Musei Civici del Castello Visconteo, inv. p.95

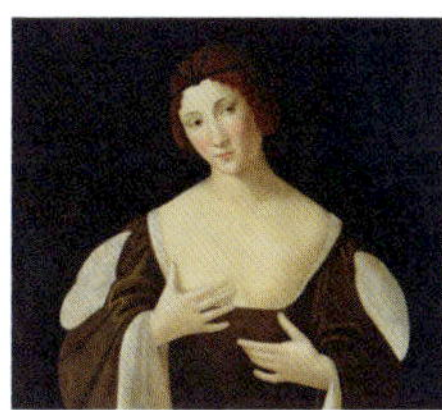

Attributed to Giovanni Antonio Boltraffio
Female Figure
16th c.
Oil on canvas
63 × 51.5 cm
Pavia, Musei Civici del Castello Visconteo, inv. p. 111

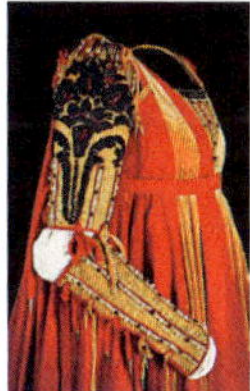

Danilo Donati
Juliet's red dress for *Romeo and Juliet* by Franco Zeffirelli (1968)
Pugnano, Fondazione Cerratelli

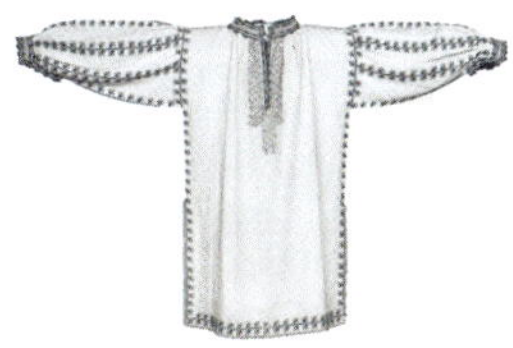

Men's shirt
16th c.
Embroidered linen, needlepoint and bobbin lace
92.5 × 150 cm
Prato, Museo del Tessuto, inv. n. 76.01.19

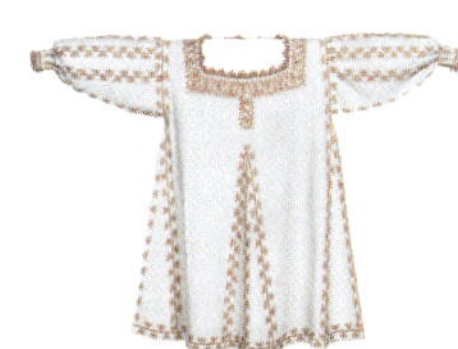

Women's shirt
16th c.
Embroidered linen, needlepoint and bobbin lace
110 × 159 cm
Prato, Museo del Tessuto, inv. n. 76.01.15

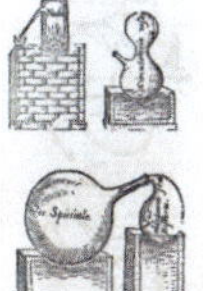

Girolamo Cardano
De subtilitate
16th c.
Printed text
17.3 × 11.3 cm
Tours, Centre d'études supérieures de la Renaissance

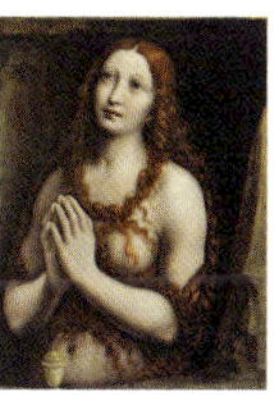

Attributed to Giovanni Pedrini, also known as Giampietrino
St Mary Magdalene
16th c.
Oil on wood
55 × 43 cm
Pavia, Musei Civici del Castello Visconteo, inv. p. 121

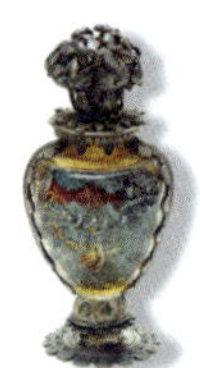

Reliquary bottle depicting a triumphal scene
16th c.
Gold and silver painted rock crystal
9 × 4 cm
Turin, Palazzo Madama – Museo Civico d'Arte Antica, inv. 107/VD

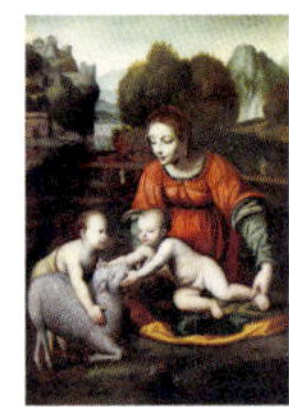

Milanese school, disciple of Bernardino Luini
The Virgin and Child with Saint John the Baptist and the Lamb in a Landscape
ca. 1600
Oil on canvas
91 × 63.5 cm
Amboise, château du Clos Lucé

SECTION 5 – PERFUMES AT THE COURT OF FRANCIS I

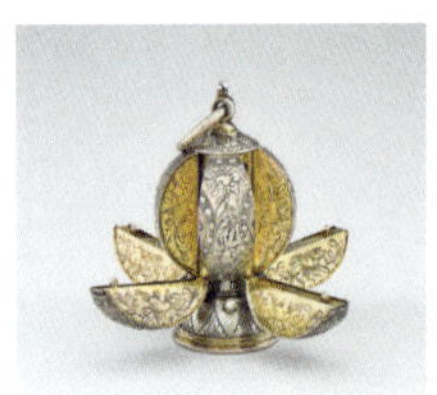

Pomander
17th c.
Partially gilded silver
6 × 3.3 cm
Écouen, musée national de la Renaissance, inv. E.Cl.12521

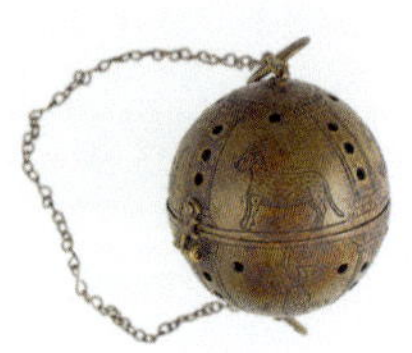

Hand warmer
16th c.
Copper
8 cm
Écouen, musée national de la Renaissance – château d'Écouen, inv. E.CL. 2825

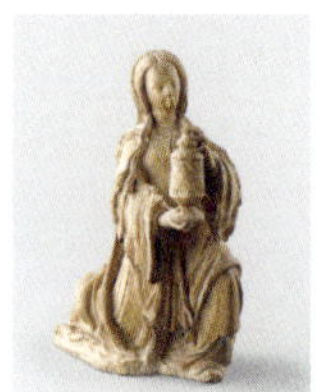

St Mary Magdalene kneeling
16th c.
Polychrome marble
44.5 × 33 cm
Paris, musée de Cluny – musée national du Moyen Âge, inv. Cl. 19382

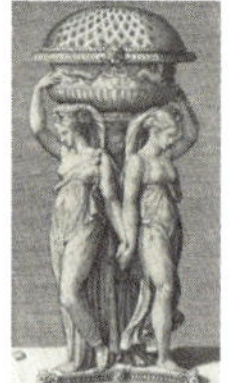

Marcantonio Raimondi after Raffaello Sanzio
Perfume burner
16th c.
Engraving
30.1 × 16.8 cm
Pavia, Musei Civici del Castello Visconteo, inv. St. Mal. 1764

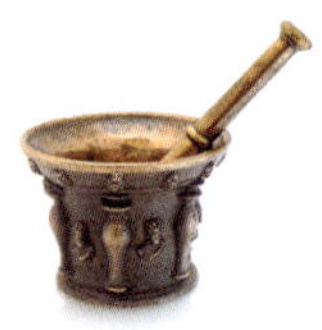

Pestle and mortar
Late 15th–early 16th c.
Cast and hammered bronze
20.7 × 3.2 cm
13.5 × 10 cm
Grasse, musée international de la Parfumerie, inv. M0877.01 95 and M0877.01 96

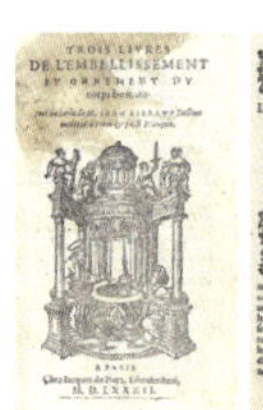

Jean Liébault
Three Books on the Embellishment and Adornment of the Human Body
1582
16.7 × 11.1 cm
Grasse, musée international de la Parfumerie, inv. M0877.01 49

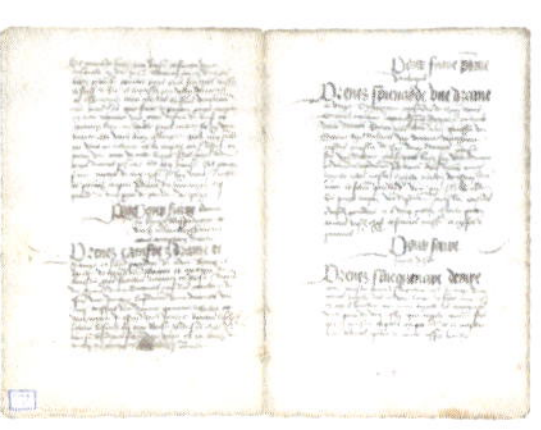

"Pommes pour faire odourer en temps d'espydeme et vault merveilleusement contre corruption d'aier",
Register of empirical, therapeutic and household formulae
15th–16th c.
Manuscript
19.5 × 27.5 cm
Le Mans, Archives départementales de la Sarthe, booklet no. 8, f. 9v and booklet no. 9, f. 1r

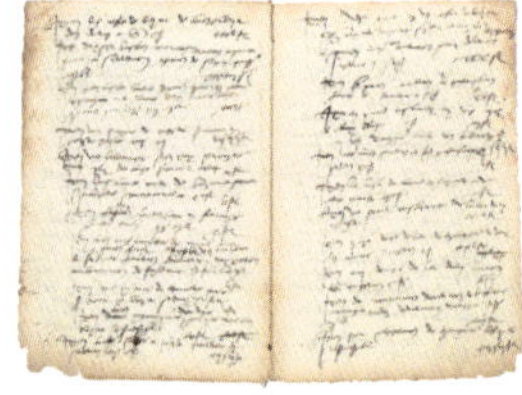

Pierre Poutrain
Post mortem inventory of François d'Escobart, Valet de Chambre and Perfumer to the King, dated 1st October 1539
16th c.
Manuscript
29 × 20 cm
Paris, Archives nationales, MC/ET/LXXXVI/89, f. 5v-6r

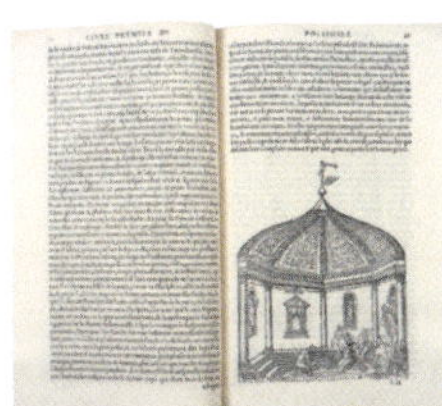

Francesco Colonna
Hypnerotomachia Poliphili or Poliphilo's Strife of Love in a Dream, describing as Love the struggle for Polia. Wherein he showeth, that all human and worldly things are but a dream, and but as vanity itself
Late 15th c.
Bound paper work
33 × 22 cm
Tours, bibliothèque municipale, Rés. 7873, f. 26v-27r

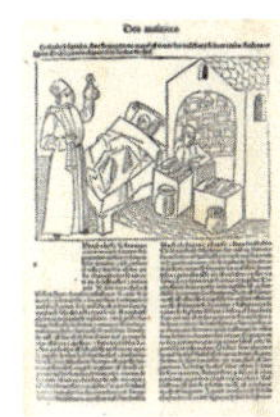

Bartholomaeus Anglicus
Le Proprietaire en françoys
(French translation of *On the Properties of Things*)
15th c.
Bound paper work
35.5 × 26 cm
Tours, bibliothèque municipale, Rés. 7573, f. 111

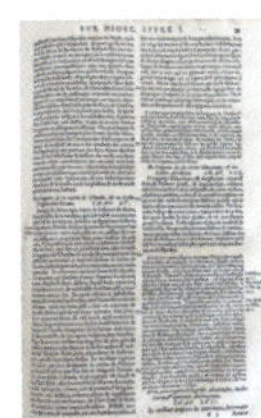

Pietro-Andrea Mattioli
The Commentaries of M.P. Andre Matthiolus, Senese Doctor, on the Six Books of Pedacius Dioscorides Anazarbæan of Medicinal Matter
1605
Printed text
33.3 × 22.5 cm
Romorantin-Lanthenay, centre de documentation du musée de Sologne, inv. FM 255, f. 39r

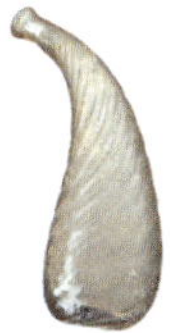

Ribbed perfume phial
17th c.
10.6 × 6 cm
Coll. Rigal, château du Cheylard d'Aujac

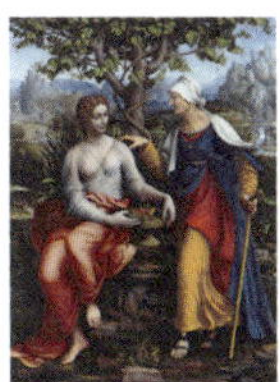

Francesco Melzi
Vertumnus and Pomona
(reproduction)
16th c.
Oil on canvas
186 × 135.5 cm
Berlin, Gemäldegalerie

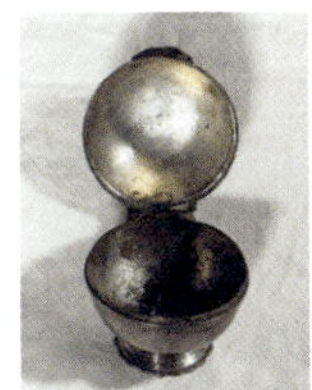

Soap box and sponge
16th c.
9 × 9 cm
Blois, musée diocésain d'Art religieux, inv. 84.1.736

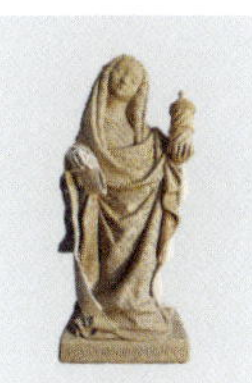

St Mary Magdalene
Late 15th c.
Carved stone with traces of polychromy
61 × 28 cm
Commune de Souvigny
Work classified as a historical monument on 7 April 1902

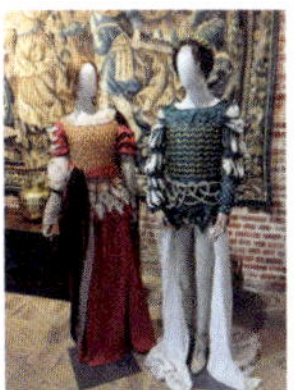

Atelier Bas et Hauts
Festive costumes
Reproductions after two drawings from Leonardo da Vinci, Windsor, RL 1276 and 1277
1518
Silk, cotton, leather, gold braids and linen
190 cm
Amboise, château du Clos Lucé

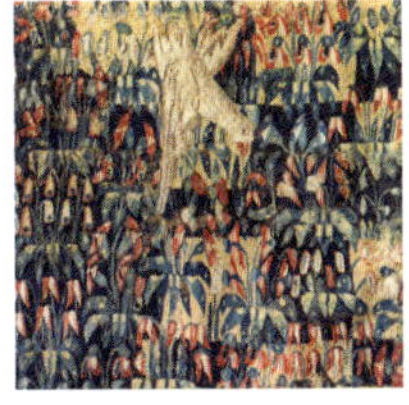

Fragment of a woollen tapestry decorated with millefleurs and a bird
15th c.
66 × 68 cm
Amboise, château du Clos Lucé

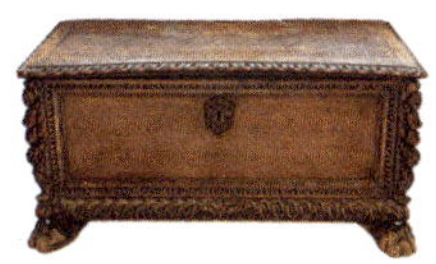

Tuscan *cassone*
16th c.
Walnut
95 × 46 × 50 cm
Amboise, château du Clos Lucé

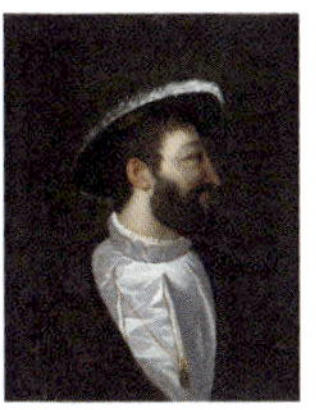

Pierre Révoil
Portait of Francis I of France
Early 19th c.
Oil on canvas
81 × 65 cm
Amboise, château du Clos Lucé

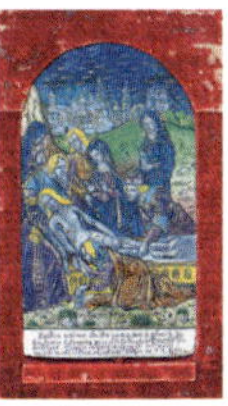

Attributed to Jean I Pénicaud
Large curved polychrome plaque in painted enamel, with a depiction of the Entombment after an engraving by Jean Ypres
ca. 1480–1530
25 × 14.6 cm
Amboise, château du Clos Lucé

—

Rosary crown
16th c.
Silver and brass thread
30 × 30 cm
Florence, Musei del Bargello, inv. 1065 Carrand

PHOTO CREDITS AND COPYRIGHTS:

© Klassik Stiftung Weimar, Bestand Museen/Olaf Mokansky: p. 26
© Léonard de Serres: p. 123 (right), p. 161 (top), p. 182, p. 185, p. 187
© MIC – Museo Internazionale della Calzatura "Pietro Bertolini" – Vigevano: p. 183
© Michel Campana: p. 176
© MIP/Photo: Carlo Barbiero, p. 169, p. 183, p. 184, p. 186
© MIP: p. 45 (right), p. 186
© Metropolitan Museum, New York: p. 70, p. 143, p. 144, p. 145, p. 147
© Musei Civici del Castello Visconteo di Pavia: p. 83, p. 87, pp. 128–129, p. 136, p. 163, p. 166, p. 183, p. 185, p. 186
© National Gallery of Art/Ailsa Mellon Bruce Fund: p. 18
© Patrick Turini: p. 23, p. 187
© Pinacoteca del Castello Sforzesco – © Comune di Milano/Lacitignola 2018: p. 134
© Royal Collection Trust/© His Majesty King Charles III, 2024: p. 10, p. 15, p. 29, p. 52, p. 108
© Staatliche Museen zu Berlin, Gemäldegalerie/Dietmar Gunne: p. 173, p. 187
© The ALBERTINA Museum, Vienna: p. 133
© The Cleveland Museum of Art: pp. 114–115
© The Directorate of National Palaces, Topkapı Palace Museum, Istanbul: p. 66, p. 69, p. 73
© The Huntington Library, San Marino, California: pp. 58–59
© Veneranda Biblioteca Ambrosiana/Metis e Mida Informatica/Mondadori Portfolio: p. 32 (right), p. 36, p. 51, p. 90, p. 93, p. 99, p. 185

Courtesy of the Ministry of Culture – Photographic Archives of the Gallerie Estensi: p. 132
Per gentile concessione della Fondazione Giorgio Cini: p. 81 (left)
Reproduced by permission of the Fondazione Torino Musei/photo: Paolo Robino 2016: p. 149, p. 186
Su concessione del Ministero della Cultura – Biblioteca Nazionale Centrale di Firenze: p. 102, p. 103, p. 116, p. 118, p. 184
Su concessione del Ministero della Cultura – Biblioteca Nazionale Marciana. Divieto di riproduzione: p. 80

G.A.V.E – Archivio fotografico – "su concessione del Ministero della Cultura": cover

ÉDITIONS SKIRA PARIS
14, rue Serpente
75006 Paris
www.skira.net

Senior Editor
Nathalie Prat-Couadau

Project Manager and Editorial Coordinator
Juliette Chambon

Commercial and Editorial Project Manager
Meryl Mason

Editorial assistant
Roxanne Rebours

Interns
Alexandre Hervé
Paul Bonete

Graphic design
Luigi Fiore

Layout
Juliette Gresland

Translations
Martin Lewis (French to English)
Pascal Brioist (Italian to French)
Marcelline Delbecq, Laurence Gravier, Barbara Vial (English to French)

Copyediting and Proofreading
Laure Barbosa (French)
Timothy Stroud (English)

Colour Separation
Litho Art New, Turin

ISBN 978-2-37074-245-2

Printed in June 2024 by Graphius in Ghent, Belgium.
Legal deposit June 2024.

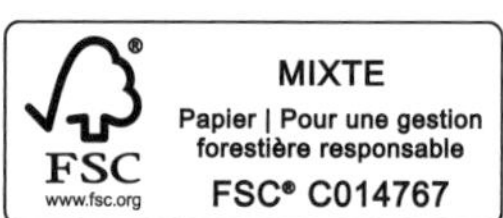